Calling for Justice throughout the World

Catholic Women Theologians on the HIV/AIDS Pandemic

edited by MARY JO IOZZIO

with MARY M. DOYLE ROCHE
and ELSIE M. MIRANDA

continuum

NEW YORK • LONDON

D0005582

2008
The Continuum International Publishing Group Inc.
80 Maiden Lane, New York, NY 10038

The Continuum International Publishing Group Ltd.
The Tower Building, 11 York Road, London SE1 7NX
www.continuumbooks.com

Printed in the United States of America

Library of Congress Cataloging-in-Publication Data

Calling for justice throughout the world : Catholic women theologians on the HIV/AIDS pandemic / edited by Mary Jo Iozzio with Mary M. Doyle Roche and Elsie M. Miranda.
　　p. ; cm.
　　Companion to: Catholic ethicists on HIV/AIDS prevention / edited by James F. Keenan ; assisted by Jon D. Fuller, Lisa Sowle Cahill, Kevin Kelly. 2000.
　　Includes bibliographical references and index.
　　ISBN-13: 978-0-8264-2863-9 (hardcover : alk. paper)
　　ISBN-10: 0-8264-2863-0 (hardcover : alk. paper)
　　ISBN-13: 978-0-8264-2864-6 (pbk. : alk. paper)
　　ISBN-10: 0-8264-2864-9 (pbk. : alk. paper)
　　1. AIDS (Disease) in women. 2. AIDS (Disease)—Religious aspects—Catholic Church. 3. Medical ethics. 4. Christian ethics—Catholic authors. 5. Catholic women. I. Iozzio, Mary Jo. II. Roche, Mary M. Doyle. III. Miranda, Elsie M. IV. Keenan, James F. Catholic ethicists on HIV/AIDS prevention.
　　[DNLM: 1. Bioethical Issues. 2. HIV Infections. 3. Catholicism. 4. Religion and Medicine. 5. Women's Health—ethics. WC 503.7 C161 2008]

RA643.8.C35 2008
362.196'97920082—dc22
　　　　　　　　　　　　　　　　　　　　　　　　　　　　　2008029829

Calling for Justice
throughout the World

THE CONTRIBUTORS DEDICATE THIS WORK TO:

The poor all over the world

The community of Kilbride Centre

Women collaborators

*Each person who suffers because of AIDS, especially women,
children, and those wounded by violence and indigence*

*The children living with HIV and AIDS at Mary's Child Centre
and Martha's House, and Mustard Seed Communities, Jamaica*

AIDS hospice workers

Alec and Rosemary Hepburn

Tran Van and Bui Nhu Chau, and Ed Vacek, SJ

*Anthony K. Byenkya, Francisca Bwala,
and Mother Mary Mukanyangezi*

*Amirtham, my loving father, who taught me
to work for the empowerment of women*

Pat, with thanks

Robert J. Vitillo and Margaret Farley

Alphonse Bambi, Godelieve Katuta, and Brigette Syamalewe

Ms. Dolzura Cortez, the first Filipina with AIDS

Ann Sheehy

Stewart Sykes and Crystal Felicia Sykes

*Jolly Nyeko and Lydia Nyesigomwe, founder
and director of Action for Children, Uganda*

Eileen Hogan, Alison Munro, and Anne Nasimiyu

Carlos Manual Egaña

*Stefan Hippler and all the people in Project Hope,
Cape Town, South Africa*

Sandra Moolu Gayer

*Pétronille, Josée, Julie, Margaret, Hope, Mumsey, Renate, Miranda,
and Valérie: Thank you for the hospitality. Long life!*

*The NCAN community living and deceased, Sr. Mary V. Annell, MD,
Rev. Bryan Massingale, and Raymond Jasper*

*My beloved mother, Mrs. Mary Joseph,
a valiant and compassionate woman who had a special corner
in her heart for people suffering with fatal diseases*

Robert Valentis and Michael W. Sieczkarek

Norman P. Iozzio, MD

James F. Keenan, SJ

Contents

Part Two: Challenging the Church

Part Three: Migrants and Immigrants

Part Four: Invisible and Vulnerable

Part Five: The Female Face of AIDS

Conclusion

Mary Jo Iozzio

Preface

A Companion to Catholic Ethicists on HIV/AIDS Prevention

In 2002, Continuum published "the first book in moral theology to engage Catholic ethicists from around the world in addressing a singular moral issue."[1] *Calling for Justice throughout the World: Catholic Women Theologians on the HIV/AIDS Pandemic* appears to be the second such book. This collection continues what may become for contemporary audiences and the teaching traditions of the Catholic Church a vehicle for the voices and concerns of Catholic theological ethicists on HIV/AIDS—and theoretically many other subjects—as they reflect on the lived experiences of our sisters and brothers in the world.

Some may argue that a second collection on HIV/AIDS is redundant or superfluous. Others may think this subject has been sufficiently addressed in the 2002 collection and in many other texts by sociologists, psychologists, physicians, nurses, and policy makers, and that the problems and concerns raised there have been resolved and presumably relieved. Still others contend that HIV/AIDS is but one among multiple symptoms of a larger global crisis.

This book expands the work of the first collection by bringing the voices and perspectives of Catholic women to a pandemic that shows little sign of abatement, especially as it reaches ever more threateningly and globally into the lives of the most vulnerable populations: women, children, people of color, homosexual and bisexual persons, migrants, elders, and people with disabilities. Moreover, this collection follows *Catholic Ethicists on HIV/AIDS Prevention* in its recognition, along with Jonathan Mann,[2] that the pandemic is a social problem—a call for justice especially for those whose voices often go unheard. Additionally, this collection enlisted authors who speak to the moral ramifications of the pandemic in order, like the 2002 text, to move consciousness beyond awareness toward action that can thwart the steady global progress of HIV. The first collection presented 33 essays, 6 by women; specific case studies introduced its part 1; and its part 2 engaged the fundamental moral issues of prevention. This collection presents 24 essays, all authored by women, who integrate contextual details with fundamental moral issues as part of their scrutiny. These women illuminate the challenges of the pandemic anew for the Church and its teachings and practices, for health care access and prevention programs, and for God's people everywhere.

Focus and Rationale

The extent of the HIV/AIDS pandemic cries out for responses from our academies, churches, and communities. Since the Catholic Church is committed to providing ministerial outreach and affordable health care to persons with HIV, and since a number of Catholic theologians have spoken boldly on the demands of justice and loving care for persons with HIV and AIDS and their families, these essays offer theological reflection and critical reasons for the continued urgency demanded by the pandemic. The collection reminds the Church and those who serve God's people how to wrestle with a crisis of global proportions and to relieve human suffering, especially of those who are outcast and oppressed, in accordance with the justice mandate of the gospel and the Church's social teachings on solidarity and the common good.

This project developed from a panel presentation on "When God's People Have HIV/AIDS: Ethical Approaches" at the annual meeting of the Society of Christian Ethics in January 2006 and follows from the opportunities presented for collaboration with scholars who met at the First International Cross-cultural Conference for Catholic Theological Ethicists in July 2006 (Padua Conference).[3] That conference proved a watershed of talent and common vision[4] as it cleared the way for dialogue and the means to continue discussions begun there among Catholic colleagues separated by distance and culture. In addition to the introductions this face-to-face event provided, all participants received contact information to facilitate the kind of collaboration this collection demonstrates is possible. This collection offers a critical call and reminder of the work of justice for people worldwide and examines issues crucial to both local and global realities by considering the moral ramifications of the pandemic as it relates to poverty, gender, education, stigma and discrimination, and access to health care. These essays are decidedly praxis-oriented and written from the social locations of women in solidarity with those infected with and affected by the pandemic.

In varying degrees, essayists draw upon their formation in moral theology, present a critical-historical review of the social location of concern, and analyze materials collected and developed over the course of their own research.

To date, no singularly focused text on the HIV/AIDS pandemic has been both developed and written by Catholic women moral theologians. As this collection continues the seminal work of *Catholic Ethicists on HIV/AIDS Prevention* among other texts that engage Christian theologies and the

Church's responses to the pandemic, some concerns previously overlooked, especially in regard to the female face of AIDS, are here brought to the fore. Moreover, the Padua Conference confirmed—in plenary and applied ethics sessions—that women worldwide disproportionately bear the weight of infection, care, and stigma that surround the pandemic.[5] In fact, considerable talk over the course of the conference acknowledged women as key for the relief of many contemporary social, political, and ecclesial ills; from the voices of women and men a clarion call for justice was heard. This collection raises the voices of women in solidarity with their sisters and brothers throughout the world.

Content

In this book women from many parts of the globe consider the specific and local experience of HIV/AIDS for the geographic region where they live and work or have firsthand knowledge from extensive visits. Essayists explore the moral ramifications of the pandemic through the lens of women in solidarity with all those infected with and affected by HIV/AIDS. Scholars from Africa, Asia, Europe, Central America, the Caribbean, South America, North America, and Oceania bring the pandemic to greater consciousness in the hope of igniting activism for prevention and care programs.

Like the 2002 collection, this companion follows the organization of essays by their principal thematic concerns rather than according to the geographic regions under consideration. Many similar concerns are explored as authors write about the justice that is all too often denied to people infected with and affected by HIV/AIDS. And each author considers how the Church, either through its teachings or its local response to the pandemic, promotes or obstructs the gospel of liberation and restorative justice for the people in its care and those beyond its reach. Unsurprisingly, the five substantive themes raised in the 2002 collection are found here too: (1) a lack of women's empowerment, (2) religious scrupulosity on the use of condoms as a critically important preventive, (3) a failure to recognize non-Western and/or developing nations' cultural traditions, (4) the co-morbid stigma of AIDS and homosexuality and bisexuality, (5) and the vulnerability of children. In addition to these themes, authors recognize problems associated with the invisibility of marginalized people and of immigrant/migrant populations, the sadness of the loss of loved ones and of their futures, and the persistent interpretative assignment of culpability as deserved punishment for presumed wrongdoing.

This collection is divided by theme into five parts; many of these themes rise with greater or less emphasis across the essays. The collection begins with an introduction on solidarity to situate collaborative work. Recognizing also the absence of voices from Eastern Europe and the Middle East, and the limited number from Latin America, some consideration of these unrepresented and underrepresented regions are included in the introduction as part of the global initiative.

In an introductory chapter, Bernadette Mbuy Beya (RD Congo) offers consideration of the contextually sensitive ramifications of the pandemic as she prays, "Show Me My Face, O Lord." Part 1 presents work that challenges simple notions of justice: Lisa Sowle Cahill (USA), Y-Lan Tran (Vietnam), Maria Cimperman, OSU (USA), Margaret Farley (USA), and Carolyn Sharp (Canada) invite us to consider the ways governments, institutions, programs, initiatives, and faith and religious teachings support, engage, or thwart positive trends in responding to prevention and care. Part 2 provides a look at some of the ways that church or local politics and ideals combine to move relief forward or reverse course: Agnes Brazal (Philippines), Elizabeth Hepburn, IBVM (Australia), Elsie Miranda (USA), and Anna Kasafi Perkins (Jamaica) consider questions of Church interventions, influence, and popular theologies in need of prudent design if relief and justice are to have effect. Part 3 exposes the often ignored concerns for the care of migrant and immigrant populations: Marie-Jo Thiel (France), Hille Haker (Germany), Gillian Paterson (UK), and Suzanne Mulligan (Ireland) reflect on the desperation and the vulnerability to health crises, stigma, and abuse that people away from home and ken experience at the reach of others more powerful than they. Part 4 continues the theme of vulnerability of invisible others: Mary Doyle Roche (USA), Mary Jo Iozzio (USA), Emily Reimer-Barry (USA), and Shawnee Daniels-Sykes, SSND (USA) explore the infection risk for children, elders, people with disabilities, and minority women and how ideologies of innocence, desert, and disbelief fail them. Part 5 illustrates in full force the female face of HIV/AIDS: Christina Astorga (Philippines), Maryanne Confoy, RSC (Australia), Metti Amirtham, SCC (India), Therese Tinkasiimire, DST (Uganda), and Pushpa Joseph, FMM (India) retell in rich contextual detail experiences that demand revision of global responses to the pandemic. Finally, Maria Clara Bingemer (Brazil) navigates a quasi-exegetical and tender interpretation of leprosy and AIDS as she draws the precarious line between the earlier and contemporary stigmatization over the total embrace by a world and a people that is called to care.

I draw your attention to successful and proposed strategies presented in what follows for collaboration: the positive initiatives of Doc-on-a-Box, HealthStore, and Action for Children in Africa, and the Circle of Concerned African Women Theologians and Sister-to-Sister projects; points of engagement that invite brainstorming, planning, and doing; evaluation criteria for the Church's public policy positions; examination of discourse to stigmatize or empower; integration of Catholic social teaching into a social bioethics; principles to guide women-centered prevention and empowerment; and a relationship-based spirituality using indigenous/traditional therapies to rehabilitate the moral agency of people stigmatized by HIV. These and other strategies engage the wisdom of the Catholic moral traditions at their best—with mercy and love in the service of human dignity, solidarity, and the common good.

Admittedly, this collection has shortcomings. Along with my coeditors, Mary Doyle Roche and Elsie Miranda, and our colleague Maria Cimperman, OSU, we contacted more than fifty women by e-mail or phone asking if they would be interested in writing an essay for this text. Wanting to be as inclusive as possible, invitations by e-mail were sent with text in English, French, Italian, Portuguese, and Spanish.[6] Some did not answer the invitation or responded with regrets. Many were failed by intermittent access to communication technologies; others experienced personal illness or the death of a parent. I have become far more sensitive than previously to the difficulties surrounding a project that attempts to present global perspectives, and I am more mindful of the personal expense involved with each woman's own experience and obligations to family, friend, and work. The most obvious shortcoming is the limited number of essays from Africa, Central America, and South America, and the lack of essays from Eastern Europe and the Middle East. I hope that as the network begun with the Padua Conference strengthens and grows, we will find ways to collaborate with scholars from these underrepresented regions.

Gratitude

On behalf of Mary Doyle Roche and Elsie Miranda, I thank James F. Keenan, SJ, for supporting this collection, for leading the cross-cultural international movement among Catholic ethicists with the Padua Conference, and for mentoring many of us through the development of our respective work. Our thanks go also to Andrea Vicini, SJ, and Tony Mifsud, SJ, who helped us to extend invitations to their women colleagues in Europe and South America. We extend our sincerest thanks to Frank Oveis of Continuum for encouraging the volume and accepting the project as a companion to the 2002 collection for which he was also responsible, and to Burke Gerstenschläger and Ryan Masteller, also of Continuum, for seeing the project to completion. Thanks also to Agnes Brazal, Maria Cimperman, and Margaret Farley, who put us in touch with some of their sister-colleagues in Africa and Southeast Asia. Finally, we acknowledge all of our contributors and the women who work in the field but who could not submit an essay here. We stand with you in solidarity and in thanks.

In addition to the concrete and personal faces of the pandemic presented here, we are mindful of the work the Church undertakes on behalf of those infected with and affected by HIV. We are encouraged by the support of the Church for its health care, prevention, and sanctuary programs, especially those serving the most disadvantaged and those in rural locales. And we recommit to the work of the gospel in clothing the naked, comforting the sick, visiting the dying, giving bread to the hungry, proclaiming a year of salvation, and loving with the passion of the God who stands with us and for us against the forces that threaten peace. This call for justice barely touches the surface of the systemic and institutionalized power to oppress on account of HIV and/or AIDS. We hope this collaborative effort and the exhortations of the Church Catholic inspire others to work likewise. In the words of Benedict XVI, we must do more:

> The God of Jesus Christ must be known, believed in and loved, and hearts must be converted if progress is to be made on social issues and reconciliation is to begin, and if—for example—AIDS is to be combated by realistically facing its deeper causes and the sick are to be given the loving care they need. . . . When we bring people only knowledge, ability, technical competence and tools, we bring them too little.[7]

Mary Jo Iozzio with Mary Doyle Roche and Elsie M. Miranda

Introduction

Globalizing Solidarity

Calling for justice, globalizing solidarity, one human family or one earth community, one God over all, one moment in time when she said yes *and the Word became flesh*. When she said yes any lingering questions of God's intent for humankind were answered definitively: God is for us.[1] This posture, this answer, this incarnation should dispel any thinking that God wills pain, suffering, or punishment; as you will see in the pages that follow, some still think that HIV/AIDS and the suffering and oppression frequently associated with it is God's will—but they are wrong. As Teresa Okure, SHCJ, affirms:

> A consequence of [God's entering into human history at the margin of the margins with Mary's fiat] for globalising solidarity today is that we need to take into serious consideration the women question. . . . Today we need to find ways of being in solidarity with God who saw it very good and necessary to create humanity as male and female. . . . Humanity also needs to reclaim the woman in all walks of life if it is ever to achieve wholeness. . . . [The] time has come to align ourselves with God in reclaiming the unique gifts which God offers through the woman for the work of reconciliation and globalising solidarity.[2]

Okure's reflection calls for a reckoning of the Church's identification of a "solid method for participating in God's project of globalising love, salvation and total human liberation" in light of the urgency to attend to justice for all. Commentary upon part of the theme of the 2003 General Assembly of Caritas Internationalis (CI), Okure challenges the Church to hear the extent to which women and other marginalized people disproportionately carry the burdens of poverty and the burdens of infection as well as the care for all of God's people infected with and affected by HIV and AIDS. The CI theme followed the call of John Paul II on the globalization of solidarity,[3] the essentially interdependent condition of all human life and the demands of justice

1

exercised through the principles of communion, respect, and subsidiarity in human affairs. Moreover, CI identified global trends that illustrate the dehumanizing effects of poverty on women and the critical need to stand up for women's rights. In his closing remarks, CI's president, Msgr. Youhanna-Fouad El-Hage, charged the 2003 General Assembly with the "resounding call to bring social and economic justice to the world's marginalized by working in solidarity with the poor. . . . We leave . . . with a mandate to act not only on behalf of the poor, but to enable people to deal better with the forces that oppress them."[4] This collection is one response to that mandate.

Globalizing solidarity announces an urgent call to action. Three areas of special concern come to the fore with respect to the Church's response and our response to HIV/AIDS as members of the communion of faith: (1) the *imago Dei* that grounds respect for life and human dignity, (2) the common good that ensures the distribution of resources for the sake of human flourishing at the margins and the centers of power, and (3) the preferential option for the poor that seeks justice on behalf of those whose voice, experience, and need have been too long ignored. Following an exploration of these concerns in light of the pandemic, consideration of the state of the pandemic in regions absent from the text is presented to provide a glimpse of its extent in the hope that collaboration and solidarity may be achieved with the Church of these regions in the near future.

Imago Dei

What does it mean to be made in the image and likeness of God? What are the implications of being *la imagen y semejanza de Dios*? The Spanish is deliberate; it denotes intrinsic relatedness to the other as inherently good. In a world with HIV and AIDS, something is at stake for the human community that lives in the tradition of an *imago Dei*.

Classical theology, buttressed by Scripture and tradition, considers creation the revelation of a fundamental truth regarding the relational existence of God in whom human beings are created: "God said, let us make human beings in our image and likeness." God speaks, and the creative Word brings forth life from God's relational integrity and sexually differentiates the human being as male and female, naming them *imago Dei*.[5] This text and the traditions that emerge from it provide the basis for the transcendence and relationality of *imago Dei* by the tri-relational God.[6] The *imago Dei* legitimizes the unity and diversity of humanity by allowing gender, race, culture, and other self-defining variables confirmation as inherently good in the tri-relationality that includes self, God, and other. In this context human beings are called to go forth and be the active presence of God in the world, for the world. Grounded in the Trinity, the essence of *imago Dei* reflects the fundamental relationships within God's self. Thomas G. Weinandy writes, "Our creation in the image and likeness of God involves all three persons of the Trinity. . . . The relevance of being created in the image and likeness of God resides in who we are in our deepest essence—because our lives are intrinsically ordered to and lived within the very life of the Trinity."[7] Living out the tri-relationality of God for us, human beings discern the responsibility that comes with being *imago Dei*. This responsibility requires conscious action for justice with care: to stand in solidarity with the poor and oppressed, to uphold the dignity and sanctity of life, and to recognize God as the source of human transcendent and relational integrity.

The implications of being *la imagen y semejanza de Dios* extend to the fundamental responsibility to be in relationship.[8] In a world plagued by HIV and AIDS lies the danger of negating the transcendent good, true, and beautiful of relationships. Without the beautiful, we will no longer be able to love; without the good, evil will rise in its stead.[9] Daring to be transformed by relationships, the human community stands in solidarity and lives in the consciousness of the joyful and painful narratives and the one narrative of incarnate love. Consider the motion: "The body of Christ has AIDS. . . . What will you do for him now?"[10]

What is at stake for a community that lives with the *imago Dei* tradition? Some would respond, the very glory of God. In countering the heresies of the second century, Irenaeus declared that the spiritual and material dignity of the human being was rooted in the *imago Dei* tradition, wherein the glory of God is the human being fully alive.[11] For Irenaeus, the essence of our humanity clothes us with a near inconceivable dignity that pertains to our created estate.[12] Sharing in God's tri-relationality, we are to celebrate the fullness of our humanity in triune relationship with God, self, and other. As human beings fully alive, we walk in relationships accompanied by love, we witness truth, beauty, and goodness in the often uncharted journey of life.

Recognizing that what is at stake is the glory of God, we are heartened by the words of Benedict XVI in his 2008 World Peace Day message. The pope urged the global community to respect human dignity as a foundational measure of promoting "the human family, as a community of peace. . . . The peoples of the earth, are called to build relationships of solidarity and cooperation among themselves, as befits members of the one human family."[13] As Christians and members of one human family, we recognize in our own lives and in the lives of others the passion of the living Christ. Our transcendent dignity hinges upon the revelation that we are created by God to participate in salvation history with God, for God, in the world.

The Common Good

The commitment to intrinsic human dignity, located in the *imago Dei*, is the foundational principle of the common good and its effect on human flourishing. Though dignity redounds to each unique individual, this dignity can only be understood in light of tri-relationality and interdependence. Reflecting on the common good in light of this interdependence and its increasing complexity in the modern world (long before "globalization" made its way into everyday parlance), the Second Vatican Council, in *Gaudium et spes*, is instructive:

> As a result the common good . . . the sum conditions of social life which allow social groups and their individual members relatively thorough and ready access to their own fulfillment, today takes on an increasingly universal complexion and consequently involves rights and duties with respect to the whole human race. Every social group must take account of the needs and legitimate aspirations of other groups, and . . . the general welfare of the entire human family.[14]

While attending to the well-being of distinct communities, the common good has in fact gone global.[15] With enhanced movement of peoples, resources, information and, yes, epidemics like AIDS, our world becomes smaller and the opportunities for solidarity in the human community grow whether we take advantage of them or not. The aspirations of all peoples, particularly for humane living conditions and human flourishing, become the concern of all people of goodwill. The many linked causes of poverty and flourishing are brought to sharp relief in light of the common good.[16]

The conditions of social life are inextricably linked to basic human rights, as *Gaudium et spes* describes: "food, clothing, and shelter; the right to choose a state of life freely and to found a family, the right to education, to employment, to a good reputation, to respect, to appropriate information, to activity in accord with the upright norm of one's own conscience, to protection of privacy and rightful freedom, even in matters religious."[17] These rights are widely recognized and enshrined in the United Nations' Universal Declaration on Human Rights and form the basis for the UN's Millennium Development Goals so crucial to the fight against AIDS.[18] In contrast to the contemporary logic of free market capitalism, the common good recognizes that these conditions, these basic human needs, are only achieved through the cooperation of the many institutions of civil society.

The common good in the Catholic tradition has a number of distinctive features that bear highlighting. Grounded in individual human dignity, the common good cannot be reduced to a form of utilitarian calculus where the greatest good for the greatest number is achieved even at great cost to the few. The fruits of the common good belong to everyone, and the burdens of sacrifice, when sacrifice is required, are to be distributed according to the norms of justice. In an unjust world, women, people of color, those who are poor, the elderly, and children are asked repeatedly to assume burdens for the benefit of others. These benefits frequently flow only to the few, in positions of power and privilege, and to those who have mistaken their personal well-being for the common good. For example, while the market may have a role in the distribution of pharmaceutical, prophylaxis, and care resources, this role must be shaped by a commitment to justice tempered by an option for the poor and vulnerable. As research into effective treatment protocols, prevention measures, and vaccines continues in areas hardest hit by the pandemic, the scientific community must attend also to the exploitation of peoples in the developing world. At the very least, those with a share of the burdens of research, which must be commensurate with anticipated benefits, must share in the fruits of the research irrespective of any ability to pay.[19]

The common good includes but is not limited to the just distribution of the world's material and social resources. Constitutive of the common good for persons and communities is *participation*. All members of the local and global communities should be allowed and encouraged to participate in creating the goods of social life in accordance with their age and ability. Charitable initiatives will continue to play a vital role in meeting the needs of communities impacted by the pandemic, but to the extent that they perpetuate relationships in which one party "has" and "gives" to the party that "has not" and "receives," these initiatives will fail to realize relationships of solidarity striving toward mutuality where the voices, talents, and unique resources of all are heard and recognized.

The common good calls us to think and act beyond private goods and goals. While we need not abandon these pursuits altogether, they must be understood in light of the goods and goals of the community. Participation of those who are poor and most vulnerable in determining these goods reflects the general axiom that what is good for one will be good for all, and what is good for all will be good for the one; this participation demands that any pursuit of an individual desire be made with regard to others. Moreover, some of those with power and privilege neglect to recognize that their success was achieved with the help of (many) others; this neglect is intolerable. Limits on the pursuit of private goods for some are necessary for the advancement of the basic means of flourishing for all.

What then are the implications for this rich tradition in the context of HIV/AIDS? Human flourishing requires nutrition, security, health care, education, and access to needed information, as well as basic freedom to follow one's conscience. The implications for HIV prevention were illustrated well by the contributors to *Catholic Ethicists on HIV/AIDS Prevention*. Education about HIV is crucial if we are to advance successful programs and reduce the stigma that still shadows the disease. Information must be accurate and conveyed in ways that realize practical effects on behalf of those infected with and affected by HIV/AIDS. The requirement that all people have access to the goods necessary for flourishing demands also that the Christian community challenge those practices and institutions that leave people on the margins.

This book moves toward widespread participation by incorporating many voices often pushed to the margins, namely, the voices of women. The exclusions that arise from gross gender inequality must be redressed. Moreover, women are often marginalized in the theological disciplines of the academy and the pastoral leadership of the Church; an adequate Christian response to HIV/AIDS will not emerge without them. Again, the common good makes clear that full participation requires certain social, economic, and political conditions. This level of participation will not become a reality if the basic infrastructures of health care and education are undermined or left in ruins. Public health is a global common good. Public health crises like AIDS highlight our common human vulnerability and the ways in which this vulnerability is exacerbated in the contexts of poverty, gender inequality, and political instability—contexts wherein the common good is destabilized. The pursuit of public health and human flourishing more generally will only be successful when everyone is involved.

Preferential Option for the Poor

The Church has taken to heart and to the streets the *aggiornamento* of the work of the Second Vatican Council to read and interpret the "signs of the times" in light of the gospel and to carry the message "especially to those who are poor or afflicted in any way."[20] Following this mandate, Paul VI called for action on the urgent needs of equitable development among the peoples and nations of the world. In *Populorum progressio* (1967), recognizing the great strides of the twentieth century for human weal, the signs of the times are read, interpreted, and exposed as so many unjust structures and policies that thwart the progress of peace and the dignity of all peoples; alternately, Paul VI reminds us that the gospel challenges the faithful to stand in solidarity and identify with those who are materially poor so all will prosper and thrive. As these teachings provide the impetus to action in the modern world, the members of the Conference of Bishops in Latin America (CELAM) moved forward and committed themselves to solidarity and justice for those who are poor.[21] Within ten years of their 1968 conference in Medellín, Colombia, the theology of liberation developed a more systematic consideration of the "preferential option for the poor" that had only been hinted at earlier. This engaged critical theological reflection on concrete pastoral realities and the concerns of those most affected by injustice. By the CELAM meeting in Puebla, Mexico, in 1979, this preferential option was raised as a central axis for any discussion by the Church on the questions of justice the gospel demands.[22]

Although the Vatican hierarchy did not always agree with the direction CELAM took regarding the more left-leaning politics of some liberation theologies, the insight of God's affection for those who are marginalized took effect. In particular, the identification of those who are marginalized today with those who were marginalized in Jesus' time gave theological power to the Vatican's vigilant concern for relief of the suffering that accompanies poverty and its co-morbid conditions, especially the poverty that results from the exploitation of some over others. Moreover, liberation theology gave voice to the Church's political will for justice in our day.

What does this option look like? This preference does not suggest that God's affection for those who are poor relieves the responsibility to provide succor where it is lacking. It is not God's will that some shall be poor and suffer in this life while others batten on spoil. Rather, this affection has at least three causes: First, among the people of the world who know God, those who know God best are most dependent upon and grateful for God's comfort. Those who are poor cannot (and do not) depend upon the largesse of the wealthy, for them God's care is steadfast and sure. Second, those who are poor, vulnerable, and otherwise marginalized have keen insight into the assignment, use, and abuse of power. Third, among the people whom God could have chosen to dwell, God chose to be incarnated among the *anawim*, not the mighty, of Palestine. These causes demand a response from the rich faithful on behalf of and with those who are poor to stop the violent exercise of power over others. Concretely, this response gives preference to the poor in meeting the demands of justice for food, clothing, shelter, education, and health care, and it gives way to an epistemological privilege that empowers moral agency[23] among those brought low everywhere on account of the social and personal sins, for example, of complacence, private wealth, and supremacist structures and systems of oppression.

This option for the poor is inextricably linked to solidarity. Taking the theme of CI on globalizing solidarity and preferencing those who are marginalized even at the margins, people caring for someone or who are themselves living with HIV or AIDS would require that—regardless of sero-status—everyone the world throughout stands with and for everyone the world throughout infected with and affected by HIV/AIDS. Globalizing solidarity requires a rejection of the personal and social sins that have divided the human family and more. When solidarity is coupled with both the preferential option and epistemological privilege of the poor, every individual is honored with the respect due to persons as sisters and brothers of the one human family, the goods of the earth and of human hands are distributed according to need and the common good of peoples, and the children of oppression lead. Moreover, this globalizing solidarity is inextricably linked to the Church, the Body of Christ, and the preferences and privileges of those who, like Christ, stand before a power greater than themselves and triumph over evil likewise.

How then can the preferences and privileges of those infected with and affected by HIV/AIDS take root and bear the fruit of liberation if not by the means of globalizing solidarity? The theme of the 2007 World AIDS Day, "Take the Lead. Stop AIDS. Keep the Promise," and the ongoing work of CI can help. The globalizing solidarity movement is a local movement with global ramifications; CI continues to respond to the pandemic by providing information and educational programs; promoting the work of Caritas and other faith-based organizations and national and international relief efforts; advocating for comprehensive laws, policies, and access to health care, treatment, and prevention; and rejecting stigma and discrimination.[24] To the extent that CI cooperates with international agencies, the mobilization of the international community against HIV witnesses that solidarity has taken effect. The next step in realizing justice will be to locate efforts that have asked and followed—preferenced and privileged—those who are both marginalized and most vulnerable to HIV. How ought local, regional, national, and international communities proceed to relieve your burdens and those of others infected with and affected by HIV/AIDS?

Beyond This Text:
Regions Absent from Consideration

As noted, this collection of essays has shortcomings, one of which can be remedied only on the surface by a woman born, raised, and educated in the United States. While it may be more honest to leave this shortcoming untouched, to the extent the collection represents collaboration among Catholic women authors who stand in solidarity with and for our sisters and brothers throughout the world, the globalizing agenda of our efforts includes the justice demands to recognize those who are absent, even when their own voices, experiences, and needs remain unrecorded here. The one remedy, itself flawed and limited, is consideration of the reach of the pandemic to China, Japan, Eastern Europe, Central Asia, Central and South America, Hispaniola, the Middle East, Arab League and North Africa.

China

In a country of 1.32 billion people, China leads the world in population. (India is second with 1.13 billion, and the USA is third with 303 million.)[25] Contrary to what one might think given these statistics, the rate of HIV infection in China is relatively low, with 650,000 people reported.[26] This number represents a mere 0.5 percent of China's population. Unlike most countries and perhaps owing to its size, a predominantly nonindustrialized economy, and a widely dispersed population, most infection occurs in rural areas.

The overwhelming causes of infection in China are needle sharing among and sexual relations with injecting drug users (IDUs) who are HIV-positive. China reports an alarming rate of IDU in 2,148 of its 2,863 counties. A 2002 count by the National Narcotic Control Commission shows a one-year increase of 11 percent to over 1 million people then registered as drug users (50 percent of these registered drug users are IDUs and 50 percent of these share needles). To thwart further spread of HIV, China initiated its drug registration and needle exchange programs in 1999. Nevertheless, while silence and stigma surround illicit drug use, an unsuspecting population has been put at risk: the "dragon" of China is awake and spreading its fire through ignorance of the dangers of heroin use, needle sharing, and unprotected sexual relations.[27] As could be predicted, once IDUs become infected, transmission soon results from unprotected heterosexual and homosexual relations.[28]

Women in China are vulnerable to HIV for many of the same reasons as women elsewhere: poverty and lack of access to education and health care. Although China has instituted a number of prevention and treatment programs, and to good effect, many women remain outside the reach of government-inspired "Four Frees One Care" and "Face-to-Face" media campaigns.[29] Many women have been caught off-guard with respect to the risks of unprotected sex.

Japan

In a country of 127,433,500 people, Japan ranks tenth in world population. As in China, the rate of HIV infection in Japan is low, with approximately 17,000 living with HIV or AIDS, representing 0.1 percent of the general population. The predominant cause of infection is related to commercial sex workers, submissive demeanor of women to men, and a lack of prevention education programs for young people.[30] Others claim that "official apathy is [to be blamed] for much of Japan's situation."[31]

Health experts in Japan are concerned that prevalence of HIV/AIDS could increase dramatically in the next few years as the result of a lucrative sex trade that is estimated at $13 billion annually (Japan is on a Tier 2 Watch List for sex slavery),[32] inconsistent or no use of condoms, little government support of programs to increase risk awareness, more risky sexual behavior among teens and young adults, and the generally lower status of women in traditional Japanese culture. Heterosexual contact leads HIV transmission factors, with male homosexual contact a close second; IDU is a distant and nominal factor (most illicit drugs used in Japan are inhalants).[33] Non-Japanese migrant nationals working as day laborers or as part of the sex industry account for more than 71 percent of all HIV cases in Japan.

Women in Japan, regardless of their nationality, are at greater risk of infection than men as a result of cultural constructions of gendered power and poverty-relief attempts through commercial sex trades. With a culture of institutionalized paternalism, the people of Japan depend upon their government to protect them.[34] Unfortunately, their government has not prioritized HIV,[35] little money has been allocated to develop adequate responses to thwart infection, and nonprofit work is just beginning to impact social affairs. The media underreport HIV, owing to cultural perceptions of propriety[36] and AIDS-related stigma; HIV is usually considered to be someone else's problem.

Eastern Europe and Central Asia

While hesitant to group these regions, I follow the lead of UNAIDS but report only on the Russian Federation, Ukraine, and Uzbekistan. Covering a geographic region larger than any other nation, and with 143,450,000 people, the Russian Federation ranks eighth in world population; among other Eastern European nations where HIV prevalence is high, Ukraine ranks twenty-sixth in world population, with 46,300,000 people. Though the number of new cases remains stable, the largest epidemic in Central Asia and the most alarming increase of incidence in one year belongs to Uzbekistan, forty-second in world population, with 27,780,000 people. Why these three countries? Because in the population of these three countries alone (approximately 217 million), close to 2 million people, 1 percent of the population, live with HIV or AIDS,[37] the near arithmetic, *not geometric*, equivalent of the approximate total for North America, Western Europe, and Central Europe combined. (This total is more than 850 million people, with 2.1 million to 3 million—or 0.3 percent—living with HIV or AIDS.) Of new infections in 2005, 62 percent can be attributed to IDU and 37 percent to unprotected heterosexual intercourse. Poverty and a lack of meaningful employment are clearly a driving force behind these numbers.[38]

It is difficult to envision a way out of this trend except through combined national and international efforts to rehabilitate the economy through job creation, which would very likely reduce recourse to drugs and imprisonment.[39] Young people are especially at risk: with dismal prospects for employment, high secondary school dropout rates, increased sexual activity, and IDU, young people between 15 and 29 account for most new cases of HIV and other STDs.[40] By most appearances, Eastern Europe and Central Asia attribute the concentration of HIV to IDUs and to prisoners or former inmates; what they underreport is heterosexual transmission that often follows if not accompanies IDU. Complicating these conclusions is an unreliable monitoring system, especially regarding commercial sex work, migration, and homosexual transmission. Where governments provide some services for people with HIV, "these services are compromised by inadequate quality, a lack of confidentiality, and widespread discrimination and stigma."[41]

Women comprise 40 percent of East European and Central Asian people living with HIV. With an alarming increase of infection through heterosexual intercourse, mother-to-child transmission has also increased.[42] Like their male counterparts, many women lack sustainable employment; they resort to commercial or informal sex work and succumb to IDU and needle sharing.[43] Without a stable economy, even to the extent that some will not become themselves IDUs, women who have sex with HIV-positive men—former prisoners, IDUs, or new partners or sex customers[44]—remain vulnerable. Overall, HIV in Eastern Europe and Central Asia represents the failure of governments to respond appropriately to increased migration and the social, political, and economic upheavals that have unfolded over the past twenty years.[45]

Central America, South America, and the Caribbean

In a region that accounts for more than 568 million people,[46] estimates from Latin America (Central and South America and the Caribbean) indicate that between 1.6 million and 2.5 million people live with HIV[47]—a prevalence of between 0.3 percent and 0.45 percent of the total population. Surveillance depends upon the cooperation of 28 offices reporting to the Pan American Health Organization (PAHO), which works to monitor and improve health and living standards of people in the Americas.[48] The predominant route of transmission occurs with the commercial sex trade, and unprotected heterosexual and homosexual intercourse.

The World Bank identifies four social conditions contributing to the progress of HIV in Latin America: poverty and unequal gender relationships, political and economic instability, stigma and discrimination, and a lack of prevention programs.[49] As in Eastern Europe and Central Asia, the epidemic in Latin America is driven by forces beyond the control of many of the regions' governments. In almost all countries of Latin America, where economic conditions contribute to a highly mobile though not necessarily migrant population (e.g., the transportation industry), heterosexual routes of transmission are high and must be the first order of concern in prevention and treatment efforts.[50]

HIV in Latin America is concentrated, as elsewhere, in socially marginalized populations, with women disproportionately among them.[51] The vast majority of Latin American women with HIV suffer from social stigma and discrimination: they are fired from their jobs, often find themselves managing family dynamics and care of their children, and have limited access to health care and medicine.[52] To the extent that *machismo*—with its sexually active heterosexual and bisexual men, male prowess, and the imposition of gendered role expectations—compounds marginalization, wives and sex workers are left to engage in unprotected sex with their husbands and clients with HIV.[53] Even while HIV incidence is stable in Latin America, that stability reflects a persistent threat that the epidemic will continue until the silence surrounding male-to-male sex followed by male-to-female sex and the stigma associated with other high-risk behaviors are exposed.

An Additional Word about Hispaniola

Sadly, like the political and economic destabilization of Eastern Europe, the poverty of rural Africa, and the persistent threat or presence of military conflict, war, and economic collapse in the Muslim world, the conditions endured by the people of Hispaniola contribute to the spread of HIV.[54] Haiti is not only the poorest nation in the Western hemisphere,[55] but combined with its neighbor on the island of Hispaniola, the Dominican Republic, it has the largest number of people with HIV in the hemisphere, with 210,000 to

270,000 out of more than 17 million people.[56] The dominant mode of transmission is heterosexual intercourse originating with commercial sex work. (The incidence of transmission in tourist destinations—in Haiti, Port-au-Prince, in the Dominican Republic, La Romana—remains troubling[57]). Young girls and women are particularly at risk of sexual assault.[58] Stigma is very strong and remains a challenge in Haiti both in reference to people with HIV and to the taboo of men having sex with men. Although recent US reports[59] trace HIV prevalence in the Western hemisphere to Haiti, it is no more likely that one Haitian was responsible for HIV in the West than "Patient Zero" was responsible for the pandemic.[60] Along with other academics, we reject this most recent smear of the people of Haiti.[61]

The Middle East, the Arab League, and North Africa

Almost 470 million people[62] live in a region extending from southwestern Asia to North Africa (Iran, Iraq, Turkey, Syria, Lebanon, Israel and Palestine, Jordan, Saudi Arabia, Yemen, Oman, United Arab Emirates, Qatar, Bahrain, Kuwait, Cyprus, Egypt, Algeria, Libya, Mauritania, Morocco, Tunisia, Sudan).[63] More than 380,000 people and as many as 720,000[64] in the region have HIV; these figures represent 35,000 to 67,000 new cases of infection in 2006 alone[65]—an increase of 300 percent.[66] With an inadequate surveillance system and an even less reliable system of monitoring populations at higher risk, the region lacks a methodology to track trends that could inform prevention and treatment programs.[67]

Despite the lack of a comprehensive surveillance program, regional trends identify unprotected heterosexual intercourse and IDU as causes of transmission; conclusive data on men who have sex with men is not to be found, as stigma associated with this reality among the cultures of the region persists.[68] Extreme stigma marginalizes people with HIV, prevents many from learning their sero-status, and sends others underground.[69] As Sandy Sufian says, "In a few countries in the region, people living with HIV/AIDS are placed in quarantine compounds far away from the general population."[70] Factors contributing to the recent explosion of infection include political, economic, and social instability, and an increase in the movement of people seeking safety and overall better living conditions.[71] Additionally, given the relatively new access that Arab countries have to global media and economic influences,[72] "with their young populations, unresolved political conflicts, slow-growing economies, stressed or crumbling health infrastructures, gender inequalities, population mobility and shared borders with high-prevalence regions like Central Asia and sub-Saharan Africa,"[73] this region was at risk and succumbed, as the 300 percent increase in cases demonstrates.

Perhaps more than in any other part of the world, the women of this region are silent.[74] Much of this silence is culturally imposed, and, as Dr. Suman Mehta warns, that "not a single [woman] is coming forward to say 'I am HIV-positive' says something about the fear, the scare, the discrimination and stigma attached to AIDS."[75] Women are vulnerable as a result of their lower status in society and the legal sanctions that enshrine the "patriarchal notion that women's bodies and sexuality belong not to themselves, but to their families *and society*."[76] The bodies of women are violated by marital rape, early marriages, and temporary marriages; public discussion is prohibited on sexual orientation, premarital and extramarital sexuality, honor crimes, female genital mutilation, unmarried mothers, adolescent sexuality, unwanted pregnancies and safe abortion; and taboos around women's sexuality maintain the structures supporting these violations.[77] Additionally, the behaviors that place most people at risk, like IDU, commercial sex work, and sex between men, continue in the region without recognition, surveillance, or programs that could protect them. Nevertheless, a Middle East–North Africa regional workshop on sexual and bodily rights as human rights[78] organized by the Coalition for Sexual and Bodily Rights in Muslim Societies[79] and Women for Women's Human Rights-New Ways[80] recognized sexual autonomy as part of the core of human rights, affirming that neither women's equality nor their empowerment can be realized unless their sexual and bodily rights are theirs alone.

Conclusion

With more than twenty-five years having passed since the medical community's recognition of the start of the rapid spread of HIV, the situation has reached pandemic proportions. While the term *pandemic* is often reserved for outbreaks of influenza, malaria, cholera, or the plague on account of the virulence and a geographically wide-reaching death toll, with the worldwide persistence of HIV and the demographic trends that now place all people at risk, few question today the pandemic status of HIV. And where a pandemic asserts itself, there the medical, social, political, cultural, and religious communities must respond ever more forcefully and effectively to thwart stigma and discrimination, to provide treatment and care, and to consider prevention programs protecting their immediate populations from infection and their next generation from the loss of siblings, parents, aunts, uncles, and grandparents. AIDS ranks as the fourth-leading cause of death worldwide (trailing only cancer, ischemic heart disease, and stroke, and trailed by tuberculosis, traffic accidents, malaria, and other infectious diseases).[81] The World Health Organization (WHO) projects the global number of deaths from AIDS will increase from 2.8 million annually to 6.5 million by 2030; this projection assumes that by 2012 80 percent of people with HIV will be receiving antiretroviral drug treatment. The Catholic tradition stands in prophetic witness, as do the voices of the contributors to this book. May others too hear and heed the call for globalizing solidarity and justice throughout the world.

M. Bernadette Mbuy Beya, CSU, with Jeanne Bluekens

Translated from the French by Philip Revell, CFX

Show Me My Face, O Lord

The prayer that the Lord will "show me my face" is in itself sufficient motivation to work on HIV/AIDS prevention and to care not on the level of theory but with concrete propositions that enable African women to stand up for their rights. The era of mere observation is behind us. As members of the Circle of Concerned African Women Theologians (CCAWT) who have worked with women for almost twenty years, we believe it is time to mobilize; otherwise, in the age of HIV/AIDS, we risk our own death.

With humility gained from our experiences as befrienders and companions of people in difficult circumstances, we share these experiences with you in the hope that they will echo in your hearts and the hearts of our sisters and brothers in distress.[1]

The Way of Prayer

The CCAWT is noted for numerous studies on sexuality and the violence that is inflicted upon African women. Six years ago one study explored the needs of women in the peace process. Recently the two of us examined the sufferings of women displaced by the war in the interior of our country, the Democratic Republic of Congo (DR Congo). We listened to stories that were both awful and revolting. The women and their daughters had been infected with HIV by military personnel and other armed men intent on decimating our people. Worse still, many women had been forced to commit barbarous acts upon even their own children. These women were like the living dead and awaited only the ultimate destruction of their own being that would come with the fatal symptoms of AIDS.

The context of ignorance and misery from the absolute poverty and low living standards among the population encourages the spread of HIV and the subsequent growing number of AIDS orphans. Additionally, sexuality continues to pose a problem both for greater access to education and to influence life-choices that must be made in the face of certain death. If the population cannot feed itself, how is it going to find the means to treat AIDS patients?

Concerned for our people, we choose to accompany and befriend, in prayer and in the celebration of life, women suffering from HIV or AIDS and those women who have lost someone close to them from AIDS. We remain involved in the name of Jesus Christ, who calls us to go beyond ourselves and our personal limitations. Our action is a stand for justice. We have been appalled at and must respond to the distressing treatment of women by certain so-called men of God, who inflict upon their "clients" a gospel that, rather than liberating, scandalously drives them to deny the faith of their childhood. The victim-clients of these men are subjected to processes of illusory healing, painful divisions, and hatred toward those whom these men claim are "witches" and "sorcerers" within their own families. Nevertheless, many people are attracted to these charlatans in hope of finding some strength to carry on to the end.

Fortunately, not all faith communities are so troubling. An association called "Women and AIDS" has succeeded in breaking down certain taboos and has managed to call the illness by its name. Women and AIDS helps those who are infected to fight against passivity and to prepare with courage and sensibility the future for their orphans "to be." As a result, we have seen women finish the construction of a house started by or with a now deceased husband.

"Show me my face" is a prayer addressed to the Lord by a sick woman or by one who is confronted with the imminent death of a loved one. "Show me my face" proclaims the search for truth on the part of the African woman who not only believes but who dares to address God as Mother. She knows that, for God, suffering and death do not have the last word. Faced with the suffering that preoccupies us, the attitude of non-Africans is somewhat different. In Belgium and other European countries they speak about euthanasia. Yet Africa, despite precarious means of survival, continues to struggle admirably to ensure survival; euthanasia is no option for us.

Thus, our prayer, published here for the first time, continues:

> Show me my face, O Lord, the one you gave to me the very day when you called me into life. Let me once more touch the fringe of your coat, for it is time that I find once more the passion and joy of living for and in spite of everything![2]

Someone to Love

"There is no greater love than this, to give one's life for another" (John 15:13). This Gospel illuminates the following testimony given by a fiancée in the form of a prayer to her betrothed, Emmanuel:

Lord, I love Emmanuel and he loves me. I am so happy to be chosen
when so many others hoped for him. When I think of him I am happy
to obey you and to give him all my life. What can I do about all the distrust which surrounds us? My parents talk about HIV tests before hearing of anything else. Emmanuel wants me to give myself to him as proof
of my love. If I refuse him this gift I risk losing him, and that would be
serious for me. Is the fear of AIDS stronger than love? Even if he is sero-
positive, hasn't he got a right to love?

Lord, why did you create love and ask us to love one another? Love
is becoming a weight, and I don't know what to do. Haven't I got the
right to make something of my life?

How can we respond to this sincere request? We can look to God's invitation and care:

See, I place before you today life and happiness, death and sorrow. . . .
Choose life in loving Yahweh and in obeying his Law (Deut 30:15–16).

Happy the [woman] who finds [her] pleasure in the law of the Lord.
[She] is like a plant beside the water which gives its fruit in due season
and whose leaves never fade (Ps 1:2–3).[3]

Indeed, life is the most beautiful gift that God has given us. From this gift we
can choose the best means to hand that life over to another and to be a source
of life for others.

My Husband Is Ill

Here is another testimony that summarizes the situation of the majority of
wives whose husbands are infected by HIV or have AIDS:

Lord, here I am before you, poor and unhappy because my husband has
been ill for months. The doctors tell me they can find nothing, but between
themselves they consult constantly. My family is nervous and has called
the pastor, who comes to pray and chase away the demons. He and his disciples cry out and scream as if to wake the Lord! But nothing changes, so
they asked us to find out who in the family has cast this fate upon him.

Lord! I have given all so that my husband can be cured. I have even
denied my faith because it was insufficient. But this evening, I have
learned the terrible truth. My husband's mistress has died from AIDS.
Everyone knew about my husband's illness, but nobody would talk to
me about it. So here I am confronted horribly with death. Why has Gerard done this to us, why has he brought death into the family? And me,
what have I done to deserve this?

Lord! I know it's not for me to judge my husband, and really I have
no time to waste thinking about death. We have seven children; the
youngest is only five. All our children want to live! At a very young age
I abandoned my studies in favor of my brothers. My husband is the only
support for his family, the only one to earn a living, as he says. He has
started to build a house for us, but now he is going to leave us with a
building site.

Lord! Give me the strength to fight for the life of my children. If I
have been infected, give me the time to leave something as a decent
inheritance for them. Do not let me waste my time in useless mourning!

Faced with similar suffering, the psalmist responds:

> To Yahweh, my cry, I plead.
> To Yahweh, my cry, I entreat.
> I pour out my supplications.
> I unfold all my troubles, my spirit fails within me
> but you, O Lord, know my path.
> On the path I follow they have concealed a trap.
> Look on my right and see, there is no one who takes my part.
> All help is denied to me, no one cares about me.
> I call to you, Lord, you alone are my refuge,
> my heritage in the land of the living,
> listen to my cries for help
> and I will thank your name once more in the assembly of the virtuous
> for the goodness you show me. (Ps 142)

The Prostitute

Since 1989 we have had close contacts with prostitutes in the town of Lubumbashi. Extreme poverty is the principal cause of this prostitution, all-too-often
practiced in spite of personal intentions.[4] The poignant suffering of Nicole,
whose story is presented in the form of her prayer, illustrates this paradox:

Lord! Everything started with an incurable cough. Now I am getting
thinner and I have pains all over my body. After lots of comings and
goings between my family and the hospital, I realized that no one could
do anything for me; on the contrary, everyone turns away from me. The
medical personnel put on their gloves when it is a question of treating
me, and I can sense the fear in those who approach me. What is this illness which makes the world so afraid? Given the life I lead, it could be
AIDS! But none of my friends have it. I've been generous to everyone.
The money I earned, I shared. I paid for my brothers and sisters to study.

I bought food for all the family. What then have I done to deserve this fate? And then, all the clients who used to run after me, where have they disappeared to? I couldn't have gotten this illness all alone. Why should I be the only one to have to face shame and death?

A friend, the only one who had the courage to be sincere, introduced me to the association Women Against AIDS. It's there that I got all the explanations about the illness. My first reaction was for vengeance: I couldn't die alone. How long have I got yet to live? At all costs I wanted to make other victims.

After long weeks of agony, my mother finally understood that the illness was serious. I wasn't just physically ill—my whole being was sick! In desperation my mother decided to send me to a charismatic prayer group. They were so good and welcoming that I began to understand that I was lovable and that alone was worth their putting themselves out for me—me, who had sold charm nonstop! After the revulsion came praise, and I started to witness for the team that concerned itself with prevention of sexually transmitted diseases. I know that I'm going to die, but I have decided to go with dignity without leaving troubles after me. The best way to express what I feel now is in the words of Psalm 40:

> I waited for the Lord
> and now at last he has stooped to me and heard my cry for help.
> He has pulled me out from the horrible pit,
> out of the slough of the marsh,
> has settled my feet on a rock and steadied my steps.
> He has put a new song into my mouth,
> a song to praise our God,
> dread will seize many at the sight
> and they will put their trust in the Lord. (Ps 40:1–3)

Lord! Today I go forward in life happy to know that you love me so much. All those who deride me and point at me, to them you say, "Let him among you who is without sin cast the first stone" (John 8:7). I know, Lord, that no one can face me and throw the stone, and that you say to me once more, "Go, and sin no more" (John 8:11). Yes, Lord, I feel at home in the steps of Mary Magdalene, the sinner forgiven, or yet again following the Samaritan woman, of whom you asked water to drink.

Although Nicole has committed the common error of identifying Mary Magdalene as the woman caught in adultery, that the Magdalene was a woman from whom Jesus cast seven demons brings a certain intimacy and forgiveness that belies the patriarchal limits to women's personal agency even while it places them at risk. Nicole understands now that she was an object of exploitation and of derision for others in her society. But the grace of God has refashioned her into a new being.

My Daughter Is Sick

Joan is twenty-five and has been married for two years. At the birth of her first child she showed symptoms of excessive tiredness, and since then she has never felt well. Her mother has tried everything to get her treated with traditional medicine and at the hospital. The doctors have spoken about "multi-therapy"; the poor mother doesn't even know what that means. Everything in RD Congo is in short supply, the country having been mired in wars since 1996. Workers go for months without pay, basic foodstuffs go short, electricity and water are cut off for certain clients for long-term nonpayment. How do you pay for multi-therapy? Joan's mother has broken down. Her prayer is a cry from her innermost being. She screams out her pain. She fears no one:

> Lord! My daughter is condemned. All you politicians and you who struggle for power, tell me what I can do for my daughter. Do your politics bring us a better life? Are the people happy to have you as our leaders? What are you going to do about all those who fall dead in front of you every day? What are you going to do about those evil creatures, those who rape and pillage? You who import porno films and let children into your cinemas, tell me what are the values that we can impart to our children? You who use children under ten for your pleasure to avoid AIDS infection when you yourself are ill, tell me what sort of inheritance are we going to leave to our children, yours and mine? Would you be proud to be pointed out by your children? Today, I am deaf to your speeches because my daughter is ill, perhaps because of you. I want her to get better; at least I want her not to suffer so much.
>
> Lord! Do you remember the woman who suffered a hemorrhage for twelve years and did everything to be able to touch the hem of your garment?[5]
>
> Look, I have been losing blood for nearly forty years! I live in a country that is supposed to be one of the richest in the world. Hardly had power been put into the hands of the nation when a new class began to emerge—that of the all-powerful rich, who had stolen our riches with the complicity of those who kept them in power for their own benefit. Mobutu was unmovable as far as the Western world was concerned; for us he was a catastrophe. This is the history of my people, my family and my daughter who is trembling here beside me on a

mat. This is the story of my blood, which runs and flows without stopping! I run toward you, Lord.

> I lift my eyes to the mountains, from where shall come my help?
> My help shall come from the Lord who made heaven and earth.
> Let him sleep not your guard.
> You cover me with your shadow,
> let the sun not strike me by day nor the moon in the night.
> Lord keep me from evil, save my life.
> Keep guard over me, watch over me in the night,
> that I may never betray you. (Ps 121)

My Wife Is Dead

Though women are our primary interest, there are also men who suffer alone. We met with one of them, our friend Daniel. His wife, Gloria, died of AIDS. Daniel remembers her:

Gloria was the mother of my children; I say "was," because four years ago she died. It took me time to realize that she was really gone. The last years of her life were really awful. Gloria started to become ill after a miscarriage. She bled white, and the hospital gave her a lot of blood to save her. Strangely, she did not get better. She continued to get worse, and the hospital had me going round in circles because no one could find the cause. We did the rounds of healers without result. We were at the end of our strength when a friend took us to a charismatic group where we found the strength to continue to live with our "cross." The Lord gave us a new family, a new source of support until her death. Since we continued to go to the hospital, life at the house became impossible for Gloria and for our four children. I could not always be beside my wife because I had to work to support our needs. So I called upon my mother-in-law. She came willingly, but after certain people had spoken to her she thought it better to take my wife to her home. Thus it was that Gloria died out of the hospital and away from her family after having taken all sorts of medicines.

Before Gloria died I went to see the doctor, wanting him to tell me the truth. He couldn't do it. Rather, he got a Sister friend to undertake the difficult task of telling me. Gloria was infected with HIV. The Sister asked me to take courage and have the test so that we would know where I stood alongside Gloria. The day of the results, the Sister accompanied me. We cried for joy like fools when it was pronounced that I was not infected. Gloria was an angel up to the end of her life. She protected me for our children. However, another source of suffering for me was to put up with the looks from friends. I couldn't explain to everyone how my wife became ill, and moreover I had no means of bringing a case against the hospital. I've been pointed at, been the object of suspicion, and I have been in the depths of depression till today.

So in the light of all that, I pray with the psalmist:

> Lord, in you alone is my shelter.
> I shall not be ashamed.
> In your justice free me, save me,
> turn your ear toward me and hasten to me.
> Be for me a rock of strength, for my rock it is you;
> for your name's sake lead me and guide me.
> Rescue me from the snare they have laid before me,
> for you are my strength;
> into your hands I commit my spirit, for it is you who saves me. (Ps 31:1–5)

Prayer for Healing

Each one of us carries the burdens and blessings of our life story. Although we have not always been conscious of it, we have been wounded in one way or another since our birth. We might say that each of the different people presented in this essay corresponds to one or another of our personal tragedies. And we may add to the prayer that began the essay a petition for pardon and peace.

> Lord! I come before you that you may look upon my life to heal me and breathe a new spirit in me. Send forth your Spirit, Lord, and we shall be created and you will renew the face of the earth. I know that the journey of healing wounds takes us through pardon and reconciliation with ourselves and with others. Give me, Lord, a clear vision of myself and my life story. Show me my face, O Lord.

Conclusion

Let us reread the Beatitudes (Matt 5:3–9) not as passive acceptance of life but as an invitation to struggle, that happiness might be a reality for all.

Happy are the poor in spirit. Can poverty be praised? No. Poverty diminishes the life of human beings, causes alienation, and must be fought by all means. The only poverty that merits praise is that which brings us to God and others in truth, helps us recognize our limits, and pushes us to find a way through the injustices of exploitation, alienation, and shame so that we will see our face.

Happy are the gentle. Jesus does not call us to let things be; otherwise he would not have whipped the merchants from the temple. The gentleness in question for us is our welcoming attitude, our attentive listening to those who are suffering. Women have a great capacity to respond to this call. Insofar as we are a source of life, as those who bring forth new life in and through our bodies, we will receive an ever greater life. "I have come that they may have life and have it in abundance" (John 10:10).

Happy are those who suffer. The suffering of African women pains us as sisters everywhere suffer vulnerability. Our struggle is that one day we shall stand in solidarity to face our lives more successfully and without risk of losing ourselves. It is a grace to suffer with those who suffer and to feel with them. Consider these words from John Littleton's song "Mon Ami": "When you are frightened, it is me who trembles."[6]

Happy are the pure in heart. Who can boast of being without sin? The one who is pure is the one who serves God with all the heart. To fall is the lot of humanity, but Jesus offers us everyday a new opportunity to take hold of ourselves and begin anew. Even from the bottom of the pit, the pure of heart can see that the face the Lord shows is their own.

These testimonies, expressed in the form of prayers, are but a starting point for a richer reflection and a deepening of our liturgical traditions. These traditions will be enriched when women are empowered, and they will take into account the particularities of this time of AIDS. When our liturgies fail these times, it is we, as women theologians, who can give some soul to them. We have the capacity to bring the love and the compassion of God to all and especially to those who are suffering. We have prayed that you "show me my face, O Lord" and found our prayer fulfilled in the faces of our sisters and brothers infected with and affected by HIV and AIDS.

Part One

Challenges to Justice

Lisa Sowle Cahill

AIDS, Women, and Empowerment

This essay views AIDS from the standpoint of the empowerment of people most affected and its crushing effects on families and communities. Just as socially, economically, and politically disadvantaged women are most vulnerable to AIDS, so enhancement of women's social, economic, and political resources enables women to cope with these threats. Given the right support systems, especially economic self-sufficiency, women can meet the challenges of HIV/AIDS courageously and effectively. Additionally, women's options must be considered within the larger context of communities and entire countries or regions suffering socioeconomic deprivation and lack of opportunity.

I write as a US theologian, scholar, and college professor with little personal experience with AIDS or economic disadvantage. However, like many from my context, I want greater solidarity with those in less privileged situations; it is a demand of the gospel, of Catholic social tradition, and of justice.[1] I have been in solidarity in a small personal way as a long-term result of the international adoption experience of my family, about which I will say more later. Beyond personal exposure, I believe that all of us fortunate enough to enjoy "first world" benefits have a *political* obligation to influence global policies and institutions so that these benefits are shared more inclusively. For Christians, this solidarity is also a *religious* obligation. It is important to understand as accurately as possible what policies are just and effective, and to be informed by concrete experience and evidence. Moreover, women—and all those affected by AIDS, economic inequities, or both—desire empowerment, not only solidarity; they desire sustainable self-sufficiency, not only charity.

I examine some facts about the spread of AIDS today and consider some reasons why donor aid is not very effective in empowering those affected by AIDS to reverse these trends. Then I look at some alternative uses of donor funds from the United States and other "first world" sources that could be more successful. A crucial element in devising better policies about how to implement solidarity at the concrete level is to help all affected by AIDS take control of their own situations and define their own futures.

Responding to AIDS is a matter of global justice, and the specifically Christian contribution is charity in the form of a preferential option for the poor.

This option is inspired by gospel values, but its potential appeal is not limited to Christians. In modern theories of justice, the essential equality of persons is central. Global support for justice as basic equality is reflected in movements for human rights and democratic political participation. All persons have rights to basic material and social needs, and just societies institutionalize respect for these rights and foster practices and policies that meet them.

Christ's concern for the outcast and the vulnerable inspires Christians to prioritize special regard for those least well-off; others recognize that justice requires special efforts to sustain and empower the most disadvantaged. All major religious traditions uphold ideals of compassion and of service to others. John Paul II offered "solidarity" as a bridge concept linking justice, charity, and compassion.[2] A social virtue, solidarity grounds a practical and lasting commitment to overcome structural sin. In order to know what justice, charity, and solidarity demand in relation to AIDS, the structural causes of AIDS, and the effect of AIDS on human needs, vulnerabilities, and rights must be understood.

The major route of transmission of HIV today is heterosexual sex. While the roles and power women have sexually in relation to men vary widely worldwide, women's relative lack of social power and resources is a factor contributing to the steady increase in the number of women living with HIV—now almost half (48 percent) of all adults. Teens and young adults account for 40 percent of new HIV infections, with girls and women disproportionately affected. In sub-Saharan Africa, three young women are infected for every young man. A recent report from the Henry J. Kaiser Family Foundation provides the following summary:

> Gender inequalities in social and economic status and in access to prevention and care services increase women's vulnerability to HIV. Sexual violence may also increase women's risk and women, especially young women, are biologically more susceptible to HIV infection than men. The epidemic has multiple effects on women including: added responsibilities of caring for sick family members; loss of property if they become widowed and/or infected; and even, violence when their HIV status is discovered.[3]

In 2005, there were an estimated 15.2 million AIDS orphans, 12 million living in sub-Saharan Africa. These children add to the responsibilities and burdens of women, especially in situations where the epidemic has already had devastating effects on the communities in which they live. AIDS is a serious challenge to stable economic and social function; it decimates the working-age population, cuts the number of teachers and health care workers, and creates an overwhelming demand for social services. Many nations hardest hit by AIDS are already suffering from food insecurity and civil conflict.[4]

The global response to AIDS has grown over the past two decades and includes several important new initiatives, including the UN Declaration of

Commitment on HIV/AIDS; the Global Fund to Fight AIDS, Tuberculosis, and Malaria; and the U.S. President's Emergency Plan for AIDS Relief (PEP-FAR). UNAIDS estimates that spending on AIDS rose from US$300 million in 1996 to $8.9 billion in 2006, and was projected to reach $10 billion in 2007. Yet at least twice that much is needed. Most funding comes from international donors, with the United States committing $4.6 billion for 2007, which ranks it only fifth compared to other wealthy country donors (rankings are based on the percentage of GNP donated). Affected country governments have also developed legislation, programs, and services.[5]

At its summit in June 2007, the Group of 8 pledged $60 billion to fight AIDS, tuberculosis, and malaria over the next several years. President George W. Bush has proposed contributing as part of this total around $30 billion from 2009 to 2013, a moderate increase in the current U.S. spending trajectory. The G8 aimed to bring five million patients in Africa within access to treatment by 2010—only about half of those projected to need it.[6]

Despite this surge in AIDS funding, the spread of AIDS and the social problems following in its wake are still out of control. Among the 12 high-prevalence countries in sub-Saharan Africa, only 12 percent of men and 10 percent of women have access to HIV testing, and only 11 percent of pregnant women with HIV have access to antiretroviral therapy (ART) to prevent transmission to their unborn children; only about a quarter of all those living with HIV have access to life-prolonging ART.[7] Infection and death rates continue to rise, communities and their ways of life and means of livelihood are undermined, and the effects on women and children are disastrous.

Beyond inadequate amounts of donor money, some public health analysts suggest that aid is not being spent in the most beneficial and effective ways. Specifically, donors target individual AIDS projects, but the funds do not have wide-ranging or long-lasting effects on communities, or on the ability of members to escape the burdens of disease and rebuild. Effective solidarity around the problems of AIDS cannot focus on one of the issues in isolation from multiple economic and social factors that create the prevalence of AIDS in the first place. Women in particular would have more capacity to resist HIV and to counter its effects if they had access to education, income-generating activities, and basic health and family services. But these prevention methods are lacking in what Paul Collier, former economist at the World Bank, has recently called "the bottom billion" of the five billion inhabitants of the developing world.[8] Seventy percent of this "bottom billion" lives in Africa, the continent hardest hit by AIDS and by economies plagued by continual civil war, poor governance, and corruption.

According to Laurie Garrett, most aid money is ineffectually applied—a point on which Paul Collier heartily agrees. Health funding is typically "'stovepiped' down narrow channels relating to a particular program or disease."[9] A government may receive money for an ART program for mothers and children in the capital but not have the flexibility to support basic health care or services for women and families in rural areas. Moreover, program money consigned to stand-alone projects fails to develop the basic health infrastructure. Yet a health infrastructure is precisely what is needed to provide local employment and retain the huge numbers of doctors, nurses, and other medical personnel who flee developing countries every year in search of decently paying jobs. The AIDS pandemic continues to be the primary mobilizer of global concern about health, though the top three killers in poor countries are maternal death around childbirth, and pediatric respiratory and intestinal infections, all of which would benefit by basic health care and improved standards of living. "But few women's rights groups put safe pregnancy near the top of their list of priorities," Garrett says, or target general economic conditions that put women at risk of becoming infected with HIV.[10]

As a more broad-based and community-building intervention, Garrett suggests the "Doc-on-a-Box" program devised by the Council on Foreign Relations: convert durable used shipping containers (the size of a small room) into portable clinics stocked with tools to combat infectious diseases. Each would be staffed by a paramedic and connected to nurses and doctors via wireless communication (provided there is electricity). Initial equipment and medications would be donated; clinics could operate under a franchise model, with supplies purchased in bulk from a central supplier, who would realize profits based on the quantity sold and the quality of services provided to local consumers. This model would expand low-cost, local health care while injecting the local economy with modest new opportunities.[11]

A similar model has been implemented by a U.S. foundation using donor funds to support nurses who open HealthStore franchises in Kenya. Conceived by a wealthy U.S. businessman who decided after a car accident that his Christian faith called him to do more, HealthStores reach rural areas with reliable, quality, low-cost medicines. They are seeded by a nonprofit organization that receives foreign aid and grants from the Kenyan government. The franchise chain (CFWshops Kenya) is now headed by a Kenyan director, Liza Kimbo.[12] The nonprofit provides franchise owners with low-interest loans for already low start-up costs (about US $1,700). The franchises ensure quality through uniform practices and suppliers, and aim for enough profits to support modest investments in the local economy. Charging about $0.50 per treatment, "HealthStore clinics offer nurses the potential to earn a safe, comfortable salary while serving their communities, helping to reverse the trend of 'brain drain' plaguing Africa."[13] One Nairobi HealthStore operates in Kibera, the largest slum in Africa, and is run by a nurse with an existing clinic who took advantage of the benefits the HealthStore franchise could offer her and her clients.

HealthStores or similar ventures attract the middle and lower-middle classes in countries affected by AIDS, not the poorest of the poor; some modest educational, economic, and social resources are necessary to open a franchise. Yet such businesses provide services to those lower on the economic ladder and have the potential to spin off auxiliary enterprises, such as patient transportation and food stalls, that could provide income to those with minimal resources. Health infrastructures and other types of economic development could and should move along all echelons of society.

An example of a higher-level intervention is a project of the Harvard Medical School Division of AIDS that, with grants of several million dollars from the Doris Duke Foundation, created a program at the University of Natal to expand the HIV/AIDS clinical research capacity in South Africa.[14] The binational program sponsors training, research, and collaborative efforts to enable South African clinical investigators to study the pathogenesis of AIDS, develop better drugs and treatment protocols, retain indigenous scientists and clinicians, and improve the South African medical, educational, and economic infrastructure. The program uses donor money to invest in Africa and Africans, and to build local capacity to deal creatively with problems.

An example of a more "grassroots" and more comprehensive model comes from a Christian women's organization in Uganda that partners with Western donors. It encourages community-networking and income-producing activity among the poorest, mostly women, in communities affected by AIDS. I became personally familiar with this organization as a result of the experiences of my family, which adopted three Thai children through Holt International Children's Services, a Christian agency headquartered in Eugene, Oregon. Founded to enable the adoption of Korean War orphans, Holt now provides family and children's services worldwide.

Our boys were born to women who were too poor to care for them and who were still unable to do so at the time the children were adopted, even with the offer of additional support from Holt. The boys spent their first few years in government-sponsored institutional care. International adoption is an excellent solution for children who cannot return to their birth families, and for whom adoptive families in their native land are unavailable. However, adoption is obviously not a just, comprehensive, long-term solution to the problems of poverty-related family disintegration.

In Thailand (and elsewhere), Holt affiliates provide family reunification and preservation programs, nutrition programs, and services for women with AIDS to enable families to stay together. Several years ago, Holt was approached by the head of a small Ugandan women-led nongovernmental organization, Action for Children, who requested donor assistance to serve women and families caring for AIDS orphans, mostly in very poor rural settings. In many cases, one adult, sometimes even a young teenager, is caring for several or more children (up to twenty), in a household that lacks sufficient income to provide basic nutrition, minimal health care, or school fees. Housing is often inferior, consisting of sheds, shacks, or temporary coverings. Eventually, Holt became a major donor to this organization. In January 2006, my husband Larry and I had the opportunity to travel with a Holt group to see for ourselves the incredible work of Action for Children.

The approach of Action for Children is community-based. Its essential aim is to help each head of household determine her own needs, then plan steps to achieve their fulfillment. A key step is access to income-producing initiatives that provide food and schooling. Many women grow produce for neighbors and local markets. Volunteers from both Action and Holt contribute funds, materials, or labor to improve living spaces. Action also uses donor funds to provide microgrants or microcredit to purchase animals or basic gardening equipment. Action places a few regional social workers but relies primarily on networks of women and families in and among rural villages to offer mutual support and advice. The aim is the self-reliance of each household so that it may survive and thrive in its own environment and community without further charitable assistance. Holt has funded the building of community centers, where grandmothers provide early childhood education, food is sometimes served to children, and small clinics are staffed by visiting nurses.

Action for Children serves children and youth in camps for internally displaced persons (IDP) in northern Uganda (some visited by the Holt team). Some of the young residents are former child soldiers or "brides" of the Lord's Resistance Army, perpetrator of a long civil war. In IDP camps, Action uses funds from PEPFAR to support AIDS education. Interestingly, Action applied for these funds as an "abstinence education" grant. The implementation of the "abstinence" program by Action displays a much more comprehensive and holistic approach to the problem of avoiding AIDS than that of many US activists. While Western ideologues battle over abstinence or condoms, Action sees the susceptibility to AIDS of youth, especially girls, due primarily to a lack of self-worth and of options. Action does not reject the use of condoms, but it directs its efforts more broadly and proactively. Lacking basic food and clothing, as well as education and other developmentally appropriate activities, girls in IDP camps are easily persuaded to trade sex for small benefits. Meanwhile, boys and men also lack education, employment, and entertainment outlets, and they can become violent and abusive toward young girls and women. Action for Children has begun youth groups and work projects in the camps, including brick making, sewing, and raising chickens; although these are minor income sources, they engender a sense of mutual respect and of possibilities for the future. These are mighty deterrents to AIDS transmission.

I have illustrated the need for the Christian concept of justice to include practical initiatives to empower those directly affected by AIDS. I have described three programs, directed to different levels of society, that try to use U.S. resources to enhance the agency and options of people in Africa, and to build up African social strengths as defined by Africans. These steps of solidarity concretize the "preferential option for the poor" and the Catholic commitment to the common good. They offer a model for cooperation among women and across cultures that is true to the gospel, to women's realities, and to the ideal of global justice.

Y-Lan Tran, CND

HIV/AIDS in Vietnam

Calling for Dignity, Justice, and Care

All AIDS strategies should pass the test: Does this work for women?
—Peter Piot, Executive Director, UNAIDS

A quarter of a century into the pandemic, HIV/AIDS increasingly threatens the world's stability and development despite global efforts. AIDS-related deaths have reached more than 20 million worldwide, rendering approximately 15 million children orphans. Young women and girls are increasingly and disproportionately infected with HIV; nearly half of the world's 40 million people with HIV are women.[1]

Undisputed evidence shows the primary contributors to infection are poverty, injustice, gender inequalities and traditional roles, low status of women, and women's biological and physiological vulnerability.[2] While unsafe and violent sex remain a challenge in the struggle to end the pandemic, special attention to these larger global dimensions and re-evaluating the role of mothers in the family, as well as virtues, the dignity of the human person, solidarity, and medical practice are needed.

Primary Data and Situation Analysis in Vietnam

Vietnam's first HIV case was confirmed in Ho Chi Minh City in December 1990: a prostitute who had returned to Vietnam from Cambodia. Since then, infection has spread rapidly in the south, and particularly in Ho Chi Minh City among injecting drug users (IDUs), 50 to 60 percent of whom are HIV-positive; female sex workers (FSWs), who have the second-highest prevalence at 16 percent;[3] and the clients of FSWs.[4] By the end of 2005, there were 220,000 new HIV infections;[5] the true number may be much higher, as stigma and costly diagnostics hinder people at risk from getting tested for HIV. By 2007, HIV was present in all 64 provinces of Vietnam.

As elsewhere, Vietnam's HIV epidemic today is more diverse than a decade ago. Though prevention efforts have increased,[6] HIV is found across the population.[7] Migrants, sailors, and prisoners have higher risk of exposure;[8] some wives, themselves faithful to their marital vows, are infected by their migrant husbands,[9] and more newborns are infected with HIV. More adolescents engage in sexual activities and have sex before marriage or outside of wedlock, and the number of young people with multiple sexual partners has increased.[10] Serious deterioration of the current educational system[11] and an increased breakdown of families have resulted in young adults' comprising approximately 80 percent of the HIV-positive population.[12]

Vietnam's national strategy on HIV/AIDS "adopts most international best practices on HIV/AIDS prevention, care, support and treatment."[13] However, the poverty of the nation, as well as its corruption, discrimination, lack of professional skills, and lack of goodwill on the part of a number of political, medical, and government leaders limit the care and treatment people with AIDS receive.[14] And high-risk groups remain underserved.[15]

Response of the Vietnamese Church

The Vietnamese church seems a step behind the world's efforts on HIV. Though present since 1990 in Vietnam, eleven years passed before the Bishops Conference even referred to HIV/AIDS.[16] In 2000, the Vietnamese church set up a number of HIV and AIDS-related services and trained personnel for intervention.[17] The church provides care for persons with HIV or AIDS;[18] most activities are idiopathic and inaugurated by laypersons.

Being strictly faithful to Catholic teaching, bishops rarely talk about condoms or needle exchange programs as preventive strategies. The number of theologians discussing alternatives is very small; the number of moral theologians doing so is even smaller, and most discussion repeats magisterial teachings. No credible theological essay discusses condom use and AIDS prevention;[19] the silence is troubling and puts many Catholic doctors and health care personnel, who nearly always obey the bishops' teaching, into the difficult compromise of magisterially safe alternatives for prevention. In order to engage alternatives, the church must pave a way for critical theology, establish work teams, and support thinking, writing, and responding to the pandemic. To this end, Benedict XVI has commissioned a review of condom use in the restricted circumstances of discordant spouses, an important first step toward a possibly historic shift from an absolute prohibition on condom use.[20]

Nevertheless, more than 25 percent of global AIDS care services are provided by Catholic organizations. Often the unique and sole care and treatment provider, the Church's influence is significant. Additionally, the magisterium has a great impact on moral issues, especially in developing countries like Vietnam. Taking two essential roles—as powerful HIV/AIDS care provider and authoritative moral teacher—the Church's action unfortunately results in two painful effects: either Catholic care providers ignore the teaching, or they subvert it with an anxious conscience over dissent and disobedience.[21]

Yet the tradition can sustain reasonable justification for this subversion. The principal objection is to condom use. Yet condom use by discordant couples is not contraceptive—it is prophylactic and here saves lives, the highest good to which medicine strives. To wit, if a husband who is infected with HIV and knows that without a condom he can transmit HIV to his wife by their intercourse—and that this infection once full-blown will kill her—still has sex with his wife without a condom, his seminal fluid, the "gift of the self" in this spousal act, is no longer a "gift" but a lethal weapon, a moral license to kill! Illogically and disingenuously, the magisterium endorses some contraceptive medical approaches (contraceptives for women with some ovarian or uterine tumors or menstrual disorders that are nonfatal conditions) while it prohibits condom use in the prevention of AIDS, which is deadly and highly contagious. In the pilgrim world, few norms are absolute; prohibitions against murder or knowingly and deliberately threatening life or placing another in mortal danger rank among them. "Thou shalt not kill" has generous nuance (e.g., self-defense, just war). Can this nuance extend also to the prophylactic condom?

The main routes of HIV transmission are having sex with multiple partners, prostitution, spousal sexual infidelity, earlier and younger sexual encounters, combined heterosexual, bisexual, and homosexual behaviors, and injecting drug use.[22] Indeed, related to AIDS, there exists also a kind of "moral acquired immune deficiency syndrome"[23]; officially, many HIV prevention strategies call for spousal fidelity, abstinence, limited sex with one healthy partner, and delayed start of sexual activity among youth. The Church's teaching on the spiritual values of human sexuality and fidelity can be a decisively important guide in HIV prevention programs.[24] For Vietnamese as for the Church, chastity and virginity remain treasured values and, rather than learning these values from media outlets,[25] people must learn the spiritual values of love.

Promoting Gender Equality

"The history of the epidemic has shown that the full protection of human rights is essential."[26] In Southeast Asia and Oceania,[27] the gaps between poor and rich in rural and urban areas, and the education of girls and boys are increasingly worrisome issues. In Vietnam, girls in rural poor families usually sacrifice opportunities for higher education so that their brothers may pursue study. Consequently, rural women have low social status, no stable jobs, and have to depend on husbands or fathers.

The Asian Confucian family is hierarchical, especially regarding the role of women; traditionally, women are characterized with the "three subjections" (daughter to her parents, wife to her husband, widow to her son) and the "four virtues" (proper employment, proper demeanor, proper speech, and proper behavior). To be sure, women's "three subjections" no longer exist as before, but the spirit of hierarchy remains in many rural families in Asia. Gender-related violence against women and girls occurs daily; culturally passive, women are often ignorant about finding ways to secure their health and well-being, and they defer to men for decisions and choice. Even as many girls leave their villages for the city to work, they are easily abused by their bosses or boyfriends, and abandoned when these men lose interest.

Christianity enhances the Asian family's spirituality and transforms relationships between men and women. As persons created in God's image, husband and wife are equal in their personal dignity and are endowed with equal rights; reciprocal responsibilities foster familial happiness reflecting the loving communion of the triune God.[28] Reciprocity, transformative gender roles, and gender equitable relationships newly improve women's power to understand their dignity, acquire self-confidence, and participate actively in building their own security and happiness.

Following Christian initiatives, helping rural women to have stable jobs would reduce the wave of urban migration and its risks.[29] Unfortunately, the proportion of unemployed women with HIV is high,[30] and prevention for them, and for those who are poor, is imperative. To counter women's vulnerability, some laypersons in Vietnam have opened "houses of charity" for girls to educate them, help them find jobs, and provide a loving family.[31]

Moreover, motherhood and women's roles in the family must be revalued. Although Vietnamese usually talk about the authority of the father, in reality, the mother has an equally important role in bringing about happiness for the whole family.[32] As an old Vietnamese saying observes, "Fatherless child eats rice with fish, motherless child lives on the street." Vietnamese proverbs express the prominent role of the mother in educating children: "Children's happiness depends on the mother's virtues and good deeds." This perspective is shared between Confucian values and Catholicism. Noting the trend of women working outside the home, John Paul II acknowledged women's contributions to society and family, underlining the specific roles of women as teachers. He cautioned that a woman's work in society should never take her away from the task of a mother and a wife.[33] Valuing the role of women and recognizing their work for the family could decisively cut one root of HIV infection.

An important step toward this revaluing is the just remuneration for work. This justice concerns everyone. John Paul II's teaching enlightens:

> Just remuneration . . . will suffice for establishing and properly maintaining a family and for providing security for its future. Such remuneration can be given either through what is called a *family wage*—that is, a single salary given to the head of the family for his work, sufficient for the needs of the family without the other spouse having to take up gainful employment outside the home—or through *other social measures* such as family allowances or grants to mothers devoting themselves exclusively to their families.[34]

Structural Sin, Discrimination, and Virtue

A significant number of children who resort to violence, commit crimes, use drugs, and engage in prostitution do so from poverty, ignorance, and the breakdown of traditional families.[35] The data suggests at least two things: the need for special attention to children and young people, and the value of a traditional family, which has been undermined by modern culture's social structures that draw both the father and mother to outside work. These conditions interfere with familial safety nets and care. Instilling a spirituality of a good life, ideal morality, and humanity would engender a desire for truth, virtue, and resistance to at-risk ways of living.

Particularly vulnerable to this interference, consider FSWs. Most FSWs are poor or very poor, poorly educated or illiterate, and responsible for earning a living for their families. If they had other choices for work, they would make them.[36] Compounding their poverty, ignorance, or insufficient knowledge about infection and addiction, increases their vulnerability.[37] Rehabilitation centers for them must integrate harm reduction, treat drug dependence, and teach skills that provide alternate ways of earning a living; in centers that do so, many FSWs are recovering from drug addiction, have gained self-respect, feel less self-pity, and receive formation for work in stable and safe jobs. And they know about HIV.[38]

As for many other national traditions, Vietnamese tradition emphasizes the spiritual rather than material or physical life. Educators must remind young people of the spirit expressed in some proverbs: "Hungry but righteous, ragged but good reputation," "Kind hearts are more than coronets," "Better a glorious death than a shameful life," "When people die, their good fame still lasts for generations," "A gentleman remains firm even in poverty." Vietnamese culture and traditional values have been fertile soil ready for sowing the gospel. Yet even there some have been stigmatized, seemingly condemned by God and thereby excluded; today many consider persons with HIV or AIDS similarly.

Out of misunderstanding, many family members of people with AIDS do not eat with or talk to them. Out of shame to the prestige of the family, some parents do not accept their children with HIV and do not allow them to stay at home. The story of a girl dying of AIDS strikes at the heart of a Vietnamese family's discomfort: the owner of the house rented by the parents of that dying girl threatened to take the house back after hearing about the sickness of their daughter. The parents, out of fear of being shunned by their neighbors, bought a wooden float, put their daughter inside, and let it drift on the river; their daughter would die without neighbors spreading rumors (exposing whose shame?). This one story illuminates the moral breakdown in Vietnamese society: even a sick child, regardless of age, cannot rely on her parents to advocate, care for, and love her in her greatest need.

Sadly, children infected with HIV from their mothers also suffer discrimination and stigma: their basic human rights—making friends, going to school, and having access to health care and social and development opportunities—are cut off.[39] Children affected by HIV, a majority living in poor families, are at risk of dropping out of school, going to work, and becoming themselves vulnerable to infection. These families need financial and spiritual support for the lives and futures of their children. "Actions to reduce vulnerability and to address stigma and discrimination are central to the success of responses and will continue to be prioritized, particularly in the poorest and most disadvantaged countries where the needs are greatest."[40]

Media campaigns could reduce stigma and discrimination but, above all, the witness of caring and loving persons is necessary. For Vietnamese, the authority of priests and bishops is considerable, their understanding and compassion is an inspiration to others, and their optimism is influential. Perhaps the best image to challenge stigma would show priests or bishops embracing persons with HIV and AIDS to demonstrate that it is both good and right to do so. Experiences of some Vietnamese Catholic groups caring for those with HIV are encouraging. After seeing loving care of abandoned family members by these groups, parents, spouses, and relatives of people with AIDS changed their thinking and behavior. Less fearful of family members with AIDS, they are inviting these family members to stay home and receive care.[41]

Mercy and Care

Facing despair, Vietnamese Catholics offer hope, mercy, and compassion to people with AIDS. That offer includes the loving and attentive ways of care no matter the social or physical status of the person in need.

In Vietnam, government institutions provide limited treatment and little care for patients with AIDS. Those at the last stages of AIDS are often abandoned; many die lonely, shameful deaths. Neither the Catholic Church nor religious congregations are permitted to run hospitals or clinics; in need of care for orphans, the infirmed, lepers, and people with AIDS, however, government institutions have recognized their incapacity and have called on religious, in particular Catholic, services. In response, some Catholic groups accompany people with HIV, experience solidarity with them, and gain the privileges and insights of their problems, sentiments, and feelings; this solidarity imparts care and God's power to heal.[42] Interestingly, having been healed spiritually and psychologically, in their turn, those with HIV become the most eager, helpful, and convincing companions for other people with HIV as they talk with and from their own experiences. These witnesses speak of faith, hope, and love confidently.[43]

In the spirit of the Vietnamese proverb, "Living is temporary; death is to return to eternal home," preparation of a body for burial is an honored ritual act in which the body is washed clean with a special wine and the face is slightly made up.[44] But many die of AIDS while their family dares not to touch them. A number of Catholics offer day or night at a moment's notice to come and to pray with those dying from AIDS and to help them enter this last journey with dignity. These volunteers perform the final act of washing the body of the dead. This act honors the dead, impresses the living, and changes them to become more sympathetic and sensitive toward people with AIDS.[45]

Physicians and Health Care

It is not uncommon for patients with HIV or AIDS to be refused or abandoned when they present for hospitalization or surgical intervention.[46] Some Catholic doctors step forward to accept them, but they are not the norm. Yet it is in the very calamity of an emergency, like hospitalization, that opportunity presents. In the midst of the darkness of disease, the Catholic faith provides a hope for patients and a light for the community to see the way clear to persons in need.

Fundamentally, respect for persons guides both religion and medicine.[47] Catholic teaching on human dignity, the Hippocratic Oath, and Hai Thuong Lan Ong[48] (the physician-founder of Vietnamese traditional medicine) commend duties of care and justice regardless of a patient's personal history or condition.[49] This justice includes the promotion of human dignity in the first place among health care ministries and as a source of medical ethics.[50] As a healing profession, medicine is committed to respect for persons and to their spiritual and physical integrity.[51] Never a pure technical process of healing,[52] like spiritual care, medical practice has as its object the person, the competence of professional skills, the arts of healing, and virtue.[53] From the Christian perspective, doctors practice not just a profession but a vocation. Grounding their spiritual and medical care by covenant, they follow Jesus in establishing relationships among those with whom he walked.[54]

Conclusion

HIV/AIDS reminds us that choices, decisions, behaviors, and the fate of each person depend upon a variety of factors, many beyond anyone's control. Each of us, and particularly religious, political, and community leaders, must accept responsibility for the relief of poverty, inequality, and exploitation of those who are silenced or otherwise oppressed, especially women and children with or affected by HIV. Lifting the ban on condoms could provide a reasonably practical means to relieve partly the spread of HIV. And virtue, expressed so poignantly in Vietnamese proverbs, must return to the moral life.

Maria Cimperman, OSU

Change Is Possible

Churches Reading and Responding
to the Signs of the Times

I teach moral theology and social ethics at a graduate school of theology
in the United States that prepares women and men for full-time ministry
in the Catholic Church. At least a third of our students are born outside the
United States. I present and write on HIV and AIDS, contemporary religious
life, and social spirituality. Teaching and research afford opportunities to meet
and learn from persons from various countries and cultures and also to spend
time elsewhere—in Zambia, Jamaica, Ghana, Cape Verde, and El Salvador,
among other places. I find that I cannot teach or present on any topic without mentioning a pandemic that is as devastating as it is expansive.

The pervasive reality of HIV is that it is as global as it is local. What role can
and must the church take to affect this dynamic, particularly the dynamic of
poverty and gender inequality related to infection among women and girls? We
are clearly in the midst of responding; I add to this discussion and invite further
conversation by engaging the collective wisdom of our religious imaginations.

Three particular experiences galvanized this writing. These overlapping
experiences demonstrate acknowledgment of the stark realities of women
and girls in an age of AIDS and offer some initial directions for engagement
by the church.[1]

Realities Named

A First

A few semesters ago I taught a seminar called "Ethical and Pastoral Issues in
HIV and AIDS." Students were from around the United States as well as several other countries. The first part of the course examined the global pandemic and considered narratives from around the world. Students were
surprised to find out that women represent almost half of the adults living

with HIV or AIDS and that gender inequalities in social and economic status and in access to prevention and care services significantly increase women's vulnerability to HIV.[2] News to some was that teens and young adults, particularly girls and young women, are at the center of the epidemic.[3]

At one point a conversation ensued in light of the readings on the pandemic's devastating impact on women.[4] One student from Mexico, who has lived and worked for years in the United States, expressed shock at the statistics and realities he read. He stated with some surprise, "I have a college education. I consider myself a loving husband and father of grown children, including two daughters. I periodically hear things about the inequalities of women, but I never believed it—until now."

A student from Zambia then described the reality in various parts of his country. "The boy-child will always be treated better than the girl-child. More education, better food, greater social status and more opportunities and rights are given to the boy than the girl." A classmate asked, "Can't this change? If you know that family and culture does this, can't the Church, can't your religious order, can't you make an impact here?" The student from Zambia responded, "You don't understand. This is our culture. The Church cannot make an impact. This is how families are raised. Religious orders would also have to change to make this happen. You don't understand how difficult this is!" The class was silent. After a few moments, a woman student, a physician from Nigeria, responded aloud, "Brother, I can offer you some ideas. I will share with you some of my experiences. Change is possible."

Another moment illuminating the difficulty of acknowledging realities in order to galvanize change occurred later in the course when a student presented some of his research on sexual practices that position women and girls at particular risk for HIV: female initiation rituals, drying the vagina with herbs to make the sexual experience more pleasurable for men, and widow cleansing.[5] The student was from sub-Saharan Africa. After he spoke, students from the African continent he was considering challenged him on most points and put great effort into distancing their countries and cultures from these examples. The presenting student invited his student-colleagues to read the resources themselves.

A Second

While researching for a presentation to the 2007 Catholic Theological Society of America Conference, I planned to assess three bishops' conferences across three continents on their responses to HIV/AIDS. One of the conferences was the Catholic Bishops' Conference of India (CBCI). In August 2005, the CBCI's Commission for Healthcare published its *Commitment to Compassion and Care: HIV/AIDS Policy of the Catholic Church in India*, which presents a dauntingly accurate description of women's realities in

India and claims that "they are powerless to protect themselves against HIV."[6] It says further:

> Traditionally, sexual, economic and cultural subordination of women has taken a serious toll on women's health and HIV has worsened this situation. . . . The striking feature in dealing with women and HIV/AIDS is that it often categorizes women as mothers or as sex workers and rarely considers women as a whole. . . . Women who are newly infected have contracted their infection mostly from their husbands. In short, faithful housewives are getting infected. . . . Unequal rights to property result in women losing their homes and access to productive resources when found HIV positive or, are widowed. Due to biological factors, cultural norms and socio-economic inequalities our girls and women have limited access to sexual and reproductive health education, information on HIV/AIDS and health services. At the same time, Indian women shoulder the primary burden of caring for people living with HIV/AIDS. Indian women's vulnerability to HIV/AIDS and its impact is further adversely affected by class, caste, urban/rural location, religion and culture.[7]

The document commits the Church to work for gender equity in all areas related to prevention, treatment, care, and support.[8] Prevention in an all-inclusive sense is necessary. Positively, the Church "will strive to promote male involvement in order to reduce social, cultural, economic and legal barriers to effective prevention, ensure equitable access to information, services and treatment and encourage shared responsibility for care and support."[9] As part of a response, efforts such as the involvement of men, collaboration with the CBCI's Commission for Women, and "capacity building of women through self-help groups (SHGs) and other organized structures" are significant.[10]

The emphasis here is on participatory processes for both the writing of the document and the implementation of policies and strategies. The introduction describes the process as the "fruit of partnership, collaboration and a sincere sharing of views and concerns of many. In a way, the participatory process of formulation itself was an expression of the commitment of all the members of the Church towards the implementation of this Policy."[11] Another example of participatory processes is the involvement of youth in planning and implementing education about prevention and living the moral life.[12]

Finally, acknowledging its own internal work to be done in Catholic health care and social institutions that do not yet consider HIV a priority or who discriminate by poor treatment or lack of treatment for persons with HIV, the Church sees itself as an advocate on behalf of persons infected and affected by HIV/AIDS in areas of prevention, treatment, care, and elimination of stigma and discrimination (within and outside the Church). This advocacy brings the Church more deliberately into the public sector.

A Third

The third experience is a "Statement of Commitment by Lesotho's Church Leaders," an interfaith and ecumenical document released on June 20, 2007.[13] The leaders publicly commit together and within their own communities to "work to eliminate the root causes of the AIDS epidemic including gender inequality, social and cultural norms such as having multiple concurrent sexual partners, sexual abuse, prejudice against those whose way of life or sexual orientation is different from the majority community, systemic injustice, and unequal distribution of wealth." Significantly, gender inequality is listed first and the root causes are described as extending to systemic and global injustice. Specific commitments include, among others, to "give priority attention addressing the practices within our religious traditions that increase the vulnerability of women and girls who also carry the greatest burden of response in this pandemic" and to "promote preaching and teaching about HIV in our houses of worship . . . [and] the designation of special days and/or weeks of prayer and other religious observances to focus on AIDS."[14]

The examples separately and together offer a lens from which to see the pandemic and present initial directions for response and action. The multifaceted dimensions of HIV/AIDS require multifaceted and creative responses. The Catholic Church has been involved in many ways in the pandemic and will continue to be. The Church has responded extensively in terms of care and treatment across the globe. Moreover, the Church is the largest faith-based organization responding to the pandemic. As a church community we are naming with greater depth and analysis some of the crucial, complex, and devastating dynamics of HIV and AIDS in the experience of women and girls. The growing efforts of the church to respond to this reality present an opportunity to further focus and expand these efforts.

It is in these three experiences that particular windows emerge for further action. These windows are opportunities for the convergence of the religious imagination, community, and action in solidarity with those infected with and affected by HIV/AIDS. I briefly offer seven points of engagement toward an expansion of church efforts on behalf of women and girls.[15]

Signs of the Times:
Change as Possible and Necessary

1. Religious imagination on a communal level is needed. The religious imagination is a capacity to imagine beyond the reality around us to a reality transformed by lived gospel values in persons and in the entire global community. The AIDS pandemic is so massive that, for some, even when the stage of denial is past, paralysis easily sets in. Individual efforts, while important, must be joined to community efforts. Persons must see together in order to imagine

beyond the realities they find. The student who could not see a church or religious group that could impact culture needed the experience and the hope of others to imagine another world. In fact, the conversation between the students from Zambia and Nigeria began a shift that culminated in the creation of a project that engaged the local culture and family life on practices of gender inequality. The first student could not have imagined this alone.

In order for persons and communities to imagine beyond the reality they see, to envision a world and society where the reign of God calls us to further growth as disciples, the integration of contemplation and social commitment is essential.[16] The societal impasses students found in the complex dimensions of HIV and AIDS required a different level of engagement than that to which they were accustomed. After considerable information gathering and analysis, they found it important to ponder information and insights. Needed were ways for more than one means of insight and level of consciousness to emerge. Students were asked to take ten minutes each day to simply hold the information loosely and ask a question or two: What would it look like if . . . ? How might we . . . ?

In class one day we took fifteen minutes to ponder some questions while walking contemplatively, walking without a destination but simply bodily engaging the realities. The students came with their questions, and together they started imagining some places beyond impasse. For one, the question "I wonder how I might work with women in my medical practice who are at risk for HIV and are fearful of their husbands" moved to "I wonder what it would look like to create a program so that all women are invited to conversation about relationships and assistance whenever they come to the clinic for any purpose."

As church, we find ourselves uncomfortable at times with engaging a contemplative process in the midst of social emergencies. While we can easily forget how essential this contemplative process is, the insight that emerges offers enormous potential for gospel responses.

2. The religious imagination of a community requires the participation of all. Women's voices are essential, and the pandemic will not be adequately addressed without their voices. The CBCI document and the Lesotho leaders' statement will be muted if women's voices are silenced in any way.[17]

3. The religious imagination must have a global vision engaging systems and including global efforts for which all have particular responsibilities. Two examples illustrate this vision. First, the eight United Nations Millennium Development Goals (MDG) set forth an ambitious yet possible plan for governments and peoples to build a better world for all persons by 2015. In 2000, 189 heads of state and governments committed to the MDGs. Concern for women is included in all the goals, and women are specifically mentioned in three: (1) eradicate extreme poverty and hunger, (2) ensure that all boys and girls complete primary school, (3) promote gender equality and empower women, (4) reduce by two-thirds the mortality rate among children under

five, (5) reduce by three-quarters the ratio of women dying in childbirth, (6) halt and begin to reverse the spread of HIV and incidence of malaria and other major diseases, (7) ensure environmental sustainability, and (8) develop a global partnership for development.[18] These are areas for deliberation and action within our church communities, yet years into this millennium there are many who have not yet heard about the MDGs. Second, the various church statements about intellectual property in reference to generic drug availability are a clear call for a more just global partnership for development.[19] Greater understanding of the need and implications of such actions are needed, and churches in the United States and throughout the global north are necessary conduits for galvanizing efforts for education and further responses in their local parishes for global understanding.

4. Church collaboration with many groups is necessary to engage the pandemic. The call is clearly for ecumenical and interfaith collaboration in stemming the tide of AIDS. Faith-based organizations have many skills and resources to offer within a context that brings the experience of a loving God and caring communities to bear on persons vulnerable, affected, and infected. The Church must partner in these efforts.[20] The collaboration must include sharing of information from the medical and scientific communities as they inform efforts to prevent HIV.[21]

5. There must be clear efforts to disseminate information from the global to national, regional, and local areas. The Lesotho document commits church leaders to end domestic and sexual abuse. The prevention of this kind of abuse is an area where women and the churches must clearly state the human rights violations and clear any confusion that might exist about the Church's teaching and obligations of spouses to endure abusive relationships. The United States Conference of Catholic Bishops, for example, has written very clearly about domestic violence and recognizes that no one is expected to remain in an abusive marriage.[22] However, this message is not widely disseminated in dioceses or parishes. Any and all supports that the Church on various levels can offer women must be widely distributed in many formats.[23] Such documents can be offered in parishes or even listed on walls where announcements are offered. It is essential that all documents related to the realities (and vulnerabilities) of women be placed in public and widely frequented spaces, whether the documents are from local or larger church offices or from civic authorities.

6. Local church communities are essential foci and loci for HIV prevention efforts. There are numerous venues for this intervention: First, education and opportunities for women and girls must be a greater priority and call from within the Church. Education for work in HIV/AIDS is a logical beginning. Training women and girls, who often are the primary caregivers of persons with HIV or AIDS, is important. (It is also important to provide training for men and boys who will need to offer this kind of care.) Such training would offer skills from prevention education in schools and clinics, to pharmaceutical or nursing education for care of persons who are infected, to sup-

port skills for persons living with dying and grieving members. Second, support groups for women and young girls that are connected to the church offer an important symbolic and practical effort. Third, equality of women and men can be modeled in many ways in a parish. Families and communities are affected positively by inviting couples to make announcements, to mutually head committees, and to teach catechesis. Including an equal number of women in all areas of parish life begins to engage the religious imagination about the value of women and their contributions that the church promulgates in many documents.[24]

7. Our liturgical and other rituals must name the reality of AIDS in our midst. When I ask groups if AIDS has been mentioned in homilies or intercessions in the past three years, I find few hands are raised. It is rare in U.S. parishes to hear AIDS mentioned and I continue to find this absence a challenging reality for a church that spans the globe. Stigma abounds when silence abides in churches; how will our sacramental life connect to our daily life and realities? David N. Power makes this connection:

> The celebration of the Eucharist that in truth evokes a commitment to justice fits into the life of a church that sees itself as a community of disciples, a household of God, a sacrament of the community, and reconciliation of people. The Eucharist presupposes a community engaged in action for justice, a praxis of liberation from violence and injustice. Such a community will strive to make liturgies forceful commemoration of the suffering and resurrection of Jesus Christ, into which will be gathered a memory of all the forgotten and unnamed suffering past and present.[25]

It is our call to name the suffering as we find ways to eliminate it.

Finally, the church can offer rituals in an age of AIDS to help express grief and lament. Connecting with the power of Jesus' suffering and death in the midst of grief in families and among persons, the church offers opportunities to bring suffering and the cross to a place that knows not only death but also new life.[26] Grief not dealt with bears only further grief, and the vulnerabilities of women are only exacerbated when their realities have no space to be held or time to heal. The richness of our rituals represents embodied and relational opportunities for truth, reconciliation, and even peace. We must offer them.

Conclusion

These suggestions are not exhaustive but are proposed to invite our religious imagination to develop even more ideas. As a community of faith, we can also share the fruits of our religious imagination with one another. A Web site will be created to serve as a space for further sharing of best practices if you wish to share your suggestions with others.

Margaret A. Farley

Justice, Faith, and HIV/AIDS in Africa

Challenges for the Twenty-First Century

For those struggling on all fronts against the current HIV and AIDS pandemic, the *AIDS Epidemic Update* (December 2007) offers good news.[1] The number of people living with HIV worldwide appears to have leveled off; the number of new HIV infections is estimated to have peaked in the late 1990s and to have gone down in 2007. At first glance, this is a marvelous report; the raging wildfires of the pandemic may have been contained.

On second glance, the news remains good but confusing—and not good enough. It is confusing because the accompanying *UNAIDS Fact Sheet* maintains that the downward revisions in estimated prevalence are "due mainly to improved methodology, better surveillance by countries and changes in the key epidemiological assumptions used to calculate the estimates." This difference presumably means that earlier estimates were inflated by less adequate epidemiological and demographic research. For those who have experienced the pandemic in the global south, particularly in sub-Saharan Africa, this new information is important, but it does not change the concrete experience of a dire situation. Moreover, the news is not good enough, since the data still show that in 2007 across the globe, 33.2 million people are HIV-positive (a downward estimate from 39.5 million), 2.5 million more people were newly infected, and 2.1 million people died of AIDS.[2]

My own experience of the HIV/AIDS pandemic comes, first, from journeying with a beloved nephew of mine through infection, disease, and finally death as a result of AIDS. With this good and wise young man, I learned with clarity and certainty that AIDS cannot be justifiably connected with moral judgment, that it is not a "respecter of persons," that it can strike God's beloved people everywhere, and that the church must find better ways to interpret the pandemic and to offer a healing word. This experience has been confirmed and massively expanded in the past six years through my participation in two projects with women in faith communities in sub-Saharan Africa.

One of these projects, the Women's Initiative: Gender, Faith, and Responses to HIV/AIDS in Africa, was begun in 2001 by women faculty and African women students at Yale Divinity School, in consultation and partnership with the Africa-based Circle of Concerned African Women Theologians.[3] The African women in the Circle represented various faith traditions, with a majority of them Protestant Christians. The project evolved in 2003 into a program co-sponsored by Yale Divinity School and Yale School of Epidemiology and Public Health. Through this program, African women theologians were able to study public health research methodologies and to develop protocols for their own empirical (and theological) research.

The second project, initiated in 2002, is the All-Africa Conference: Sister to Sister, an organization that works with communities and networks of Roman Catholic women religious and their lay coworkers to respond to HIV and AIDS throughout sub-Saharan Africa. This project now has over seven hundred fifty African women implementing action plans in twenty-three sub-Saharan countries. With these projects, African women have come together to break the silence surrounding AIDS, do social analysis, and explore not only medical and epidemiological questions but also issues of gender, sexuality, faith, and culture.

With these experiences, including more than a dozen travels to various parts of sub-Saharan Africa, I know that we have sisters and brothers everywhere, but especially in Africa, who are threatened with severe illness or who are already sick unto death. Lives are disrupted, families are devastated, and ordinary hopes and expectations are challenged in every way. Although some significant progress has been made in the struggle against HIV infection, the pandemic continues to rage across southern Africa.

In this essay, I aim to do three things: (1) describe something of the medical and social situation as it is today, (2) identify major justice issues that are part of this situation, including issues of justice facing world religions and their faith communities, and (3) describe the characteristics of a response to the situation that I and my colleagues (in the United States and in Africa) have found through the Circle and Sister to Sister projects. Although the AIDS pandemic stretches around the world, my focus is on sub-Saharan Africa, with special attention to the challenges facing women and their faith traditions.

The Situation

It is difficult to imagine a more dire situation in our time or in any time than the HIV/AIDS pandemic. In 2001, almost twenty years after the pandemic began, more than 65 million people were estimated to have been infected, and more than 25 million had already died.[4] Of the 33.2 million persons estimated to be living today with HIV or AIDS worldwide, approximately 22.5 million live in sub-Saharan Africa. Moreover, sub-Saharan Africa accounts for 1.7 million of the 2.5 million new HIV infections worldwide and 1.6 million of the 2.1

million deaths from AIDS.[5] Whole generations have been wiped out: parents, teachers, doctors, nurses. In some villages it is still possible to find no one alive over the age of fourteen.

A few countries in these regions have shown declines in infection prevalence—for example, Kenya (where for some years it was estimated that 700 people died every day) and Zimbabwe (where 33 percent of the population was at one time infected). Gains and losses have not yet been finally explained, and there are disputes over what has worked and what has not. Nonetheless, no one denies that the situation remains dire. A Kenyan woman with whom I worked, for example, shook her head in puzzlement over the reported decline in numbers infected in her country, and said simply, "It may be because we all have died."

Women bear a disproportionate share of the burden of this pandemic, a fact that is now widely recognized. As other essays in this volume show, women are the primary caregivers for the sick and the dying, and women are also at greater risk than men when it comes to infection and death. Most women are infected by their spouses, but young girls are also more likely to be infected than young boys. In situations of military conflict, women are targeted for sexual abuse and hence infection. Many factors compound this disproportionate risk and injury, but most of them come down to the ways in which African women and girls are socially subordinate to and dependent upon men (not so different a story from other parts of the world).

Some things have improved in the last five years. The silence that surrounded sexuality and sexual behavior has to a great extent been broken by the media, by new African governmental strategies, and by groups dedicated to providing education. Yet in many villages, people still remain in silence and ignorance about sexuality and AIDS. Anti-retroviral therapies (ARV) are now available at lower prices than before. As an example, Catholic church-sponsored programs in South Africa managed to provide ARV to upwards of 4,000 individuals in 2005.[6] Still, there are millions upon millions who need ARV but have as yet no access to them. The Global Fund to Fight AIDS, despite some notable successes, is running low on money. The U.S. President's Emergency Plan for AIDS Relief operates in only fifteen countries, with many strings attached. And the pandemic goes on.

Issues of Justice

Almost everything in my description of the "dire" situation involves underlying issues of justice. A major part of the problem is the ongoing poverty of persons living in sub-Saharan Africa. Religious and political leaders in the global south have not neglected the connections between poverty and the spread of AIDS. Yet the relationship between poverty and lack of education and medical care is everywhere visible. And deficiencies in nutrition, safe water, and control of diseases such as malaria and tuberculosis render people vulnerable to HIV infection and a quick conversion to AIDS. Moreover, AIDS itself exacerbates poverty when, for example, farm workers are no longer strong enough to cultivate the land. But the poverty in Africa is an international problem, whose causes have much to do with the consequences of past colonialism, international debt structures, present exploitation of Africa's rich resources, and unfair trade practices.

Poverty and its causes are not the only justice issues, however. As I have already suggested, gender bias is central to the pandemic, and it is surely an issue of justice. Women are increasingly at the center of community, city, district, and national responses to HIV and AIDS. Yet women's continuing lack of economic, social, and political power remains a constraint in the prevention of HIV transmission and the care of those living with AIDS. The United Nations declared a Year of Women in 1975 and a Decade of Women 1976–1985; the African Union has tried to articulate women's rights that must be respected and secured; particular countries have introduced measures to protect women from abuse and to assist them with their children. But women remain blatantly excluded from leadership and decision-making roles in tribes, in civil government, and in churches, temples, and mosques. Patterns of gender discrimination are perpetuated through cultural and religious reinforcement of economic dependence and passive rather than active roles for women in both the public and the private spheres.

Without power in society, or in their own sexual lives, women who could hold the key to stopping the AIDS pandemic are all too often rendered powerless. Practices differ from country to country, region to region, and tribe to tribe in Africa, yet it is not uncommon for women to be coerced into marriages and into marital sexual relations without condoms, even if they suspect that their husbands are HIV-positive. The continuation of traditional practices such as ritual initiation of adolescent girls into sexual activity and "widow cleansing" (in which a widow is "purified" by having sex with a relative of her dead husband or with some man designated as a "cleanser") transforms what were meaningful practices in the past into dangerous practices in the present— fraught, in a time of AIDS, with high risk of infection. Women live all too often in contexts where their subordination to men determines their health or sickness, life or death. As powerful as women may be in some spheres of their familial lives, they are often powerless in persuading male spouses and partners to engage in safe sex, or in refusing sex when it is demanded on traditional religious and cultural grounds. South African theologian Isabel Phiri provides a partial explanation of this power differential: "Girls learn from their mothers that they are created to serve their brothers. Boys also grow up believing that they were born to be served by girls and women."[7] African sexual practices, then, while oriented toward the good of the community and its preservation, are nonetheless lodged in gendered patterns of relationship that put women at particular risk.[8]

There are also justice issues that belong in particular to the churches.[9] There is no doubt that churches, temples, and mosques have been in the forefront of responses to HIV/AIDS. Indeed, recent statistics suggest that in some countries, faith-based communities today provide more than 40 percent of the care for the sick and dying, and that in the last five years they have made important strides in education, counseling, and multiple forms of support for those affected and infected by HIV and AIDS.

Yet more is needed, specifically from religious traditions and institutions. For example, if there ever was a situation in which the principle of preferential option for the poor was relevant and crucial, here it is. Considered either as a strategic priority or a religious command, this principle includes the moral imperative of turning to those most in need, whether because they are relegated to the margins of world concern and power, or because they are exploited, forgotten, shamed, or sick from whatever causes. Preferential option is clearly operative in much of the work of the Christian churches in response to the AIDS pandemic in sub-Saharan Africa; it is especially visible in their care of the sick and of orphans. But action based on this principle appears not to have reached the needs of women as a group or individuals whose sexual behavior departs from uncritically accepted norms.

A growing number of African women theologians are saying that the traditions of world religions in which many of them now stand must find better ways to address problems of stigma, discrimination, and gender bias. The favored response of religious leaders has all too often been simply and vehemently to reiterate moral rules that, if they could be adhered to, might guard people against risks. Ironically, the simple repetition of traditional moral rules has frequently served only to heighten the shame and stigma associated with AIDS and to promote misplaced judgments on individuals and groups, especially women. The perpetuation of unreflective taboo morality and its accompanying stigmatization of people reinforces the sort of divine punishment argument challenged in the book of Job. Moreover, it ignores the genuine requirements of justice that extend to sexual relationships. Even in response to their own members, churches have been as likely to stigmatize those infected with HIV or sick with AIDS as they have been to deny their urgent needs.

The AIDS crisis presents a clear situation in which faith traditions must address their own traditional teachings about sexuality and must rethink the gender bias that remains deep within their teachings and practices. It would be naïve to think that cultural patterns which make women vulnerable to AIDS are not influenced by the teachings of world religions (and vice versa), whose presence is longstanding in their countries. Questions must be pressed about the role of patriarchal religions in making women invisible, even though women's responsibilities are enormous, and their own agency can be crucial and strong. Questions must also be pressed about sexual mores once imposed by missionaries as if Western sexual practices were part of the Christian gospel.

I have learned from African women that there are many layers of life and influence in which Africans live: the layer of traditional indigenous culture and religion, the layer of Christian or Muslim beliefs and practices, the layer of colonialist imposition of gendered practices (reinforced by missionaries), the layer of modern (largely Western) cultural forces, the layer of growing post-colonialist critiques. The work by African women leaders and scholars is crucial now as potentially formative of the work of the churches.

Response to the Situation and to the Claims of Justice

If space allowed, I would outline many more justice issues involved in the AIDS pandemic, but I move now to my third task: to share the clues I and those with whom I have worked in Africa have discovered regarding needed characteristics for organized responses to the pandemic. Drawing from my experience in the Circle of Concerned African Women Theologians and with the All-Africa Conference: Sister to Sister organization, I identify four such characteristics or elements of response that have guided us along the way.

First, we decided from the start that *women are key if the AIDS pandemic is ever to be stopped.* This claim does not mean that no significant responses should be addressed to men; indeed, all responses should in some way take account of women, men, and children. But we had in the beginning profound experiences of the power that is unleashed when women come together to share their experiences of HIV and AIDS, the power whereby women empower one another. Women who before had no safe place to share these experiences of AIDS—not in their families, communities, parishes, or villages—broke the silence among themselves and discovered paths along which they could together commit themselves to go. They could rise up not only among themselves but through these projects in partnership with women across the world.

Second, our way of working together in both projects is never to work alone, but only *in partnership with African women.* For example, the All-Africa Conference: Sister to Sister is not a "missionary" project. It is not we in the West who interpret African women's experience; it is not we who impose judgments on churches or mosques; it is not we who call for changes in personal or communal behavior. We work in partnership with our African sisters—with the Circle and with religious communities of African women. Partnership means, however, a commitment to giving primary voice in the ongoing shaping and implementation of project agendas to those most affected by them—that is, to our African partners. We have gradually learned from them that we not only can help to provide space for African women to speak with one another and to act together, but that we too must participate with them in active dialogue, colearning, and action that includes us all.

Third, the work of both projects has been by its very nature *cross-cultural*. This kind of work has always been difficult, and many mistakes have been made in attempting it in the past.[10] Our only way of bridging the boundaries between cultures is through the sustaining of genuine partnerships. In part, differences have been recognized and respected, and they have not yielded insurmountable obstacles. We have discovered that we can, across borders, experience awe before one another; we can laugh together, weep together, and labor for common goals. And we have learned that we can stand in solidarity with those who critique, in their own culture and ours, practices from which people die.

The fourth element that has characterized our work is recognition that particular kinds of action are required based on our understanding of *Christianity as a world church*.[11] Some people may understand "world church" to mean that the Christian gospel has been taken to the far corners of the world. But ours is a time when the concept of world church can be given a different content and require even more than what is commonly thought of as "inculturation." We now recognize that the Christian gospel was never meant to be only or even primarily a Western European or North American gospel exported like the rest of Western culture to other parts of the world. At last we realize that God's self-revelation not only can be *received* in every language and culture, but that this revelation can be *given* and *spoken* out of every language and culture. We stifle its possibilities when any one culture claims nearly total control over its forms.

Two consequences follow from our understanding of what it means to be within a world church. The first of these follows from the fact that the church has not always thought about itself in this way. In the past, Western Christianity exported teachings regarding, for example, sexuality and the status of women that are now part of the problem with HIV/AIDS. Imposition of attitudes and practices shaped by Western culture at the very least destabilized traditional cultures in Africa. These attitudes and practices now intermingle confusedly with tribal practices, together contributing to the spread of HIV and reinforcing stigma and shame. Recognizing this problem gives a wake-up call to all Christians (even all religious traditions) to reexamine certain teachings and attitudes in the light of what is needed to stop the relentless sickness and death from AIDS. Insofar as some teachings of the church are part of the problem, Christian co-believers all have some responsibility for part of the remedy.

The second consequence of our present understanding of "world church" is that it is now clear that all of us, whether in the United States or Europe or China or Africa, are all equal sharers in the one life of the church, partakers in the one Life of the Spirit of God. We are all therefore called to bear the burdens of one another when the church in one part of the world is in dire need. It is often said in this regard that the church has AIDS; or in other words, the Body of Christ has AIDS. Christians are not spared this devastation—neither the faithful nor their priests and religious, nor their bishops. Insofar as

HIV/AIDS is a problem for the church of Africa (or of China or India or Latin America or the United States), it is a problem for us all. We who stand in the tradition of our church as "world church" cannot look upon such situations as simply "their" problem. The gospel comes to us and is received by all of us, together across the world; it calls us not just to assist one another but to stand in solidarity with all, especially with those who suffer the most. Today when AIDS is a challenge for the whole world, it is surely a challenge to the whole of the church.

I have already observed that the church is part of the problem as well as part of the remedy in relation to HIV and AIDS. The clearest way in which it is part of the problem is the way in which it has shaped stigmatizing beliefs about human sexuality. A sexual ethic that remains too much in the form of a taboo morality has led to an interpretation and rejection of some means of HIV prevention—in particular, the use of condoms—because they are also forms of contraceptives. This interpretation, however, tragically misses the point that their use in this context has nothing to do with a contraceptive goal; it has only to do with preventing people from dying.[12] A tradition that does not hesitate to rethink moral rules in other spheres of human life—social, political, economic—when situations demand it, can be much too complacent about its rules in the sexual sphere.[13] Taboo morality depends precisely on resisting critical examination, perpetuating fear and shame, and hence either preventing change or the deepening of traditional beliefs regarding rules. This is why the mere reiteration of longstanding sexual rules can appear moralistic, unresponsive to the needs as well as the responsibilities of human persons in their present circumstances.

The African women whom I have come to know are on the ground everywhere—in clinics, schools, tiny villages, large cities—attempting to heal and companion the dying, challenge systems of shaming, educate their people, and prevent and treat the elusive infection and disease. African women theologians now focus on the causes of the pandemic, attempting to find out what kinds of sexual education are being given to young girls and boys, what cultural practices lead to infection, and what women themselves say they need in order to be safe and to keep their families well.

With and from these women, I have learned that if religious traditions have anything at all to say to situations like the pandemic, they must speak of God and of human responsibilities to one another in relation to God. Words of hope and deeds of love will be true insofar as they are shaped by accurate understandings of the situation and plausible identification of claims of justice. The great human and religious goals of mutual respect, solidarity, fairness, and compassion come slowly. But in some contexts, where responses to human suffering become urgent, where abandonment and death make slow progress "too late," it may be possible to find the ways whereby at least Christian co-believers can labor together to stop the dying.

Carolyn Sharp

Loving Embrace

Sexual Flourishing and an HIV-Positive Humanity

Erotic desire, pleasure and ecstasy, sexual intimacy, companionship and commitment, human fecundity, reproduction, child raising, and connectedness are moral goods that significantly contribute to human flourishing.[1] To be deprived of these goods may substantially impoverish the life of persons. To be excluded from the community of relationship through which these goods find embodiment can be dehumanizing, with an ultimate consequence in the diminishment of the exclusionary community itself. Because of the importance of sexual transmission, the AIDS crisis has repeatedly drawn attention to questions of sexual ethics. Much of the discussion has concentrated on public health and prevention issues, with a great deal of debate about morally appropriate norms for risk reduction and behavior change. The interrelations between the spread of infection and patterns of sexual abuse, violence, and exploitation have been identified as foundational issues.[2] However, little attention has been paid to how the experience of loving embrace might enrich and strengthen us—individually, collectively, and as a species—to meet the challenges of HIV/AIDS.

As the work of justice makes inroads in facilitating access to treatment, the chronic character of HIV is increasingly visible. The virus can be present for years without making its presence felt, in terms of overall health or capacity to live life as normal. Greater understanding of the relationship between general health and the impact of HIV on the life of infected persons means that it is possible for someone who is HIV-positive to live even longer and without experiencing negative consequences. On the other hand, the increasing treatment capacity, most notably through the use of anti-retroviral treatments (ART), means that even after the onset of AIDS, an infected person can live an active and productive life, fully engaged in community and loving relationships. Justice Edwin Cameron of the Supreme Court of Appeal of South Africa, himself HIV-positive, stresses that "AIDS no longer has to be a fatal illness. Life-saving combinations of anti-retroviral drugs have shown that illness and death from AIDS can be contained. Under the right conditions, HIV is now a chronic, manageable infection and AIDS a treatable disease."[3] In light of effective ART, ethicists must move beyond prescriptive modes of thinking about sexual behavior in relation to HIV and begin to explore the meaning and place of sexual flourishing in an HIV-positive human community.

A widespread and perhaps the most commonly held view understands that the proper moral response to an HIV-positive status is compulsory and complete abstinence, the burden of which is to be shouldered by those infected.[4] This view submits the infected and those close to them to a regime of self-policing condemnation designed to protect the uninfected from stigmatized desires; it amounts to a sexual injunction not to be.[5]

Stereotypes

In a highly controversial 1992 United Colors of Benetton advertisement, a loving and caring family surrounds an emaciated AIDS patient; the controversy pointed to at least two concerns: that the face of patients with AIDS is always emaciated, and that in spite of that horror this family remained loving and caring. Such images dominate the popular imagination.[6] As attention has turned to the plight of the millions of Africans and other peoples in the global south caught in the grip of the pandemic, images of dying women and orphaned children have stirred international compassion and mobilized global solidarity. These powerful and poignant images play an important role in raising awareness of the crisis. In the earliest stages, when the disease was barely understood and treatment a mere hope, such images challenged the scandalous stigmatization of those who were infected and the shameless callousness toward the sick and dying, including by those involved in pastoral care.[7] So too, as the global demographics of the pandemic became clearer, such images disputed the indurate withholding of preventive measures and treatment, whether in the name of sexual righteousness or international trade rights or other purposes.[8]

However useful they may have been, such images themselves perpetuate stigmatizing mythologies whose pessimistic reductionism obscures the more complex reality where persons with HIV continue to thrive and those with AIDS meet the challenges of life with a debilitating chronic illness.[9] Advocating access to the means of prevention and treatment is crucial; so is publicizing the growing understanding of self-care and social support, and what it means to live well with HIV. Access to knowledge, treatment, and care are liberative. Narrative accounts of individuals with HIV attest to "the transformation in the way of life at the moment when the illness is discovered or in the time that follows. A painful change . . . heralds a new life, a sort of resurrection. Not only will nothing ever be the same again, but the inner revolution commands a strength that manages to stave off the announcement of death."[10] Numerous testimonies affirm the recovery of health and vitality when ART becomes available to those physically devastated by the disease.[11] This resurrection effect does not merely concern the individual, as James R.

Cochrane explains: "The person who has risen from the dead has not done so for herself alone but for a phalanx of others . . . who gain strength, hope and vitality from it."[12] The restoration of dignity through a full range of care that embraces psycho-affective, social, economic, spiritual and existential, and physical and medical needs can affect radical shifts in the well-being of those whose lives are most impacted.[13]

Alternatives

In Khayelitsha, South Africa, a group of women called the Bambanani, who are receiving ART under the sponsorship of Médecins Sans Frontières (Doctors without Borders), have produced a series of photographic self-portraits. The photos show their pleasure in caring for their health and their deeply personal engagement in relationship with others. "I love myself," one accompanying testimony reads. "I took a picture of myself at nighttime. . . . I take the picture in my bedroom. And you can see a lot of flowers. It means that there is a lot of love in my house."[14] A documentary recounting an HIV-positive South African woman's successful climb of Mount Kilimanjaro speaks also to this facet of the complex reality of HIV: the mustering of courage and commitment to conquer the physically daunting climb provides a potent metaphor for the mobilization of energy and self-love required for living in the face of this devastating threat to personal well-being. Nor are these death-defying, life-affirming images limited to the personal; calling upon a political tradition which understands that an injury to one is an injury to all, the Treatment Action Campaign has asserted and indeed celebrated the ongoing value of the lives of all those who are infected. In commenting on a painting of hers, one woman explains, "When I look at my body, it reflects the life of activism. That is why one foot is up in the painting. It shows the strength that I have everyday to fight for my life and those who cannot fight for themselves."[15]

Unfortunately, such positive images remain marginal to the general perception of the pandemic. A sexual ethics captivated uniquely by dire images will continue to generate precautionary and even condemnatory responses to the desires, pleasures, intimacies, and reproductive activities of an HIV-positive humanity, albeit expressed as justifiable prudence or compassionate concern. Only stretching beyond pessimistic clichés will sexual ethics open its scope wide enough to dare the question of an inclusive sexual wholeness and flourishing. Turning its attention to the "conditions of the possibility of loving in the time of AIDS,"[16] such an ethics can inquire into the role of sexuality in living positively and facing the suffering that can be caused by the disease. "The fact is that we all have bodies," says Gillian Paterson. "We are all born and die and bleed; and whether we are sexually active or not, we are still sexual beings. We are all vulnerable, all (to some extent) disabled. For the real, lived body is not perfect: it is human."[17]

Sexual embodiment is central to our connection to the world. "The ecstasy of lovemaking frees us to understand our want: how alone, how incomplete, how broken we are without participation in ecstasy. . . . We are erotically connected to the world."[18] Our being in the world finds a privileged expression in and through our experience of self and other in lovemaking. Recognizing this privilege allows us to ponder differently the longing to enter into and to remain in relationship, even when the risks of infection are known. Fassin tells of a woman who, upon discovering that her new husband was HIV-positive and may have infected her, responded by saying, "Even if you are like that you are still Mesias, you are still my lover and I am still going to be your wife."[19]

Such experiences speak to the profound relationship between suffering and sexuality. Clearly, the experience of illness and the threat of death transform sexual being. However, it is human to experience a need for sexual connectedness in the face of illness, death, and loss.

Erotic pleasure, sexual companionship, reproductive joy, and sorrow all mark the moments of existence. In the face of a grave threat to well-being, this marking becomes all the more powerful. So too, in and through sexuality, humans encounter an ability to comfort one another and to discover the power to love as a life-giving force. Similar dynamics exist with regard to reproduction, as one woman explains: "When I want to have a child, [the doctor] said I must tell him. If I take AZT and my CD4 cell count is non-detectable, there is a great chance that my child will be negative; but it can be a big risk for my body. It is also a risk for my partner because of course you cannot use a condom to make a child."[20] After a period of serious illness, the feeling of well-being associated with ART may increase the desire to have a child as an affirmation of a hold on life.

In her discussion of stigmatization, Gillian Paterson highlights three phases of the Christian churches' response to the HIV/AIDS pandemic.[21] The first involved becoming aware of the epidemic and organizing the appropriate compassionate response to those affected, especially those who were sick, dying, and orphaned. In the second, the impact of HIV and AIDS on church membership and their clergy forced the churches to recognize that the virus did not only infect those outside of church communities, but also faithful and practicing Christians; hence the saying "the body of Christ has AIDS." In the third phase, awareness grew of how the dynamics of stigma, denial, and fear hardened the disease's impact, and the call arose for the churches to combat stigmatization. Throughout these phases, the ethical controversies surrounding prevention and treatment swirled ad nauseum. Divisions among and within the churches diminished their capacity to act, and controversies and divisions reinforced the very stigmatization that the churches sought to counter. According to Paterson, "AIDS has acted as a magnet for all the negative meanings that Western Christian tradition has attached to the body: meanings which underpinned its ethics and ecclesiology, and which influenced the culture of Christian churches."[22]

Understanding HIV as a chronic infection and AIDS as a manageable, although debilitating and life-shortening, condition requires a fourth phase in our reflection. The life expectancy of those who are infected is unknown. Recognizing that they remain sexual persons whose lives are impoverished when they are denied their sexuality and that humanity itself is diminished when any are stigmatized and excluded from sexual community, we must speak frankly and openly about the meaning of erotic desire and pleasure, sexual intimacy and companionship, human fecundity and connectedness for an HIV-positive humanity. Moreover, this reflection involves more than the generation of moral guidelines for individuals. Indeed, a narrow focus upon individual behaviors, whether prescriptive warnings for those with HIV or prudential counsels for those who are sero-negative, risks a rules-based ethics of proscription and blame.[23]

Sexual Flourishing

Rather than norms and rules, reflection must ask about the necessary conditions and possibilities of an inclusive and life-affirming sexual flourishing in an HIV-positive humanity. Its mode of inquiry works out of an ethical vision through attention to the actualities of lived sexual experience within a framework affirming sexuality as a vital and necessary dimension of human life.[24] It grants, moreover, a privileged place to the voices of those most deeply wounded by the pandemic, preserving their status as agents of their own lives, as full members of the human sexual community, and valuing their understanding of the complexities of living in this time of HIV/AIDS.[25] Calling for a discourse of hope, Jill Olivier recognizes how essential is the lead of people with or affected by HIV and AIDS:

> It is essential that everyone should have the same opportunity and power to define their future for themselves. . . . Christian discourse of hope in the time of HIV/AIDS must be a participatory process, and not the church leadership prescribing its hopes onto its members. It is important that PLWHA are given the space to define their own hopes and social imaginary, instead of being silenced by what the dominant discourse believes they should be feeling.[26]

To some, however, the need for such a reflection may not be evident. In those contexts in which HIV prevalence remains low and infection is primarily associated with marginalized and stigmatized groups, the question may appear abstract and distant: the sexual exclusion and condemnation of the few can seem like a small price to pay for the protection of the larger community, and as infection is associated with culpable personal choice, this price may be a just and justifiable consequence of imprudent behavior.[27]

In contexts where prevalence rates are higher, the inaccessibility of treatment may make the proposal for reflection appear premature, as a distraction from the more immediately pressing struggle to gain access and provide appropriate care as well as from the equally urgent task of prevention, including combating the gender, racial, and economic inequalities that greatly facilitate the spread of the disease. The culture of scarcity can create the illusion that treatment itself is a privilege whose value outweighs the sacrifice of one's sexuality; the intersection of HIV risk with patterns of sexual exploitation, gender-based violence, oppressive family structures, and abuse of power may discredit discussion of sexuality as a conduit of personal wholeness and fulfillment, human love, and relationship; conscious that the lives of millions remain in peril, those involved in international pressure campaigns may perceive reflection on the meaning and place of sexuality to be strategically imprudent; fragile gains in recent years can easily be lost if a fickle public opinion comes to believe that concerted action is no longer necessary.[28] This complacence or failure to consider the meanings of sexual intimacy for human flourishing mirrors the concern that the alleviation of the fear of the disease through widespread access to treatment has led to an increase in risk-taking behaviors.

However, such a reflection is both timely and necessary. The emergence of an understanding of the chronic character of HIV requires attention to the embodied sexual experience of infected persons and a careful listening to their hopes and aspirations, fears and troubles, happiness and sadness.[29] Such a listening affirms their place as fully sexual members of humanity. Moreover, since the beginning of the pandemic, a generation has come of age sexually. Their awareness of themselves as sexual persons, their understanding of sexual relationship, and their hopes for parenthood has been profoundly shaped by the presence of HIV/AIDS. While enormous cross-cultural and individual differences exist with regard to erotic desire and fulfillment, sexual intimacy and relationship, human fecundity and parenting, the globalized character of the pandemic invites an active commitment to embracing present and future generations within the circle of embodied human loving. Finally, the crisis that is HIV/AIDS reveals much about who we are as sexual beings and sexual communities, our suffering and brokenness, our courage and resilience. As Dorothee Soelle explains, "To receive bodily consolation from our partner after undergoing a loss or trauma is an experience that shows how wrong it is to split off eros from agape. Love indeed bears, believes, hopes and endures all things. . . . God needs our growing capacity to love to continue creation. In the socio-political struggle against death . . . God will make use of all of our passions and our undivided love for life."[30] Being attentive to what we can learn about human sexual flourishing in the wake of the pandemic, including our need for conversion and reconciliation, lays the groundwork for a deeper understanding of human wholeness and solidarity.

Part Two

Challenging the Church

Agnes M. Brazal

Information, Sex Education, and Church Intervention in Public Policy in the Philippines

Since the United Nations Conference on Population and Development in Cairo, Egypt, in 1994, the hierarchy of the Catholic Church has been actively intervening in global policy making regarding issues of reproductive health.[1] The right to reproductive health of all individuals and, in particular, of women and adolescents, has been recognized in several international human rights organizations. In particular, the International Conference on Population and Development's (ICPD) Programme of Action (principle 8, par. 7.46) has been proactive in establishing this right, despite "grave concerns" from the Holy See that this right would be interpreted as sanctioning extramarital sexual activity, particularly among the youth.[2] As signatory to this document, however, the Philippine state has the corresponding duty to protect the right to reproductive health care for all Filipinos.

In other Asian countries where the Catholic Church is a minority, the hierarchy is oftentimes compelled to adopt a more pluralist and tolerant perspective on the government's reproductive health programs. In a state like the Philippines, where the Church continues to be a dominant political and cultural force, pluralist tolerance has not held sway. The Philippine national episcopate exerts pressure on the government to adopt the Catholic position on reproductive health issues.

This pressure brings to the fore the question of whether other religious groups in the country are deprived of their right to information and sex education necessary to adequately respond to life and death issues, like HIV. While the Philippines remains predominantly Catholic (82.9 percent), there are other religious groups whose views should be considered (mainline Protestant, 5.4 percent; Philippine Independent Church, 2.6 percent; Tagalog Iglesia ni Cristo, 2.3 percent; Muslim, 4.6 percent; and others, 1.8 percent).[3] Linked to this diversity is the need to closely examine the existence of a plurality of perspectives among Catholics themselves, who are deprived of their right to information and education on reproductive health and HIV.

The Catholic Church is challenged by progressive NGOs and conscientious politicians to re-examine its intervention in public policies affecting the HIV/AIDS issue, from a more traditionalist to a pluralist perspective informed by the principles of justice and peace in the Catholic social tradition. I offer this theological reflection as a Filipina and a faithful daughter of the Church.

Low Prevalence in the Philippines

The Philippines has a low HIV prevalence rate at 0.1 percent.[4] Since the first AIDS case was diagnosed in 1984, the country remains at "first stage" of incidence. Several factors related to transmission explain this low prevalence rate. First is the relatively late age at which Filipinos first engage in sexual intercourse. One survey of 15- to 19-year-olds in fourteen countries worldwide showed the Philippines to be the most sexually conservative state, with less than 20 percent of respondents reporting experience with sexual intercourse.[5] A second factor is the seeming dislike or fear that Filipinos have of needles. This apprehension contributes to low prevalence from injecting drug use. The major means of HIV transmission is unprotected sexual intercourse (86 percent).[6]

The increasing trend since 2001, however, is disturbing. The HIV/AIDS Registry (January 1984–December 2006) reveals a drop in the number of new cases (asymptomatic) in 1999, which may be the fruit of increased information campaigns about AIDS to vulnerable groups and efforts to monitor STDs, including HIV, among sex workers. In 1998, the Philippine Aids Prevention and Control Act of 1998 (Republic Act 8504) was promulgated. The drop, however, was not sustained, as the data for 2001–2006 shows an increase in the number of cases, indicating certain gaps in the way HIV is reported.[7]

Danger signs and cultural factors could still trigger an epidemic in the country. After all, high-prevalence countries at the moment, such as South Africa, showed low prevalence at the start.[8] One danger is the limited knowledge about HIV and AIDS and safe sex among the general population and, in particular, among the youth. This lack of information is due largely to cultural and religious traditions that prevent open discussion of sex and situations of risk.

Lack of Effective Knowledge

In 2002, a Young Adult Fertility and Sexuality Study (YAFS) of 19,728 women and men aged 15 to 27 was conducted.[9] The third in a series of regular surveys initiated by the University of the Philippines Population Institute,[10] the survey revealed an increase of premarital sex in adolescents from 17.8 percent in 1994 to 23.1 percent in 2002.[11]

The study also showed that while awareness of HIV and AIDS is high (95 percent), knowledge about transmission and effects of the disease is limited. Almost one-third (28 percent) believe AIDS is curable, and most of the youth (73 percent) think they are safe from HIV infection. This illusion of invincibility operates even among those who engage in premarital sex; a majority of them fail to avail themselves of any protection (70 percent of the men, 68 percent of the women). Only 9 percent of sexually active youth have used a condom at one time or another.[12] A 2003 National Demographic and Health Survey showed that only 50 percent of the general population is aware of the usefulness of condoms as a method of HIV prevention.[13]

In general, women are at risk of contracting HIV from their boyfriends or husbands. This risk stems from sexually active young men, who engage in casual sex and sex with multiple partners (49 percent of men, 11 percent of women).[14] Also, 20 percent of sexually active men pay for sex, and 12 percent of sexually active men had been paid to have sex with men.[15] Among women, the prevalence of commercial sex is negligible. For those who engage in commercial sex, a little more than 50 percent use condoms with various levels of consistency.[16] These data indicate that monogamy or fidelity on the part of women alone will not necessarily protect them from HIV.

Church Opposition to
Sex Education in Schools

Young adults (15 to 24) are among the most vulnerable segments of the population. The prevalence of gonorrhea and chlamydia are higher among youth, indicating both high-risk sexual behaviors (especially among young men) and ignorance of reproductive and sexual health.[17] Schools can be a strategic site for a holistic approach to HIV prevention via education programs in responsible sexuality.

For decades, however, the leaders of the Philippine Catholic Church have stood as the sole opposition against sex education programs in schools.[18] In 2006, a trial sex education program was to have run that would have integrated the lessons in many subjects within the school curriculum, including health and science, Filipino history and culture, and livelihood education.[19] This program was lauded by the UN Fund for Population Activities as a positive move. Teachers were to educate about overpopulation and the dangers of premarital sex; this was to be a venue as well for education in sexually transmitted diseases. The trial, however, was suspended because of the opposition by the Catholic bishops.

The head of the Catholic Bishops' Conference of the Philippines Episcopal Commission on Family and Life argued that the sex education of youth should be left to the parents alone and that "no excuse or alibi can justify the public teaching of sex education by strangers."[20] While the prelate is right that sex education must not be detached from parental responsibilities and family values, his reinforcement of the privatization of sexual discourse that the Church advocates is unhelpful. There is no guarantee that parents—many of whom are uncomfortable discussing sex—would be better equipped than professionally trained teachers to handle their children's education on sexuality. Moreover, a 2005 study on Filipino youth showed that, generally, young people are not comfortable discussing sexual matters with their parents; only 32.6 percent prefer to discuss sexual matters with either their mother or father.[21] The 2002 YAFS also showed that 76 percent of young men and 48 percent of young women already had exposure to pornographic materials either in film, video, or literature.[22] If the schools do not provide sex education, youth will learn it from other sources, with the greater danger of improper guidance.

Church leaders also object to sex education on the proper use of condoms and contraceptives. Thus, the country's law on AIDS Prevention, Republic Act 8504, legislated the integration of instruction about HIV/AIDS in intermediate grades, provided "it shall not be used as an excuse to propagate birth control or the sale or distribution of birth control devices" and "it does not utilize sexually explicit materials" (art. 1, sec. 4).[23] The implementation of a school-based AIDS Educational Project in 2000 by the Department of Education and Culture was actually stopped when Catholic schools, echoing the Church's opposition to condom use, organized a demonstration protesting the integration of AIDS prevention in several subject areas. Is it merely coincidental that, since 2001, the Philippines presents a more rapid increase of asymptomatic cases annually?

Re-evaluating Church Intervention in Public Policy

The Catholic Church in the Philippines wields strong influence in national politics. It has used this power on issues of education in reproductive health. The Church's intervention in the Department of Education's sex education program in public schools is just one among a series of active and successful efforts against bills promoting reproductive health, especially the health of women.[24]

Democratic societies like the Philippines uphold religious freedom; in this context, the Catholic Church has the right to lobby for its values and norms. However, this right should be exercised in a manner respecting the rights of members of other religious communities too. As Frances Kissling, president of the US-based Catholics for a Free Choice, notes, "When the Catholic Church puts forward a public policy position . . . to prevent sexual education programs in public schools, or to refuse to provide information about condoms as a preventive measure against the transmission of AIDS—it is not just Roman Catholics who are affected if policy makers enact such positions. Every woman, every man, and every child would be subject to these laws."[25]

While the Philippine Catholic hierarchy has been very active and leads in interfaith discussions on social conflicts among Islamic and non-Islamic groups in the southern part of the Philippines, it has yet to adopt the same pluralist perspective in its intervention in public policy issues pertaining to sex education and reproductive health.

Nevertheless, during the term of Protestant president Fidel Ramos and his Protestant health secretary, Dr. Juan Flavier, family planning became a key health program of the government. As the book *Sex, Church, and the Free Press* argues, the Catholic Church "attacked without letup [the government's] every stride towards moves to advance sexuality and reproductive health issues—from sexuality education in the high school curriculum to contraception to proposed reproductive health care."[26]

The four transcultural criteria of Kissling and Clifton-Brown can be used by lawmakers to evaluate recommendations by any group, including religious groups on public policy positions.[27] Here I examine how these criteria correspond to the basic principles of the Catholic social tradition and argue that adherence to these criteria are at the heart of the Church's teachings on justice.

Criteria for Public Policy Positions

Whom does this group represent, who is their constituency, and does that constituency agree with them on this issue? This criterion is underlined in the Catholic social principle of participation. John Paul II stresses how "every democracy must be participative."[28] The *Compendium of the Social Doctrine of the Church* further elaborates that "the different subjects of civil community at every level must be informed, listened to and involved in the exercise of the carried-out functions."[29]

According to a 2007 survey conducted by Pulse Asia, 89 percent of Filipinos think that government should allot a budget for modern methods of family planning, including access to the pill, condoms, and other means of regulating births. Seventy-five percent of Filipinos indicate they would vote for a candidate who supports this budgetary allocation.[30] Granted, these data cannot be interpreted as favoring sex education in public schools, but they indicate that the Catholic bloc is not of a homogenous mind on reproductive health and that government policy has not considered the voice of this majority. Data like these can likewise allay fears of politicians that they will lose the Catholic vote once they support reproductive health issues. For Catholic legislators and the hierarchy, this support need not mean simply succumbing to the majority. We have rich theological resources such as the *sensus fidelium* and "reception" of a teaching to help guide discernment on these issues.[31]

Are those presenting recommendations honest? Do they present accurate and valid facts? This criterion is linked to the people's right to objective information. The *Compendium of the Social Doctrine of the Church* stresses that "information is among the principal instruments of democratic participation. Participation without an understanding of the situation of the political community, the facts and the proposed solutions to problems is unthinkable. It is necessary to guarantee a real pluralism in this delicate area of social life."[32]

In lieu of this disclosure, the agenda must be examined closely to discern what may be propagated by various Church groups regarding proposed public policies. Among the claims of some, HIV can enter through rubber lattices and therefore the condom is not an effective prophylactic against transmission; it simply gives people the illusion of security and has not really prevented AIDS from reaching pandemic proportions.[33] While condom use is not 100 percent foolproof, a U.S. Centers for Disease Control and Prevention study of persons vulnerable to HIV showed that 98 to 100 percent of those who correctly and consistently used latex condoms were not infected.[34] Jon Fuller, Jesuit priest and physician, also cites studies that show the promotion of abstinence and condom use has likewise helped to significantly reduce HIV transmission in Uganda and Thailand.[35] It is important, especially in the life and death context surrounding HIV/AIDS, that the information disseminated is validated by the scientific community.[36]

Does this policy position promote the common good?[37] From a pluralist perspective, the commitment to the good attends not only to the benefits one's group can receive; it attends also to how public policy promotes the good and respects the rights of the whole society. In general, other religious traditions have a more open attitude with regard to condom use not only for family planning but also to prevent HIV and other STDs. The World Council of Churches, representing 324 Protestant and ecumenical churches, acknowledged at the Cairo Conference how the "increased use of condoms reduces drastically the transmission of HIV/AIDS" and stressed the importance of access to various means of fertility regulation to protect reproductive health.[38] As Kissling and Clifton-Brown underline, "Given . . . the separation of church and state and an obligation not to seek laws that would limit people of other faiths or no faith in the practice of their beliefs, . . . [a] legislator who would work for laws that would limit these religions from exercising their freedom by legislating the Roman Catholic view would violate the value of tolerance at a very basic level."[39]

Will the policy position work? This criterion may be a utilitarian norm understood in terms of the values of effectiveness and efficiency, which the Church has underlined in relation to economic institutions: "Resources in society are quantitatively scarce, which means that each individual economic subject, as well as each individual society, must necessarily come up with a plan for their utilization in the most rational way possible, following the logic dictated by the 'principle of economizing.'"[40] In the context of HIV/AIDS, we ask whether the integration of sex education in public schools will effectively delay sexual intercourse among youth and prevent HIV transmission when they become sexually active.

The Church's insistence on relegating discourse about sex to the private sphere seems motivated by the fear that sex education in the public schools will lead to sexual promiscuity and experimentation. On the contrary, based on more than fifteen years of research by the American Psychological Association, rather than promoting premarital sex, "comprehensive sexuality education programs for youth that encourage abstinence, promote appropriate condom use, and teach sexual communication skills reduce HIV-risk behavior and also delay the onset of sexual intercourse."[41]

In the context of the Philippines, current data puts into question the effectiveness of information and education programs conducted in recent years. Knowledge about AIDS and its prevention in general among youth is both grossly inadequate and shows no improvement. Moreover, it is alarming that the percentage of those who think that HIV or AIDS is curable has more than doubled among those 15 to 24 years old, from 12.5 percent in 1994 to 27.8 percent in 2002. Likewise alarming, not for the increase but for the degree of ignorance revealed, is that among youth engaging in premarital sex, 73.4 percent think there is no chance for them to get AIDS—an increase of 1.4 percent since 1994.[42] This statistic should motivate a change in the way that children and adolescents are informed about sex and sexuality.

Conclusion

The Philippines still has the gift of time, which many other countries no longer possess, but complacence is not an option. The youth, in particular, should not be deprived of their right to be informed and educated, especially when it involves this and other matters of life and death. The Church, leaders and laity alike, need to draw on the rich resources of the Catholic social tradition to respond more effectively to the challenges posed by the HIV/AIDS pandemic.

Elizabeth Hepburn, IBVM

HIV/AIDS in Australia

When we in Australia first heard of AIDS we believed it was a "gay" disease, and our approach was naïve in the extreme. Twenty years since then we have begun to see things differently: we see sexuality more holistically, and questions of disease transmission as more complex. We also see issues of care and relationships between medical practitioners and patients differently: questions of privacy, disclosure, and respect in the clinical setting are now more carefully described. In short, we owe the people living with AIDS a great deal for awakening us to see them and their rights in more clearly defined ways. Their struggle has become an impetus to forward movements in health care and outreach to people in need, and for this change we are in their debt. Medical practice has changed as a result of their efforts, and the emphases of overseas aid programs have changed as well.[1]

Speculation about why this has happened has no answers. AIDS initially struck specific populations of predominantly young people, either members of the gay or the injecting drug using (IDU) communities. The results of infection in the first years of the pandemic were devastating. Gay community members were galvanized into action and information gathering. Soon after, patients from the gay community knew as much or more than their physicians did about the disease, causing havoc in well-ordered services, where the patterns of deference to medical practitioners were well established.

Then questions were asked about how to care for predominantly gay people close to death residing in institutions that were designed for the needs of older heterosexual folk, and how a physician who cared for both partners was to treat information about one patient that could be life threatening for the partner-patient. The resulting changes in hospice and hospital care have revolutionized our approach to end-of-life issues. In many Catholic hospices new arrangements have been made and rooms have been adjusted to accommodate homosexual partnerships if desired. This accommodation has proved helpful also for heterosexual couples. The Australian Medical Association amended its code of ethics to reflect specific exceptions to the general rules of patient confidentiality. The current code reads, "Maintain . . . confidentiality. Exceptions . . . must be taken very seriously[:] . . . where there is a serious risk to the patient or another person, where required by law, or where there are overwhelming societal interests."[2] Questions of confidentiality were raised in a way that focused on life-threatening risks to vulnerable others. The resolutions to these questions have benefited the relationships between physicians and patients generally and have alerted us to previously unknown issues or issues about to we turned a blind eye.

However, many issues remain unresolved, and people infected with HIV still experience traumatic and singular inhospitable periods, as letters posted on the People Living with HIV/AIDS (PLWHA) Web site attest.[3] The isolation and despair many feel is palpable, and the readiness of the community to reach out to them remains a matter of critical concern. The situation of IDUs seems much more desperate than that of the gay community, primarily because drug users are less closely bonded, less likely well-educated or able to articulate their concerns, and they are less likely to easily share their personal anguish.

In spite of the apparent growth in understanding of the multifaceted predicaments that people with AIDS face, a recent survey showed that many Australians are not altogether comfortable about gays living in their neighborhoods. According to a University of Queensland study, a quarter of Australians would not be happy to live next door to homosexuals. The study explored the attitudes of 31,625 people in 26 countries; results were pretty uniform for Australia, the USA, and the UK. However, as one spokesperson for the Gay and Lesbian Rights lobby noted, "75% would not mind living next door to a gay or lesbian couple."[4] For the journalist reporting, the 25 percent who would mind living next door to a homosexual couple was an important issue; to the lobby group, that 75 percent did not mind was seen as a positive reaction. One's sexuality seemed to determine what was taken as noteworthy. This reaction reveals an interesting dimension to the myths surrounding heterosexual presumptions about what other heterosexuals think about people who are gay or lesbian.

The once widely believed myth that AIDS is a gay disease has been debunked by global statistics but not by consciousness. On our doorstep and within a largely heterosexual population in the Asia Pacific Region (including Asia and Oceania), an estimated 8.3 million people are HIV-positive. In Australia, members of the gay community present more than three-quarters of the infected population. Unless we take drastic action, UNAIDS projects that the Asia Pacific Region will reach 20 million cases by 2010.[5] Accordingly, Australia has committed $1 billion AVD from 2000 to 2010 to fight the pandemic.[6]

Living with HIV and AIDS

So what is it like to live with HIV or AIDS now that many people have access to anti-retroviral drugs, which can extend life and keep the acute phases of AIDS at bay? A recent study carried out by the Australian Research Centre in Sex, Health, and Society at La Trobe University explored this question in depth.[7] Some of the findings important for ethical consideration indicate demographic data as well as health, disclosure, employment, and relationship concerns.

The Research Centre surveyed 982 people, estimated to be about 6.4 percent of the total HIV population in Australia.[8] Of these 982 people, 80.6 percent were gay men, 8.1 percent heterosexual women, 5.3 percent heterosexual men, and 3.7 percent bisexual men. Of these 982 people, 24 percent were tested for HIV when they became ill, 15.8 percent were tested as part of a routine health check, 13.2 percent were tested following a particular risk episode, 11 percent were tested because they belonged to a risk group, and 2 percent were tested without their knowledge.

A total of 68.1 percent reported that their general health was good or excellent, although 44.6 percent also reported having another major health condition (hepatitis C, cardiovascular disease, or asthma). However, more specific questions revealed that in the previous twelve-month period, 81.8 percent experienced low energy or fatigue, 65.8 percent reported a sleep disorder, 48 percent experienced confusion or memory loss, 43.7 percent reported weight loss, and 36.8 percent had lipodystrophy, known as "wasting" (a disturbance of fat metabolism resulting in loss of subcutaneous fat). When compared to the general population, these results reveal significant compromises to overall health.

The question of HIV-status disclosure continues to be a difficult matter to negotiate, especially since disclosure can evoke aversion. In the survey, 76.9 percent indicated their chief source of social support was a partner or spouse (frequently the only persons outside of the medical team to know their status), while 60.1 percent reported a chief source of social support was from a pet. Almost all had disclosed their HIV status to at least one person but, disturbingly, 51.8 percent had their HIV status revealed to another person without their consent. Such disclosures violate privacy standards and indicate that a trusted individual did not keep delicate information confidential. Concerns about privacy and employment in turn tend to limit the pleasure of intimate touch. Nevertheless and despite normative nondisclosure, 87.5 percent had used a condom when having sex with an HIV-negative partner, while 65.8 percent reported feeling that having HIV made sex less pleasurable.

The impact of HIV on working life was marked: 34.1 percent reported full-time employment, with a total of 51.2 percent in paid employment of some kind; however, about the same proportion (51.6 percent) said they had stopped work, some temporarily and others permanently, due to symptoms of HIV. Despite reporting feeling well, when questioned a little more searchingly, they admitted that the negative impact of HIV on lifestyle and work was considerable. The impact of the disease on financial matters was also marked, with 28.3 percent living below the poverty line and about half of the total sample reporting difficulty meeting the standard costs of living. Further complicating the provision of basic needs, the average expenditure on medication was reported at $53.07 per week.

The Research Centre report offers the following summaries: The potential to develop new relationships remains an important issue for PLWHA. While much has been done to reduce stigma and discrimination in formal settings like workplaces and health care settings, the more intimate domains of sex and relationships can still be a site of anxiety and uncertainty for people who are HIV-positive and HIV-negative. A full 61.8 percent of respondents agreed with the statement "Few people would want a relationship with someone who has HIV." A slightly smaller group (54.7 percent) agreed with the statement "I am afraid of telling potential partners of my HIV status in case they reject me."[9]

PLWHA experience less favourable treatment in many domains of their lives. While more detailed research is needed to assess adequately the specific impact of negative treatment, the impact goes beyond the direct outcomes of action and is detrimental to both health and quality of life. Additionally, the anticipation of discrimination may limit people's life choices in subtle but sustained ways.[10]

The experience of being HIV-positive has social and psychological ramifications that affect every aspect of life; without immediate knowledge of life with HIV/AIDS, we can only guess at how shattering the complex of experiences can be.

An Ethic of Compassion

The plight of PLWHA calls us to an empathic understanding and to deliver a particular kind of care, care that responds positively to what the situation demands. Stephen Schmidt, who is suffering from Crohn's disease, a chronic disorder of the small bowel requiring endless surgical resections, shares many of the sentiments as PLWHA. He describes what he wants from his caregivers in the closing lines of his meditation "When You Come into My Room."[11]

> When you come into my room, you need to sustain my hope.
> You need to know that I believe that love wins over hate,
> hope over despair, life over death
> that I hope against hope
> that I pray and believe prayer heals
> that some days I am able to make meaning of suffering
> that I am more gentle, more compassionate, better with dying,
> more loving, more sensitive, deeper in grief and joy. . . .
> When you come into my hospital room, promise me presence,
> promise me a healing partnership
> to keep hope alive
> it is all I have.

It strikes me that this attention to a patient is precisely the sort of attitude described in the gospel as typical of Jesus. In many stories Jesus is presented as a healer who does not stop to take a case history but looks into the eyes of the suffering person and asks, "What do you want?" In many cases the desire of the person Jesus addresses is similar to what Schmidt seeks: "a healing partnership to keep hope alive."

In the account of the cure of the woman with the hemorrhage (Luke 8:43–48) is a woman with a chronic condition that would have precluded normal sexual relationships and incurred social stigma and isolation. In many respects similar to the impact of HIV/AIDS on the lives of those infected, this woman was excluded from social commerce as a result of the fears others had concerning contamination. The whole scene presents the woman as so shamed and lacking in self-esteem that she does not even approach Jesus; she merely seeks to come close enough to touch his clothing. She has suffered this ignominy for twelve years: twelve years of isolation and derision, twelve years cut off from all that might be life sustaining.

The initiative is entirely the woman's, while the disciples scorn at Jesus' claim that something significant occurred in the crowded street. The healing is enough for the woman to forget twelve years of ignominy and timidity; trembling, she came forward to identify herself as the recipient of Jesus' power. Still, Jesus is reluctant to take the credit, insisting that it was a healing partnership and that is was the woman's faith that cured her.

The healing encounter between Jesus and this woman and those between caregivers and their patients with HIV and AIDS demonstrate that compassion is the appropriate response to those who seek to be understood, welcomed, and made whole. With her healing, this woman could return to a life-affirming place in the community. Following R. M. Zaner, "Compassion is, I think, the fundamental form of availability to the other, and solicits trust,"[12] which can lead to reconciliation.

I would add that compassion also engenders hope. Margaret Farley writes that compassion is a cognitive emotion with decidedly moral content involving a voluntary move to appreciate what the other is feeling and a commitment to do something to relieve that person's suffering.[13] Compassion involves both initial sensitivity and vigilance to notice the suffering of the other, and then an imaginative move to the space occupied by that other to see what care might be most helpful. Compassionate respect requires listening to and hearing the other so that the hope of just care is realized.

Martha Nussbaum also writes on the relationships that compassion forms like a bridge between ourselves and others.[14] It involves a decision (Farley's concrete turn) not to stand apart from another's need. Nussbaum recognizes that compassion needs to be tempered with respect so that responses will be both rightly measured and nonsubordinating. This compassionate respect is the heart of Jesus' response to the woman with the hemorrhage: she takes the initiative, and he makes no attempt to wrest it from her. Further, compassion does not seek to know who is responsible for unwelcome conditions confronting those who suffer; the fact that another human being is in need of something I can supply is, in and of itself, sufficient to engage a compassionate response.

Our Response to People with HIV and AIDS

The ethical code used in Australian Catholic hospitals and facilities for the aged urges that "Catholic healthcare services . . . promote the dignity of people living with HIV and AIDS by ensuring . . . access to appropriate medical, nursing and pastoral care, regardless of how they contracted the infection, and by ensuring that they enjoy the same opportunities as people afflicted with any other serious disease."[15] This promotion is consistent with the gospel, but that it needs to be codified suggests some lingering doubt that not everyone would see things this way. The code reminds health care workers that "great care must be taken to ensure that the social and personal complications of the disease do not jeopardise the provision of supportive, compassionate care."[16] The code accepts that a person's social and personal world may be stressed by the disease and urges providers to take this stress into account when caring for those affected. Their care should be characterized by compassion and support. In fact, the earlier chapters of the code deal specifically with the attitudes that ought to characterize Catholic health care, that is, the compassionate respect that Jesus of Nazareth modeled throughout his ministry—genuine attention to persons, respect for their dignity, and recognition of their own initiative to want to be whole and hale.

The code encourages the integration of thought and feeling that together engenders a holistic response to individuals and is appropriate to meeting their needs. This integration echoes the work of Aristotle in recognizing that the emotions should occupy a vital, humanizing place in our moral judgments. Moreover, to do things for the right reasons and with appropriate feeling was to Aristotle and Aquinas the mark of a virtuous person.[17] This is surely one of the underlying purposes of the code, if not an explicit reminder of the distinctive characteristics of Catholic health care.

Conclusion

To act out of compassion is to act out of love moved by justice. That a diagnosis of HIV could so easily be given to me or my sister raises in me a sense that the situation demands action. Motivated by kinship with others, this action is always a movement away from myself and toward the other. In our scriptural tradition, the Hebrew texts make little distinction between love and justice, compassion and action: love God, do justice. Compassion unites love and justice and leads to action. Compassion does not simply look on misfortune with sympathy; rather, compassion begets acting for justice. It was this capacity in Jesus, to see what a situation called for in the way that God would act, which set him apart from other teachers and healers. Jesus communicated and witnessed unconditional love and concern; to the recipients of his attention this concern was far different and removed from pity. In meeting the woman with the hemorrhage, Peter's mother-in-law (Mark 1:29–31), or in telling the story of the Good Samaritan (Luke 10:29–37), Jesus models the simple gestures of reaching out and doing what is required to restore health and wholeness, no questions asked; this is a ministry and a response that is readily available to and required of each of us. As Matthew Fox reminds us, "In the Biblical tradition all experience of God is to lead to creative compassion to neighbour."[18] Right understanding of compassion provides the necessary ground for all healing: at the heart of compassion is the struggle to have just relations restored. Despite the obvious inequalities of the sick approached by the hale, the relationship that actually heals is the one wherein the healer assumes the stance of the one in need, vulnerability is recognized as integral to the human condition, and the care there offered reflects compassionate respect.

The HIV/AIDS pandemic demands from all of us action born of this kind of compassion.

Elsie M. Miranda

Hope, Lament, and a Prophetic Imagination for a World with HIV/AIDS

When the AIDS crisis broke out in the late 1970s and early 1980s, Western society did not know what to make of it or how to name it.[1] People were dying fast, most of the dead were men, and many of them were young, educated, talented, and gay. After the determination that the virus was transmitted primarily through sexual activity with an associated blood element, men suddenly found themselves cast into a mythological evil paradigm reserved previously for women. Emerging from the mythological narrative of Eve as temptress, seductress, and responsible for the fall of man, gay men found themselves in the inadequately critiqued history of original sin often taught as sexual in nature. For the first time on a wide scale, men were treated sociologically as women. Regardless of socioeconomic and cultural location, gay men with AIDS were expendable, objectified, blamed, and dehumanized. Shame became and continues to be the order of the day, while truth is sacrificed for the sake of pretense, and the virus continues to claim power over humanity.

This moment in the Church's history requires serious lament while it simultaneously offers profound hope. The implications generated by this crossroads call out for justice in the form of dialogue, solidarity, and action in regard to the HIV/AIDS pandemic. The Church is in a position to forge alliances of hope, care, and social reconstruction that will renew the earth, as called for in Catholic social teaching and modeled by ecumenical methods and practices.

As Benedict XVI declared in his "2007 World Day of Peace Message," "Many unjust realities still tragically present in our world are the origin of many tensions that threaten peace."[2] In regard to HIV and AIDS, many of these "unjust realities" are centered in the context of prevention and treatment, and often our responses are in effect sinful. For example:

- false teachings and myths promulgated by particular religious and cultural leaders that consider infection as a punishment from God, or a fit consequence for immoral behavior;

- denial, in the form of an unrealistic acknowledgment of the vulnerability among unsuspecting populations at risk;
- lack of availability or access to testing, medication, appropriate care (most significant in rural areas and places without refrigeration);
- apathy disguised as a self-righteous resistance to recognizing suffering in the here and now;
- lack of commitment to the promotion of education, empowerment, social responsibility, or social change; and
- ineffective preaching, teaching, and practice on the part of lay and ordained leaders to promote a sacred human dignity.

In stark contrast to many of these unjust realities are hope and a call to lamentation that yields social action. I argue as well for communication and evangelization that promotes dialogue and seeks effective transformational education to impart knowledge and power. These transformative mediums challenge and correct the unjust realities that threaten human dignity, justice, and peace throughout the world.[3] Regarding HIV/AIDS, communication and evangelization allow for communities to give voice to their experiences and provide a forum to listen authentically to the hard truths and harsh realities of the other; dialogue allows the community to locate its struggles and hopes within the narrative of its traditions. These articulations generate the knowledge/power discourse that French historian Michel Foucault deems is ultimately transformative. To generate honest articulations, however, the question of sex from both a political and religious context has to be openly discussed so that all sides are capable and willing to engage in authentic discourse.[4] This broadly inclusive method allows strategies to emerge from the collective body that, if separated, would be unreachable for individuals and fields of study.

At some level, this model of discourse already exists within the Catholic Church. From the Second Vatican Council (1962–1965), the work of the Latin American bishops (CELAM) in Medellin (1968), and the 1972 collaboration with the World Council of Churches (WCC), true dialogue and social change generated new levels of meaning and empowerment among Christian communities. Pope Paul VI's Justice and Peace Commission also provides a model through which bishops, priests, ministers, lay leaders, health care workers, and others could collaborate in fostering social change, by being a prophetic voice and promoting global solidarity in regard to HIV/AIDS and other issues of justice.

To date, however, many of these commissions are little more than superfluous arms of Catholic Charities offices that function as separate offices with an economic "bottom line" and failing to reach the justice goals of their mission. The Archdiocese of Miami, for example, has the third-highest rate of infection in the United States.[5] Our populations most at risk are Hispanic, African-American, and gay white men. The Church closed its outreach offices on the premise of "fiscal responsibility," displacing the community involved with HIV/AIDS ministry and those needing care into the public sector; this reality requires lament and begs for prophetic indictment.

Considering Forty Years of Catholic Social Teaching

Pope Benedict's "2007 World Day of Peace Message" reiterates some of the basic principles of justice and peace outlined in *Populorum progressio* (1967), built on John XXIII's *Pacem in terris* (1963) and *Mater et magistra* (1961).[6] These encyclicals continue the tradition begun with Leo XIII's *Rerum novarum* (1891), which addressed the need for justice and equity as measures ensuring the dignity of the human person. John XXIII advanced the foundations for Catholic social teaching in support of the United Nations' Universal Declaration of Human Rights (1948). By 1967, Paul VI established the Justice and Peace Commission in the Church's central administration to awaken "in the People of God, a full awareness of their mission, so that they may further the progress of poorer nations and international social justice, as well as help less developed nations contribute to the development of all [hu]mankind."[7] This initiative continues in the Justice and Peace Commission to this day, but to what end? Although HIV did not exist when these teachings were declared, adequate education and social action does not preclude consideration of the meaning and value of the teachings in regard to justice, human dignity, and the promotion of the common good threatened by the pandemic.

Nevertheless, forty years later, the people of God continue to lament and to hope for justice and peace. As a community committed to the promotion of justice and the empowerment of the poor, we are proud of many of the prophetic insights of the Church and its leaders in the creation of the Justice and Peace Commission and for the many organizations, such as Catholic Relief Services, the Catholic Agency for Overseas Development, and Caritas Internationalis that promote and support in word and deed human development. Still, we lack the prophetic imagination and will to challenge the structures and policies that hinder the implementation of a transformative praxis.[8] Without effective transformative praxis, the insights and mission of Catholic social teaching remain little more than lofty words. Recall that John Paul II proclaimed, "The battle against HIV/AIDS ought to be everyone's battle." Note the hinges on the word "ought." In fact, John Paul II's battle cry can remain pure sentimentality unless we take seriously what it means to be a Christian by raising arms (as a human community) against a disease that threatens all. As a Church ordered to be a priestly, prophetic, and royal people, we must take personal responsibility for being informed and committed to transformative praxis of a society that works for world justice and peace.

Ecumenical Dialogue, Global Education, and Imagination

The implications of ecclesial renewal for the people of God generated by Vatican II can impact positively a world living with HIV/AIDS, specifically in relation to participation and solidarity with all God's people. How has this renewal legitimized the voices and discourses of a scattered universal Church that yearns for leadership and authentic Christian discipleship? How has the Christian imagination been provoked to find equitable partners for providing a means of transforming oppression and degradation to liberation and fullness of life?

First, consider some of the methods used by CELAM, which met with the WCC to create the Faith and Order Commission and produced the ecumenical document *Baptism, Eucharist, and Ministry*, which proved to be instrumental in moving ecumenical conversations forward. CELAM adopted a strategy to create social change by providing education and what it calls *concientización* among the people, building bridges between otherwise disparate groups. CELAM confirms "that it is indispensable to form a social conscience and a realistic perception of the problems of the community and of social structures. We must awaken the social conscience and communal customs in all strata of society and professional groups regarding such values as dialogue and community living within the same group and relations with wider social groups (workers, peasants, professionals, clergy, religious, administrators, etc.)."[9] This *concientización* must be integrated into pastoral action, including a proactive address of HIV/AIDS for the entire human family. The bishops continue to advocate for the evolution of Christian consciousness:

> For our authentic liberation, all of us need a profound conversion so that "the kingdom of justice, love and peace," might come to us. . . . The uniqueness of the Christian message does not so much consist in the affirmation of the necessity for structural change, as it does in an insistence on the conversion of men and women, which will in turn bring about this change. . . . There will be no new continent without new people, who know how to be truly free and responsible according to the light of the Gospel.[10]

And for a people to be both free and responsible requires education and *conscientización*. The Church too must transform its ecclesial self-understanding to include a prophetic imagination for solidarity with the poor to yield the kingdom in the here and now.

Today the Church has the institutional power to call for a global ecumenical, interdisciplinary, and interfaith commission on world health that could significantly impact the pandemic as well as other diseases that inhibit the safety and well-being of the human community. Such a commission could generate a proactive action plan that educates and empowers people, promotes prevention, and delivers the science and technology necessary to reverse the course of the pandemic worldwide.

Using Paul VI's Peace and Justice Commission and the CELAM's Faith and Order Commission as models, a "Global Health Commission" (GHC) could emerge in the Church. The GHC would work collaboratively with other organizations to establish facts, trends, and areas of greatest concern. Delegates would be appointed and serve a minimum of two years in research and compiling data, narratives, and other relevant information about HIV that promote or thwart its spread. This research would investigate testing, counseling, treatment plans, access and delivery systems for health care, and concerns of pediatric formulations of anti-retroviral treatments, male circumcision, sero-discordant marriages, condoms, marital fidelity, HIV-positive pregnancy, HIV-positive children, AIDS orphans, shame and stigma, and IV drug use. Delegates would represent the regions of the world, interdisciplinary perspectives, and diverse faith traditions; they would gather for a meeting in Africa (because it remains the continent most adversely affected by HIV). They would each and together offer their contribution to world health; the GHC would engage in the prophetic work of justice for all.

Dialogue among the delegates would require respectful listening, a commitment to truthful and honest research, and a pledge of fidelity to the processes set by the GHC. The goal of this process would not necessarily be agreement so much as to legitimize the diverse voices and perspectives often overlooked or silenced by insulated institutions. The proceedings of the GHC would be published, and recommendations for a global action plan would be set in motion by all the contributors and their allies in the field.[11]

A global education plan would be developed to protect those most vulnerable, namely, women at risk of abuse and assault and sexually exploited children. This plan would require the commitment to teach the inherent dignity and worth of every human being and to hold accountable any person who violates the bodily rights of another for profit or personal gain. The educational model requires a revision of the paradigms that question or diminish the dignity of women and children or tolerate their reduction to human chattel by objectification, commodification, and/or abuse. Alternatives to the sex trade must be provided, and legitimate forms of survival in a global marketplace located. The education plan would include provisions for (1) *concientización* that takes personal responsibility for empowerment, for knowing our HIV status, and for protecting ourselves and others from infection, and (2) plans for implementing a program that supports education and personal and communal responsibility for transformative praxis.

The Church's desire to promote the transcendental dignity of humankind, as well as to promote peace and work for justice, can be advanced greatly by the model of leadership utilized by the Justice and Peace Commission. Imagine the Church initiating an interfaith, interdisciplinary, gender-inclusive, GHC made up of ordained and lay persons committed to the work of HIV/AIDS care, prevention, education, and research, for the love of God, neighbor, and self. Imagine these people working together to create a vision and practice grounded in the awakening of the people of God, the fullness of their human dignity, and their *conscientización* and responding to the call of the present day.[12] Imagine bishops working together to promote the transcendent dignity of all humanity—and listening wholeheartedly to what dignity means in the context of communities of faith and of a global common good.[13] Further, imagine that the contributions of this GHC could generate a commitment to promote global solidarity, ensure justice, and establish peace throughout the world. Perhaps these musings are utopian, perhaps cynicism and skepticism have hardened our hearts and stripped our imaginations—or perhaps not. Perhaps what we as individuals, as Church, and as global community can do is commit ourselves to believing that we can be part of the solution and work for it—and get one other person to commit to the same. The prophetic imagination can once again be the foundation for the reality of a kingdom that is at once here and not yet.

Power and Knowledge, Sex, and Discourse

Among the elements of the kingdom not yet realized are the religious, political, and social fractures that prevent advancing dialogue and render certain human lives invisible and/or disposable. Michel Foucault examined history for the narrative discourses that capture particular constructions of truth.[14] He engaged the imagination in generating renewed possibilities for matters central to the human condition that include issues relevant to sex and sexuality. When questioned on the search for truth in regard to sex, he responded, "Since Christianity, Western civilization has not stopped saying, 'To know who you are, know what your sexuality is about.' Sex has always been the center where our 'truth' of the human subject has been tied up along with the development of our species."[15]

Throughout his life, Foucault critiqued the productive power of discourse in the context of human development and the capacity of sexual discourse to generate truth claims that, more often than not, promoted death.[16] He located this conclusion in his consideration of sexuality as a life force that, when embodied, fights to defend itself against death. Elaborating on Foucault's construction of power and sex, Judith Butler contends that "when sex becomes a site of power, it becomes an object of legal and regularity discourses" out of which normative standards for monitoring and regulating sex and sexuality emerge.[17] Given the reactions that the HIV/AIDS pandemic has generated from various political, religious, and cultural contexts, and respecting feminist readings as a first critique of his theories, Foucault's critical work on normative truth claims regarding power, knowledge, sex, and sexuality provide an educational model that promotes liberation and moral responsibility. Following Foucault, power works on sex to form knowledge. This knowledge-power generates positive, intelligible, and dignified constraints on sex and sexual discourse that reconcile freedom and responsibility to love. Education directed toward the true meaning of love as "the fundamental law of human perfection, and source of the transformation of the world,"[18] is the dynamic power motivating justice in the world.

In 1984, Foucault died of AIDS. Despite his ruminations on the discursive power of sex, sadly, Foucault did not address the disease that took his life, nor did he challenge the apathy of others in reference to prevention or human dignity in light of HIV/AIDS. Using poetry as a means of illuminating my use of Foucault in conjunction with Catholic social teaching and in relation to all whose lives are affected by HIV/AIDS, my hope is that contexts may be transcended and the imagination may mediate the convergence of the seemingly incongruent. Adrienne Rich's poem "The Photograph of the Unmade Bed" names the unconscious cruelty, silence, and apathetic violence that allow the pandemic to exercise its wrath on the human community. For Foucault, as for many others, perhaps their silence was "intentionless," the harm already done. Perhaps they died hoping that the cruelty of unconsciousness might yet be transformed.

> Cruelty is rarely conscious
> One slip of the tongue
>
> one exposure
> among so many
>
> thrust in the dark
> to see if there is pain there
>
> I never asked you to explain
> that act of violence
>
> what dazed me was our ignorance
> of our will to hurt each other. . . .
>
> In a flash I understand
> how poems are unlike photographs
>
> (the one saying *This could be*
> the other *This was*)
>
> The image
> isn't responsible
>
> for our uses of it
> It is intentionless
>
> A long strand of dark hair
> in the washbasin

is innocent and yet
such things have done harm. . . .

mere indifference? I tell you
cruelty is rarely conscious.

The done and the undone blur
Into one photograph of failure.[19]

New Paradigm

Maintaining myths and false teachings generates irreversible consequences adversely affecting millions of human lives every day. One careless slip of the tongue can carry much cruelty. Consider the lies that maintain the status quo and perpetuate the vulnerability of those at risk:

- HIV/AIDS is a punishment from God.
- AIDS is a gay disease.
- Condoms have tiny holes in them. They don't protect against infection.
- The availability of medications for HIV means no one dies of AIDS anymore.
- People who contract HIV/AIDS deserve it.
- Intercourse with a virgin will cure AIDS.
- The only sure way to protect oneself against HIV is through abstinence and fidelity.
- Insects can carry the AIDS virus.
- HIV can be transmitted by kissing or sharing a drink with a person who is infected.

If we are not participating in dismantling these myths, we are silent conspirators in their harms. To avoid such a charge, the global Church must become ever more "concienticized" in its efforts to debunk the myths and repair their harm they have caused. It is our individual and corporate responsibility, said Paul VI, to work for the "progressive development of peoples . . . especially those trying to escape the ravages of hunger, endemic disease and ignorance."[20]

In order to continue the work of transforming ignorance, generating a positive effect on human understanding, and raising consciousness, consider the theology of the *imago Dei*. As we begin wholeheartedly to act on the consciousness that all are created in the image and likeness of God, as relational beings we recognize our moral responsibility to choose life.[21] Faced with the complexities of life and death, of vulnerability and risk, we must stand together in solidarity to choose life and promote the common good.

This solidarity can be promoted by word and deed. The Church as a sovereign power can engage with those upon whom it exercises domination and control by providing opportunities for discourse. Without due consideration of the legitimacy of truth claims that emerge from outside the sovereign realm, the Church itself will lose its power. However, the dynamic between the sovereign Church and the people of God needs to move toward more collaborative and empowering paradigms, where the dignity and respect now offered its princes is recognized as belonging also to the people most often neglected and abandoned by the sin of the world. In other words, the time is long overdue for the pope, bishops, cardinals, and priests to step into the communities they shepherd and come to know their flock with the intimacy the metaphor was originally intended to portray[22] and to work with lay leaders for justice, peace, and the promotion of human dignity for the common good.

When bringing the tradition to bear on the human experiences of those infected with and affected by HIV/AIDS, dialogue, education, and imagination will serve the fundamental building of a new methodological paradigm for peace and justice now.

Anna Kasafi Perkins

God (Not) Gwine Sin Yuh

HIV/AIDS in the Caribbean

The HIV/AIDS pandemic has caused untold suffering across the globe and "promises" to continue. The Caribbean region has not escaped the effects of the pandemic; the region has the second-highest incidence of HIV behind sub-Saharan Africa, and AIDS is the leading cause of death among Caribbean nationals aged 25 to 44. Like their sisters elsewhere, Caribbean women are increasingly at risk of infection.

The vulnerability of women to HIV results from a number of factors: biological makeup, widespread poverty, and gender injustice. "Because of poverty and gender inequality," writes Paula Clifford, "women are not only particularly vulnerable to the infection themselves; they also bear the consequences of the epidemic to a much greater degree than men."[1] Adult women bear the brunt of caring for people with and affected by HIV, many the sole breadwinner of their families. Young girls are not spared these effects; often they leave school to care for sick relatives or work to supplement the family income.

Theological reflection in a time of AIDS demands rethinking justice. Enda McDonagh finds that "many of the problems revealed by the pandemic are problems of justice, personal and social. Some of these may be adequately expressed in terms of human rights and pursued in that fashion. However, not all delicate justice problems may be translated into human rights language without considerable loss of moral impact."[2] Though many Caribbean women achieve success in business and the professions, culturally derived gender asymmetries continue to disadvantage them. Jamaican Rosie Stone demonstrates this in the following dialogue with her late husband:

> "Do you think I am seeing a man?"
> "I don't know how to answer that."
> "Well, I will answer it for you. No, No and No."
> "Remember that your actions during our marriage have sealed my fate when it comes to men. Not only will no one want to be involved with someone with HIV, but certainly you have showed me how

unevenly balanced the relationship between a man and a woman is. I went into the relationship with you, I thought on par, but men have the upper hand every time. I feel so much at a disadvantage now that you don't have to worry about me getting into a relationship with anyone."[3]

The Church has been at the forefront in response to the pandemic in the region, with care, counseling, and programs supporting abstinence and faithfulness, and advancing nonstigmatization and nondiscrimination against persons with and affected by HIV/AIDS.[4] At times, however, the Church's response to the pandemic requires interrogation, as the following incident demonstrates:

At the World AIDS Day celebration in the Roman Catholic Cathedral in Bujumbura [Burundi] in 1995, the priest said, in the course of his sermon, "We must have compassion for people with AIDS because they have sinned and because they are suffering for it now." At that point something propelled Jeanne Gapiya to rise from her pew and walk up to the front of the church. "I have HIV," she declared, "and I am a faithful wife. Who are you to say that I have sinned, or that you have not? We are all sinners, which is just as well, because it is for us that Jesus came."[5]

Persons living with HIV and AIDS (PLWHA) are often confronted by a Church that proclaims their disease is punishment from God—*God gwine sin yuh* ("God will punish you"), as Jamaicans say. This response is inadequate to people's experiences and worse for women, who are increasingly at risk even in monogamous relationships. As Rosie Stone's brave retelling demonstrates, "gendered relations of power are critical for understanding the HIV epidemic [in the Caribbean]."[6]

In teaching about HIV, the Church has both ignored its gendered nature and espoused a theology of suffering that blames the victim, many of whom are women. This position led Caribbean feminists like Jamaican Glenda Simms, former director of the Women's Bureau in Jamaica, to chastise the Church for "either fail[ing] to recognise women as sexual beings (stating that marriage/sexual relationships is for reproduction) or giv[ing] them a false sense of security by promising them fidelity in marriage."[7]

Some Christian women themselves misunderstand their vulnerability and help to perpetuate the theology of sin and suffering. Isabel Apawo Phiri relates a story from a Women of Faith group meeting in southern Africa as evidence:

On 6 March 2004, we chose to talk about HIV/AIDS and African women. One of us passionately argued that we need not worry about being infected with the virus, because as long as we remained faithful to our husbands and prayed for our protection, God was going to hear our prayers and protect us from the virus. She equated the HI-virus with punishment from God for the disobedient.[8]

This mistaken thinking calls for a theology of suffering in the context of HIV/AIDS that pays attention to the gendered nature of prevention and care and to the dominant theology/theodicy of disease as divine punishment.[9] By attending to gender, justice, and suffering, the Church could respond faithfully, while recognizing and proclaiming that HIV/AIDS is neither produced by nor the result of sin. As the Conference of Latin American Bishops (CELAM) recognizes, *"[E]n su misión profética está llamada a anunciar el Reino a los enfermos y a todos los que sufren, velando para que sus derechos sean reconocidos y respetados, así como también a denunciar el pecado y sus raíces históricas, sociales, políticas y económicas que producen males como la enfermedad VIH/Sida."*[10]

At the Sixteenth International AIDS Conference, Bishop Mark Hanson of the Evangelical Lutheran Church admitted, "We have been complicit (in the spread of AIDS) by our shaming words and deeds, by our failure to listen to and walk with and follow the leadership of people living with HIV/AIDS."[11] In response, the Caribbean church must examine how, *as church*, it facilitates the spread of HIV in the region. I question the fundamental theodicy expressed in the common Jamaican saying *God gwine sin yuh*. As illustrated by the words of the priest in Bujumbura, PLWHA are doubly stigmatized as sinners and punished.[12] This belief has particular resonances for women who are stigmatized in multiple ways by the public health discourse on HIV/AIDS as vectors of transmission to their partners, and vessels of transmission to their unborn children.

The gendered nature of HIV/AIDS throws into stark relief the interconnection between a theodicy focused on the Fall and a lack of appreciation for the meaning of innocent and not-so-innocent suffering that leads to stigma and discrimination. This theodicy calls the Church to understand its responsibility in reflecting anew on gendered justice and suffering and in influencing the course of HIV in the region.

The Female Face of HIV/AIDS

Of the adult population in the Caribbean, 1.6 percent has HIV. More than 27,000 have died of AIDS, and in 2005, approximately 37,000 persons became infected. HIV prevalence and AIDS cases in the Caribbean are thought to be underestimated.[13] The Caribbean is geographically close to Latin America and is often grouped with that region in discussions of HIV/AIDS, but the epidemic is by no means uniform throughout this large and diverse area. Within the Caribbean region itself the epidemic has a unique face in each territory. At one extreme is Haiti, with the highest HIV prevalence in the Western Hemisphere (3.8 percent); at the other is Cuba, with a reported rate of just 0.1 percent. Trinidad and Tobago (2.6 percent), Jamaica (1.5 percent), Guyana (2.4 percent), Barbados (1.5 percent), and the Bahamas (3.3 percent), countries in the Anglophone Caribbean, are all heavily infected and affected.

The numbers relating to infection rates and range have meanings beyond statistics. Each number represents a life, and also connected individuals, communities, and societies devastated by fear, rejection, death, grief, and pain. Jamaica's case makes disturbing reading: girls of 10 to 19 years and 15 to 24 years are three times more at risk of infection than boys of the same age. Between 2002 and 2004, among all HIV and AIDS cases 59 young persons tested positive for HIV, 10 men and 49 women; 203 AIDS cases were reported, 61 young men and 142 young women.[14] The reality of HIV in the region reflects, as in other parts of the developing world, a gendered vulnerability.

Gender-Based Violence

One of the factors making women more vulnerable is their physiology. This increased vulnerability is complex and derives from the fluid dynamics of unprotected sex. During unprotected intercourse the man deposits milliliters of infectious semen over the surface of his partner's vagina. The risk is increased by the heavy concentration of the virus in semen compared to vaginal secretions, and the greater permeability of the mucous membranes of the vagina compared to the penis.[15] Women across the world are united in their biological vulnerability to HIV and remain at greater risk of HIV from each sexual encounter and every sexual partnership.[16] This biological vulnerability is exacerbated by cultural, economic, and social factors. Women in the Caribbean continue to make progress; they pursue higher education, enter managerial roles, lead governments, and appear by many measures to be doing well. But this prosperity is both undermined by and masks persistent gender inequities. Michelle Davis sees this best illustrated in the many acts of violence committed against women and girls.[17] Such gender-based violence is on the increase and, demonstrated in one case from Jamaica, sexual and physical violence intersect in multiple generations of women and girls:

> After being led out of court, Henry, still professing his innocence, shouted to his weeping mother: "Mummy, dem find mi guilty! How dem fi find mi guilty fi something mi never do?" The court was told that . . . Henry sexually assaulted [a girl] child, beat her all over the body with a piece of board, and banged her head on the floor and door of the house. Henry . . . admitted in court to beating the child with a "belt" before leaving the house. However, he insisted that he never had sex with her. The incident occurred while *the girl's mother* had taken *Henry's mother* to the hospital after she fainted *during an argument with Henry.*[18]

This story exemplifies the abuse of women from an early age and throughout their lifetime. As elsewhere, the sexual abuse of girls appears with the myth that sex with a virgin can cure AIDS or another STD; consequently, girls are increasingly at risk of rape and of contracting HIV. As these girls who have been violated grow older, the abuse continues even by their own peers with whom they have relationships to which, presumably, they consent. The following account illustrates this only too well:

> To the team members' shock, the boy and his friends entered the classroom [where a session on HIV/AIDS was conducted], took off his belt and proceeded to beat one of the girls . . . his "woman." She did not fight back. In fact, she did not protest, even when [the coordinator] led the group to the guidance counsellor's office. "It's the same boy who just called them 'dutty gyal,'" [the councillor] says, visibly upset. "This is the same reason why we are not reaching them. They don't value themselves, especially the girls."[19]

As these girls grow into women, they are likely to engage in unprotected sex with multiple partners, increase their vulnerability to multiple strains of HIV, and infect others.

Social Constructions of Gender

Beyond the physiological factors lies the question of the social construction of gender.[20] This social construction accounts for much of the difference in infection rates between men and women. According to Davis, femininity in the Caribbean is associated with motherhood, fertility, and passivity. This passivity, Simms charges, is how the family structure socializes girls "to do as they are told," especially by men—as graphically illustrated in the story of the high school girl. The boy's actions expose a masculinity premised on sexual prowess, aggression, strength and, though not as evident, the ability to father offspring.

These constructions preserve unequal power, status, and privilege. Asymmetry and domination are confirmed as men and women receive different rewards, benefits, and penalties.[21] Men tend to benefit from the control of women's sexuality, as Michelle Davis explains: "The power dynamics inherent in heterosexual relations found in many societies do in fact privilege men; thereby constraining women's abilities to negotiate safer sex practices, make use of family-planning methods, and construct positive self-conceptions of their bodies and beings."[22] Furthermore, sheer economic need drives some women into risky relationships. As sex researcher Kamala Kempadoo notes, "The power that women have to insist on safe sex practices is heavily compromised by an imperative for immediate cash to feed children or themselves.

Economic insecurity is an important reason for sexual transactions in the Caribbean, yet male power and control leave women in a weak negotiating position to insist upon safe sexual practices."[23] Moreover, some women feel forced to put their daughters on the streets to exchange sexual favors for money, as one newspaper account describes:

> A 15-year-old girl in an advanced stage of pregnancy was remanded to a place of safety. The girl's mother, Diana Williams, told the court that she was aware that the child was seeing a 25-year-old man. Detective Corporal Kirk Roache told the court that his investigation revealed that the mother received constant remuneration for services rendered by the juvenile. The woman agreed. The officer told the court the mother only warned the daughter to use birth control. . . . The judge remanded both the mother and the eight-month pregnant daughter.[24]

Paula Clifford calls these girls, whose lives are put at risk by their own families and women in dangerous relationships from economic necessity, the modern-day equivalents of the widows and orphans singled out for special care in the Scriptures (e.g., Deut 24:17).[25] With scarce employment opportunities, women and girls from poor communities face many obstacles in finding legitimate work. Essentially, what such women have left to "sell" are their bodies and those of their nubile daughters, an especially attractive commodity to some men. This poverty and its oppression in Caribbean societies obliges a social response to the ancient call to care for the widow and orphan, especially where covenantal relationships have broken down in the lives of the vulnerable.[26]

Not to be ignored are the many women, either wives or common-law partners, who are infected with HIV by their husbands and partners and who in some instances have then infected their unborn children.[27] In 2004, then Jamaican Minister of Health John Junor admitted that "married women are among the groups of persons most at risk of contracting the deadly virus."[28] Recognition of the particular vulnerability of women in committed relationships has led Glenda Simms to launch an attack on the Church for increasing women's vulnerability to the disease. She notes, "Whether the status of wife is sacred or slave-like the contemporary reality is that married women are as vulnerable to HIV and AIDS as any other woman in the Jamaican society."[29]

Simms and others charge that to halt and reverse the epidemic, all vulnerable populations must be given appropriate information for prevention, treatment, and support. Nonetheless, she laments that "married women may yet prove to be the most challenging high risk group [to educate]." Simms does not mince words: "It is about time we wrestle to the ground our patriarchal society, fuelled by a strong homophobic atmosphere and permeated by religious fundamentalism which puts every man, woman and child at risk in the sexual arena."[30]

Simms's recognition that some religious communities reinforce patriarchal structures that devalue women (and men) is echoed by the Caribbean Conferences of Churches (CCC) in its call to the churches in the region to educate women about their vulnerability. The CCC emphasizes the need to educate women in faith communities especially, who believe they are safe but are vulnerable because of the risk-taking behavior of their male partners.[31] Similarly, CELAM advises *"educar para que las mujeres sean más conscientes de su condición de vulnerabilidad y pueden tomar una actitud más de auto protección y proposición."*[32]

Theology and HIV/AIDS

The pandemic has thrown the great Christian themes of a good God and the goodness of creation, love, and life into disarray.[33] It raises the question of the relation between human suffering and the divine presence—the question posed by Job and by Jean, Rosie, and millions of others: How is God present and acting in this time of HIV/AIDS? Traditional theological approaches have responded poorly and are a frequent cause of greater suffering.[34]

The tendency of some within the Caribbean to view suffering as the result of and punishment for personal sin runs deep. This view persists with typical explanations to locate misfortune in the spiritual realm, reinforced by a theodicy that ties sickness to divine punishment. In a region vulnerable to natural disasters such as hurricanes and floods, this kind of theodicy raises a constant concern. The currency of this question figures in the various appeals made to people in the region to repent and seek forgiveness in times when hurricanes threaten. The Roman Catholic archbishop emeritus of Kingston, the late Samuel E. Carter, rebuffed this belief directly in his 1988 pastoral letter on hurricanes.[35]

Many see this theodicy as particularly apropos for HIV/AIDS. At its center is the belief that AIDS is punishment for immoral living. This thinking is coupled with another belief—that a cure for AIDS will not be found because it is God's judgment.[36] Kristin Jack, country director of Servants to Asia's Urban Poor in Cambodia, charges that many evangelical Christians loudly proclaim AIDS as a judgment of God on promiscuous sexual behavior and homosexuality. This judgment is the flipside of the health and prosperity teaching held by many evangelicals that claims God only blesses, protects, or prospers those who deserve it.[37] Peruvian theologian Gustavo Gutierrez identifies a similar effect in what he calls a "doctrine of temporal retribution, where the upright are rewarded with prosperity and health, while sinners are punished with poverty and sickness."[38] Gutierrez finds here a simplistic approach to morality, susceptible to stubbornly individualistic interpretations. In fact, its power comes from its simplicity. This kind of morality is convenient for those who have great possessions in this world, while it elicits a culpable resignation in those who lack. Likewise, Jack exposes the logical extension of this health and prosperity teaching: those whose lives are blighted, suffering, and poor are outside of God's blessing. But in July 2005, the Reformed Ecumenical Council issued a document that admitted, "As church we have at times laid a much too direct link between HIV/AIDS and sin, giving the impression that those with HIV/AIDS are greater sinners than others, without keeping in mind that many of those who are today HIV-positive got the virus innocently."[39]

The Antilles bishops also addressed this "theological falsehood" in a 2005 statement on HIV/AIDS: "We declare without reservation that HIV/AIDS is not a curse from God. It is not divine judgment on individuals for their sins."[40] The lesson learned from the book of Job, that the cause of suffering is not personal sin, needs new currency in the region. While certain lifestyles and life choices place persons at greater risk, to focus simply on these factors ignores the larger number of persons, women and children especially, who are unwittingly at risk and infected through no direct fault of their own. At the same time, no one is to be abandoned to the "consequences" of sin or innocence, but should be offered the care and respect due to their dignity as human beings. Job must be read again and again to many Caribbean Christians who connect human suffering with God's punishment and who see a particular application of this doctrine with HIV/AIDS.[41] It will not be easy to shake this approach to morality; it has a tenacious hold on the religious sentiments of many.

A New Theology of Sin and Suffering

Wendy Farley maintains that Christianity's reflections on evil have been governed by the problematic of sin and the Fall that makes suffering insignificant.[42] Appealing to punishment and original sin to justify radical suffering—thereby destroying the human spirit and misunderstanding it as something deserved—betrays an ethical sensibility that generates a penal theodicy, like that prominent in the Caribbean.[43] While HIV/AIDS is destructive of the human spirit, to speak of anyone deserving punishment is ethically repugnant and pastorally fatal.

The pandemic calls us to face squarely the tragic dimensions of our human reality; it locates the possibility of suffering in the conditions of existence and in the fragility of human freedom. As Farley observes, "The very structures that make human existence possible make us subject to the destructive power of suffering. Since guilt is not the primary problem, atonement and forgiveness cannot help transcend tragedy."[44] The response to tragic suffering cannot be atonement; tragic suffering must be defied—by compassion resisting and transforming suffering into solidarity.

Jesus gave suffering a new meaning when he opened his arms on the cross in an act of co-suffering and compassionate love. He healed the sick and those whose illnesses pushed them to the margins. The Antilles bishops call for this compassion, combining a sympathetic knowledge of suffering with recognition of the dignity and value of PLWHA.

A Way Forward

A theology of suffering in the female face of HIV/AIDS calls for a forthright assessment of sociocultural realities that protract infection among vulnerable populations. These realities include the early socialization of poor gender relations and social norms that condone, even encourage, multiple sex partners for men but that expect monogamy for women, male dominance, female emotional and socioeconomic dependence, and poor communication between partners about sexual needs. Similarly, the social, cultural, and religious taboos regarding sexuality in young people preclude frank discussion and education about critically life-important communication skills pertaining to sexual behavior; these taboos must be challenged. Additionally, the early sexual initiation of many young persons, including the initiation of girls and younger women by older men, must end. Lastly, the treatment of sex in a transactional fashion must be addressed. The Church can no longer be reticent or uncomfortable in speaking prophetically about issues of sexuality and gender. Nor can it complacently frame suffering in the language of temporal retribution.

The Church can be evangelized by listening to the needs of the people, acknowledging the human condition and those factors that prevent a transformation of conscience. The Church's stance cannot be sectarian, withdrawn, or dismissively resigned to a world handed over to Satan, nor can it continue talk about sex and sexuality that does not take account of the realities of women's lives. The World Health Organization and others promote the ABCD strategy (A = Abstinence, B = Be faithful, C = Condom use, D = Do not share needles).[45] The Antilles Episcopal Conference applauds the success of abstinence and fidelity (AB) and finds a behavior change compatible with the sexual ethics of many Christian communities.[46] Jack agrees that behavior-change approaches work: "When done well, behaviour change strategies are clearly the most effective long term solutions to the HIV/AIDS crisis, both for individuals and societies."[47] However, attempting to change behavior without speaking to the individual and cultural values, beliefs, motivations, expectations, and worldviews underpinning them is foolhardy. Without evangelizing the culture, little hope exists for increasing respect for women and children; without evangelizing the beliefs about masculinity and femininity, there is little hope of respect for marriage and faithful partnerships; without a motivation to do so, there is little hope that individuals will treat their bodies and those of others with respect.

Given the level of Christian involvement in the care and treatment of persons infected with and affected by HIV/AIDS, this work must go to the roots of culture and theology, especially the "theological falsehood" that *God gwine sin* PLWHAs. The Church is challenged to move beyond a focus on care and treatment for those already affected by attending to prevention, dealing with the uncomfortableness of talking about sexual ethics, and removing the gender inequalities and poverty that fuel risk. In this age of HIV/AIDS, we are confronted with the mystery of God who entered fully into the human condition, even to the point of suffering and death.[48] This God, Jesus, presents a face that includes the woman who is HIV-positive and locked away in the bedroom by her family, the man with HIV shunned by coworkers who refuse to associate with him, the mother with HIV who fears telling the father of her baby by whom she was infected, and the child sent away from school for fear of infecting classmates. The crisis opens us to new faces of the divine presence in our midst and calls upon Caribbean Christians to recognize and respond to that face with compassion. Perhaps the message will then become *God not gwine sin yuh*, but *God gwine suffer wid yuh!*

Part Three

Migrants and Immigrants

Marie-Jo Thiel

Translated by Mary Jo Iozzio

France 2007

Always and Still the Challenge of AIDS

Infection by HIV continues to spread through the world. AIDS is a global public health problem. Still more, AIDS is a fearsome peril for women and their families. From an anatomical level, a woman's body is more susceptible to infection than a man's. Women remain in many places subject to men; they receive little education and bear an inferior social stature in their societies. They are the primary victims of violence and rape, they are too often cornered by poverty, and they use their bodies to bargain for basic needs without access to protection, prevention, or medical services.

AIDS is not simply a terrible disease; it reveals fractures that separate societies, creating wider divides—between rich and poor countries, women and men, native and foreign-born nationals—that exacerbate the cultural differences and inequalities in human welfare. AIDS is not simply a viral pandemic; AIDS unveils a pandemic of stigma, discrimination, and exclusion everywhere. Unlike the plagues of old, AIDS does not hold contagion alone as the culprit; it also blames the modes of transmission and, with transmission, a degree of personal, collective, societal, and ecclesiastical responsibility.

AIDS entered into history in June 1981 with the death of so-called patient Zero. During the summer of 1982, the disease was "baptized" with the confirmed proofs of its viral etiology. Epidemic outbreaks of HIV are recorded now throughout the world, though each local epidemic follows particular transmission routes with their own identifiable characteristics.

Epidemic Data

Infection rates in France along with Spain and Italy are among the highest in Western Europe. These rates are due principally to an inability to anticipate so many new cases and to mistakes caused by a dangerous degree of timidity regarding prevention. Most people know the risks of using contaminated blood, for example, in treating hemophiliacs. Recognized early as a matter of justice, the French courts attended to the "affaire du sang contaminé." In 1983, the Council of Europe published Recommendation R(83)8 on the prevention of AIDS transmission from the donation of contaminated blood, but France has been incapable of taking the precautionary measures proposed! The blood collected in prisons until 1992 without pretesting was responsible for more than 25 percent of infections acquired through transfusions.[1] In October 1985, people with hemophilia were warned of their risk, but drug addicts and immigrant populations, at the time also judged at risk, were not informed until 1992.[2] Seven years passed in which some could infect other people as a result of their lack of knowledge of their HIV status. The indignation and demands for justice by those who could have escaped the virus if a competent authority had informed them are legitimate.

The mobilization of associations of homosexual men, who first raised the warnings about the epidemic nature of the virus, unfortunately created an almost exclusive connection between AIDS and homosexual communities. Their warnings became the occasion for movements of discrimination against them. Nevertheless, their efforts brought HIV/AIDS to the fore and resulted in a reversal of presumptions held by the dominant French society about homosexual persons. In the meantime, the media agreed not to dramatize AIDS; however, by this decision, members of the public remained uninformed about their risk.

Where are we today? Data from the Institute of Health-Vigilance (Institut de veille sanitaire, INVS) and the National Institute of Statistics and Economic Studies (Institut National de la Statistique et des Études Économiques, INSEE) specify the contours of the epidemic: the number of persons carrying HIV have increased to as many as 150,000 in 2007, with close to 7,000 new cases each year. Almost 1,500 persons develop full-blown AIDS each year; the average age of onset is 41. The incidence of infection among women 15 to 49 years old has increased by 13 percent in only eight years (from a 30 percent infection rate in 1997 to 43 percent in 2005). Of the new diagnoses, 56 percent occurred as the result of heterosexual relations, 22 percent from homosexual relations, and 2 percent from needle sharing among IV drug users. Of the people who developed AIDS, at least 47 percent did not know themselves to be sero-positive. They became aware of their HIV status following the symptoms of opportunistic infections, such as candidiasis, cryptococcus, histoplasmosis, and their admission to or testing at a hospital for treatment or intervention. One of the keys to understanding the rapid spread of the virus is that many people who are infected do not suspect their condition, while still others do not want to know and refuse to be tested, "accepting" the risk of infecting unsuspecting others.[3]

Four French territories have been affected particularly hard: Ile de France, Provence-Alpes-Côte d'Azur, Guyana, and the West Indies. Together these regions constituted 60 percent of the cases of French AIDS diagnoses in 2004.[4]

Despite the statistics, the French media reports very little on the epidemic, except for those times of the annual demonstrations during Sidaction-sponsored events or international conferences dedicated to HIV/AIDS. Sidaction serves as a clearinghouse for all French organizations working together to provide information and relief. There are many scientific works and testimonies, yet, as Helène Jaccomard shows, few studies concern the vulnerability of or are written by women.[5] Is this lack of attention because women are looked upon with scorn? The female body, Jaccomard and others remind us, has long been considered passive and predisposed to infection—indeed, "always already contaminated" and "guilty" of subsequent transmission (to women's [innocent] partners). Bernard Paillard notes that the first French rumor on AIDS targeted a woman.[6] Paradoxically, women sometimes feel that they are protected from transmission by their status as mothers or caregivers, but too often they are infected unwittingly.

Since the arrival of tri-therapies and other antiviral drug cocktails, mobilization, education, and prevention regarding the epidemic have, unfortunately, weakened. Didier Lestrade rails against those who "use this second chance to become infected. . . . Treatments are available which facilitate the biggest homosexual defeat of the past 25 years [and] I do not want to guarantee that fate."[7] Despite the warnings, the effectiveness of new treatments contributes to thinking that trivializes infection, wrongly, as a "simple chronic pathology." This complacence is visible in studies concerning especially homosexual men (and published in *Enquête Press Gay* 2004) that have found that unprotected sexual relations have increased by 70 percent since 1997.[8]

Additionally, more than 36 European countries recently modified their laws "in the goal, recalls Déborah Glejser, to characterize explicitly a real or potential transmission of HIV as a criminal act."[9] In France, the first condemnation (Court of Nanterre, December 2006) concerned a woman who was found guilty of having transmitted HIV while she knew herself to be sero-positive. She was charged with "administration of a harmful substance that caused a disabling condition lasting more than 8 days."[10] She had known her HIV status since 1995; nevertheless, she had unprotected sexual relations with a companion, who discovered himself to be sero-positive in 2000. An enthusiastic repression of people with HIV ensued and, by the end of 2006, more than two hundred legal proceedings resulted in guilty verdicts or were headed that way. More than 90 percent of these were brought by men, with 54 percent claiming transmission as a result of heterosexual relations.

But this criminalization has proven itself to be counterproductive in terms of both the public health and the stigma associated with HIV/AIDS.[11] Criminalization advances a potential defendant's refusal of precautionary screening—an at-risk person can hold that "I cannot have charges brought against me if I do not know my HIV status." Unless someone belongs to an identifiable at-risk group, incrimination is difficult, despite the conclusions of a 2007 California Supreme Court judgment of how "reprehensible the fact of silence [is] on the risks of sexual relations to a partner."[12]

Finally, while some believe naively that the epidemic is for the moment relatively contained in France with tri-therapies, it can, with little notice, flare up and with perhaps even greater fury.

Fortunately, the French climate was unfavorable to stigmatization except in the earliest years of the epidemic. Once AIDS was recognized meandering through all societal and gender sectors, "the non-discrimination of attitudes and of solidarity progressively removed temptations to reject [people who were infected] and offer authoritarian solutions,"[13] such as quarantine to isolate transmission incidence. Some resolutions were helpful, like that of the Parliamentary Assembly of the Council of Europe (N 812/1983), which provided the first international text "on certain aspects of discrimination, stigmatization, and the inviolability of private life," influencing also public opinion, campaigns for anonymous and free screening, the firm respect for confidentiality of medical records, and the challenges to social institutions, in particular, the Christian churches.

The Catholic Church and the Epidemic

The Catholic Church has needed time, as other institutions have, to measure the seriousness of the epidemic.[14] Nevertheless, the particular routes of transmission of HIV—by contact with infected blood and by sexual relations—raised awareness quickly of the risk of stigmatization. This risk was the first point of insistence by the Church and, in France, it was the object of the text of the Social Commission of the Episcopate (June 1987).[15] Another text by the Permanent Council of the Bishops (January 1989) concerned solidarity and responsibility in both the emotional and sexual arenas of life. A final text by the Social Commission (November 1995) signaled a third trait of the Church's concern for those infected with and affected by HIV/AIDS: "In the face of AIDS, raise hope." This text takes account of the complexity of issues surrounding HIV/AIDS with an invitation "to go beyond simple opposition," to avoid "the complacence [and relativism] which supposes that all behavior is acceptable and equivalent to any other," and to reject "the condemnations that simplify the situation." As some bishops had previously taught, it is necessary but insufficient for infected persons "to preserve themselves."[16] Although regretting its late arrival, this text was greeted favorably by the media, scientists, and a number of advocacy groups.[17] Nevertheless, this "yes, but" has provoked unrest in "distant episcopates"—Mexico, Costa Rica, Chile, and even Rome.[18] Here the dissonance of the Catholic message within the magisterium and episcopal offices is palpable.

The Fight against Stigmatization

Cardinal Joseph Bernadin was among the first cardinal-archbishops to enter the debate, with a text published in *La Documentation Catholique*, the official French journal of Church documents.[19] The cardinal was clear:

Some say that AIDS is a divine punishment for what they call "the sin of homosexuality." Without putting their sincerity into question, I disapprove of this assertion. . . . Jesus, while not hesitating to proclaim a radical ethics of life based on the promise of the kingdom of God, never stopped stretching his hand toward the smallest ones and those who were excluded at that time. . . . No medical justification authorizes the exercise of discrimination with regard to those persons who are carriers of the virus.

John Paul II, the French bishops, and many other episcopal conferences followed Bernadin, encouraging the care for which the Church takes an active part throughout the world.

Prevention and Sexual and Emotional Education

John Paul II believed that the prevention of AIDS is worthy and respectful when it educates and informs emotional maturity adequately: "It is only by information and education that leads to a rediscovery, with charity and with joy, the spiritual value of the love-which-is-given as a fundamental drive of human existence that adolescents and youth will find the necessary strength to thwart at risk behaviors."[20] This insistence demonstrates discontent with laconic health messages while it respects youth and the challenges to their personal integrity seriously. Nevertheless, is this Christian ideal—of spiritual, emotional, and sexual maturity—sufficient when death and threats to life so radically test and endanger entire populations? Is this ideal sufficient when the complexity of the human will—wanting the good, as St. Paul states—cracks and transmits a mortal blow with HIV? Is there any confusion between the exigencies of health and moral perspectives? Indeed, so many perspectives intermingle with HIV/AIDS that the Church must clarify its position on prevention and care in light of the fullness of established teachings, not just its teachings on sexuality. The credibility of the gospel and the Church's evangelical message is at stake.

Contraceptive or Prophylactic? Images That Trap

The official texts of the Church in defense of traditional positions continue referencing condoms as contraceptives that encourage "casualness in the sexual behaviors."[21] Rather than first a contraceptive, today the condom is a means of protection against HIV. However, condom use, even as a prophylactic, is particularly sensitive in France, a country traditionally quite resistant to its use and where, not thinking of prophylaxis but of contraception, sexual partners prefer the birth control pill or sterilization as contraceptive means.[22] Public campaigns have attempted to reverse this resistance, even calling for condom use in addition to the pill, but with little effect.

Trust

Following the rhetorical challenge of John Paul II, is our society only a culture of death? Is it not necessary to question our sense of the responsibility for our fear of the other? Does the Church's condemnation of the sexual act (especially homosexual acts) not slip toward the rejection of the person and toward stigmatization and exclusion? I do not here endorse all manner of sexual behavior—far from it. But is the recognition of homosexual persons—on average, one in twenty persons—a source of humanization for them and society following the labeling of their orientation by Cardinal Joseph Ratzinger, then Prefect of the Congregation for the Doctrine of the Faith, as "an objectively disordered inclination"?[23] Is the recognition of this inclination necessarily the same as wanting evil? If yes, then other questions must be asked if sex and sexuality are to remain suspect aspects of the human condition: Is it necessarily evil to not follow the norms of the magisterium on contraception? Is it necessarily evil to vilify the nonreception by the faithful of *Humanae vitae* and other teachings of the Church on sex and sexuality? Is this non-reception by the *sensus fidelium* underlined as early as 1968 by Cardinal Yves Congar? Is the prophylactic-preventive against HIV the same as the prophylactic-contraceptive that condom use necessarily centers the debate? Is it not also necessary to question whether the recognition of an objective disorder would necessarily affect decisions concerning sexual relations before and/or outside of marriage? Do these suspicions not betray a fundamental lack of trust?

Many think, for example, that adolescents are erratic sexually, have no control, and are incapable of stabilizing their sexual drives. Sociologists from the University of Strasbourg show, just as do the statistics of INSEE, that this assertion about adolescent sexuality "constitutes above all a phantasm in the adult imagination."[24] The investigation suggests that, in place of an intensive ad campaign that treats sexuality as a consumer good, reflection on the sense of loving relations should be promoted. In trusting our young people, we must risk their level of emotional maturity for more adequate sex education.

An Information Objective

"It is necessary to inform," said John Paul II. The German Episcopal Conference agrees: "In face of the persistent anxiety of infection with HIV, it is necessary to disseminate information widely and accurately."[25] Since 1988, many were surprised by the news inside the Church of information having the appearance of scientific nuance in its discussion of HIV prevention; however any conclusions that the science was valid are erroneous. The magisterium insists that condoms are not 100 percent reliable, which no scientific study denies. What is important is the knowledge of effective additional means of health security; in fact, uniform and consistent condom use reduces infection risk by 85 percent.[26]

Nevertheless, some manipulate these percentages. From an article published in French in the journal *Medicina e Moral* that was broadcast widely on the Internet, translated into English in a more prudent vein, then republished, the return to a milieu demonizing condom use regained strength.[27] Patrick Verspieren considers that such writings, owing to the conjunction of apparent scientific validity with the religious authority, deceptively fail to warn impressionable spirits."[28] And what is to be said of the assumptions of responsible Catholics as revealed by the BBC in October 2003 regarding a study comparing the tally of HIV to the permeability of condoms? Their assumptions include the beliefs that condoms are ineffective in preventing HIV infection because the virus can pass through the condom membrane. "The Church is the cause of a scandal" by its failure to protect and inform accurately, a news daily charged.[29] This trajectory distorts the moral questions of the epidemic and threatens the Church's effectiveness.

The Night and Chiaroscuro of the Will

Abstinence and fidelity are certainly the best prevention against HIV; the Church has reason to support and campaign for this teaching. The suggestion to abstain and to remain faithful can, without doubt, stimulate observance. However, should this be the *only* suggestion from prevention programs, especially in places where the infection rate is high? How may the Church take ever more seriously the words of Christ before his violent death, that "the spirit indeed is willing, but the flesh is weak"? (Matt 26:41).

Consider those who travel frequently: they have needs for companionship that may lead some to take risks with sexual intimacy in the stillness of the night. Is simply asking adults to avoid temptation sufficient? Is it wise to suggest that people accept the risk of infection of a deadly disease rather than to use a preventive? Must travelers risk the moral transgression of a teaching whose purpose is to value life-giving intimacy in order to work out the connection between condoms and protection against HIV? What is the Church doing to protect the innocent and those who are vulnerable on account of their loneliness? This question is their question; the Church must consider the values at stake. The ideals of abstinence and fidelity are noble, but responsible education about prevention would provide sufficient reminders, even during dark nights, of the need for protection and to hold firm before the risk of death.

The human will is not always equal to itself. There are failures and weaknesses more or less grave in every ideal of life. Their consequences in the case of people who are sero-positive can prove tragic in scope: the transmission of certain death in opposition to the commandment "You shall not kill." Even when pastors and their entourage recite the teaching, the ambiguous attitudes of the Church offend the masses, who charge that the magisterium is guilty of not helping persons in danger. So the Catholic delegate is dealt blows in the public square.[30]

Unfortunately, the Catholic message is confusing. In fact, while certain bishops warn against all use of condoms, others put the accent on personal responsibility. Certain authorities recognize, following Cardinal Tettamanzi, that a wife has the right to protect herself by insisting that her husband use a condom, or following Msgr. Rouet, that "the stagnation of the expansion of AIDS in France is due, in part, to the condom."[31] Yet others recall that the Holy See "has not in any case modified its moral position."[32] Following Rev. Martinez Camino, secretary general of the Conference of Spanish Bishops, we are asked to consider those who seem to or could separate themselves from the official teaching without remorse.[33]

These conflicting positions injure the Church and its evangelical message. They require clarification by taking account of scientifically valid information on health and exacting the courage to oppose obscurantism, ambiguity, and questionable claims on prevention options. In this respect, it is necessary to salute the courage of Msgr. E. Piat, writing in reference to his diocese on the Île Maurice, where 40 percent of the inhabitants are HIV-positive, acknowledging "that we are political decision-makers, responsible NGOs or social workers in the field, we would all win if together we adopt the order of priority expressed by the now famous ABC initiative proposed by the World Health Organization in the fight against AIDS. 'A' is for sexual abstinence before marriage, 'B' is for 'be faithful' as applied especially to marriage, and 'C' is for the condom or prophylactic."[34]

Respect for Women

Justice and evangelical care require also a particular attention to women. ABC is one way to recall a variety of prevention methods, a hierarchy of means, and the collaboration of available resources. But violence done to women must not be forgotten. A multidisciplinary team of researchers investigated the extent of this violence and found a silent and additional vulnerability for women.[35]

The Social Commission of the French Bishops seized the challenge of this study with a September 2003 pastoral letter, which exposed two types of violence toward women: conjugal rape and prostitution. The bishops expressed their solidarity with victims of this violence and petitioned public compassion. This position illustrates the ultimate issue in the fight against HIV: the promotion of ever more respectful relations among people, particularly the most vulnerable.

Finally, the Catholic Church does not lack resources to face the AIDS pandemic and affect its course. If the Church challenges societies deliberately on the values of the gospel, then the Church too will be challenged by movements that, little by little, call for a social response. It is urgent that together we move forward in the work of justice.

Hille Haker

AIDS—An Ethical Analysis

In the field of Christian ethics, more work is needed with respect to a systematic ethical approach to a pandemic that is changing the personal and social lives of millions of people and is still underestimated where public health policies are concerned. Here a framework for the ethical analysis of HIV/AIDS from a Catholic theological perspective informed by political, social, and feminist analysis is outlined.

My Context

In Germany, where I live, approximately 56,000 persons are HIV-positive. In 2006, 2,600 new HIV infections were reported; 490 (19 percent) were women. Compared to reports from other countries, this figure is low, but, as elsewhere, HIV/AIDS impacts the perceptions that many people have of infectious diseases, epidemics, and health-related vulnerabilities in general. From 2001 to 2006, the numbers of new HIV infections grew by 80 percent, an increase that has raised considerable concern in Germany.

Contrary to global trends, in Germany the number of women with new infections is not rising but falling; this trend is due to easy access to condoms, tests, and treatments, as well as the overall higher social, educational, and relational status of women in Germany, particularly in sexual relationships.

German citizens and everyone in Germany with health insurance have access to preventive and therapeutic measures covered both by the public and private health care systems, which serve the vast majority of people in Germany. Concerns are addressed with respect to migrants without papers, but the overall health care status is considered of a high standard.

Apart from certain forms of social and workplace stigmatization, HIV/AIDS is perceived to be akin to chronic illnesses: HIV is well-observed by public health offices, campaigned against in public service announcements and education programs in secondary schools, and people with AIDS are usually treated in a medically appropriate way. Voluntary workers, together with nongovernmental and governmental organizations, have built networks of support, including care and prevention programs, and public information.

In contrast to this rather constructive situation, there are countries where HIV is closer to a death sentence than a chronic condition. Without further elaboration on AIDS in Germany, I present an ethical analysis and reflection on the pandemic. Given that I am a citizen of one of the richest countries in the world *and* a Catholic moral theologian and social ethicist, I consider it my responsibility to reflect upon an approach to theological ethics that meets the drama of HIV/AIDS more appropriately than current approaches. I present my critique of current contributions from an ethical perspective and then outline a framework for ethical reasoning that will need further elaboration and refinement as conditions change.

The Shortcomings of Current Approaches

Some Catholic approaches to HIV/AIDS are characterized by weaknesses that must be overcome; they hinder rather than help in the struggle against HIV. In criticizing these approaches, I neither forget nor underestimate that Catholic organizations are in the forefront of providing care in many countries. Once the questions of sexual morality and women's rights are removed from the concerns in this debate, the commitment of the Catholic Church to different kinds of charity is extremely important and very much welcome. Nevertheless, achievements in the practical struggle against the effects of the pandemic cannot conceal shortcomings in the ethical approach: prohibiting the use of condoms, theological "explanations" of HIV/AIDS, the social and structural impact of cultural norms, poverty and human rights violations, and the failure to address women's concerns appropriately.

The first shortcoming is the ignorance and the denial—or, in the case of acknowledgment, the toleration—that Catholic sexual ethics plays into HIV infection by advising against the distribution and use of condoms. Exemplary statements like the following, given by Zambian archbishop Telesphor George Mpundu in Germany, are unacceptable from an ethical point of view: "We say no to condoms. Condoms offer a false sense of security and are no solution."[1]

Harris Kachaso, MJ, from Malawi is of the same opinion. As director of Human Life International Malawi, Kachaso noted that for the second year the Ministry of Health had dedicated a week to urge Malawians to be aware of their HIV status. In 2006, the government targeted 90,000 people in the awareness drive; in 2007, 130,000 were expected. "The idea is good," said Kachaso, "but HIV/AIDS can not decrease if the authorities concerned and other groups continue to promote condoms. . . . The concerned authorities should stop promoting condoms because this is no different from promoting genocide in a country." He said not even HIV or STD discordant couples should be advised to use condoms. They instead "should learn to live a sacrificial love where they think of caring for the sick partner and of raising children, if any."[2]

Presented in this way, the moral teaching of the Catholic Church may bear some responsibility for the death of innocent people, and we cannot be silent about this. It is morally and theologically wrong to tacitly accept these deaths for the sake of moral teaching. Christianity is about life, not about a morality that sacrifices people for doctrine. Furthermore, Christian sexual ethics have always been oriented toward family ethics. AIDS, however, takes parents from children in such numbers that the concern for their well-being must take priority over the concern for "sexual correctness." Even within the traditional moral theological approach, it is inconsistent to emphasize sexual ethics over the right to life and the right to grow up in a family.

The second shortcoming is the moral-theological explanation of the cause of HIV. Catholic moral theology correctly recognizes sexual transmission as the origin of the pandemic, although for quite some time now, other infection routes have existed: mother-to-child infection, blood transfusion, and needle sharing. From a certain theological perspective, the real cause of HIV is an evil deed that results in an evil consequence. This ancient scheme interprets a given misfortune or disease as a punishment for doing evil and holds the person who is sick morally responsible. In the book of Job and various sequences in the Gospels that deal with illness and responsibility, this judgmental, "moralizing" attitude that points at, instead of helps, is criticized exhaustively as wrong. This sin-and-guilt-oriented ethical approach is nevertheless echoed in some current analyses of HIV/AIDS using the ancient scheme in a way that infected persons cannot but feel guilty and condemned. Thus, sexual behavior that is intrinsically wrong on moral grounds may result in sexual infections and should therefore not be practiced by Catholics.[3] Stated this way, it seems less sinful to risk the infection and possible death of another person than to use a condom in the sexual act or to engage in sexual acts that are not open to procreation. More often, however, the ethical assertion is stated in a positive way: sexually appropriate behavior—that is, morally "good" and "justified" sex within marriage—protects against HIV infection. This statement, however, is empirically wrong when one partner has engaged in sexually inappropriate behavior: the unsuspecting partner is at risk of infection without means of protection. This thinking discourages testing, since in testing positive one partner's "wrong behavior" is exposed. The Church's focus on wrongdoing and guilt may well play into the reluctance to be tested.

Third, while emphasizing the need to control the sexual practices of individuals, the structural impact of cultural norms, social contexts, even the global economic order, especially the irresponsible ignorance of global poverty and health-related deaths, is underestimated.[4] True, John Paul II stressed the unjust social and economic order and pointed to the tragedy of HIV/AIDS.[5] However, while addressing the structural injustice in an exceptional way, drawing upon and developing Catholic social teaching, John Paul II never accepted the further analysis that the moral objection to the distribution of condoms plays into the spread of the pandemic and must be corrected as part of the structural change and struggle against the injustice he correctly lamented. To claim both—a narrow sexual ethics and just structures established by international regimes—is a contradiction to many, yet it seems illogically appropriate for the Church. Archbishop Mpundu, in any way, does not hesitate to add to his statement about sexual practices: "To some extent it is indifference, but also to some extent deliberate, that so little is done. Europe and the United States must find the political will to promote Africa's development. As human beings we all belong to a single family. Do not forget Africa!"[6]

Fourth, the Church fails to give appropriate answers especially to women and, indirectly, to children. Unmarried men and women want to live their sexuality as part of their adult lives. Sexuality, including homosexuality, is not against human nature, and even though it is open to individual, cultural, and social interpretation, sexuality is—or rather should be—based upon the Christian principles of unconditional love and affirmation.[7] The problem is not sexuality as such, but social norms that may accept the double standards of male extramarital sex but condemn women involved in like practices. The asymmetry produces the need to exclude specific women or at least lower their social status in order to make them available for the male desire, and at the same time it results in many women denying their sexual welfare or sexual activities outside of marriage. As recent studies reveal, this asymmetry persists in Africa.[8]

Women often do not have the power or the means to stop men from having sex with them, be it before, outside, or within marriages. Certainly, there are women who have the power and the social status to respond in a more sovereign manner, but for the vast majority of women in, for instance, sub-Saharan countries, this sovereignty is lacking.[9] The Church has no answer to the women who cannot stop their husbands from having sex with other women, especially not in regions that have known polygamy for centuries. It does not have an answer to the women who fall victim to "sugar daddies," or men looking for sexual adventures, and it certainly has no answer to the mass rapes that have left hundreds of thousands of women highly traumatized and infected with HIV. The Church has no answer to all the orphans whose mothers and fathers die, leaving them without much more than memory books, or the children's own memory of the past. I am not talking about a "footnote" of the pandemic here; rather, an estimated 20 million children will be orphans in Africa alone by 2010.

Indeed, many grassroots initiatives changed their policies on prevention, and many priests and Church workers include the distribution of condoms (if they are accessible) in their prevention strategies—but by way of conscientious objection. Drawing on one of several organizations as an example, the Young Women's Christian Association had just confirmed its policy on condoms, before the Catholic Nyaradzai Gumbonzvanda assumed the post. In a paper entitled "Male and Female Condoms: The Time to Deliver Is Now," Gumbonzvanda's predecessor, Musimbi Kanyoro, wrote that "hundreds of thousands of lives can be saved by redoubling our investment in male and female condoms and by fully financing programs that provide women and men with the knowledge, tools and social support they need to practice safer sex."[10] The question for theological ethics today is whether we can develop a framework that (1) justifies the critique of the practices and recommendations given, especially with respect to the narrow perspective on sexual ethics, (2) acknowledges the commitment of Catholic organizations and initiatives in the struggle against HIV, and (3) proposes new ways to address the pandemic, theoretically and practically.

A Framework for Ethical Reasoning

The following basic framework aims to overcome the separation between moral theology and social ethics in favor of an integrated approach. I use common terms of ethical reflection, as shown in the columns of personal-individual ethics and institutional-social ethics. Personal-individual ethics address those dimensions that focus on actions, convictions and values, and rights respective of the obligations of individual agents. Institutional-social ethics address those dimensions that focus on social settings and social values enabling and constraining human relationships; cultural and social norms; social and political structures and constraints on individuals' actions; political, professional, and/or civil institutions enabling collective actions and social practices; and issues of social and political justice. In the two horizontal axes, I distinguish between evaluative (teleological) and normative (deontological) spheres. I am aware that different ethical traditions use slightly different terms for these spheres—here the ethics of the "good" is distinguished from the ethics of the "right"—that they are interrelated, and that both the "good" and the "right" have an individualistic and a social-collective side. The task of moral theory, moral theology, and social ethics is to develop tools of analysis in order to understand from which cultural, historical, social, and religious background—in what way and by whom—actions or practices should be corrected or changed.

This framework allows us to distinguish between different fields and the different dimensions of ethical reasoning. Personal ethics or an ethics of leading a "good life," addressing *teleological* dimensions, must reflect upon, articulate, and interpret personal choices and life-planning, and also elaborate the competence and education needed to enable individuals to make reasonable choices (in view of desires, interests, and moral convictions). This ethics must analyze requirements of psychological and/or pastoral care and counseling, and find ways for the individual to manage information, here considering the risks of infection and the burden of the disease. Social ethics, addressing teleological dimensions, must concern social imagination and social visions, the norms of social interaction, practices of solidarity and group identities.

General Framework

Status of ethical reflection	Personal-individual ethics	Institutional-social ethics
Teleological considerations with diverse and pluralistic answers to the "good"	Self-respect, self-fulfillment, well-being, happiness, convictions, values, ideas Relational autonomy	Visions of the "common good," community values, social norms, social recognition Solidarity
Deontological considerations with universalistic normative claims of the "right"	Human rights based on the respect for the dignity of others, resulting in the obligation to respect the other and support his or her flourishing	Governance and legislation based on justice: just distribution of goods, fairness and equality in participating in all relevant social practices, compensation and corrections of past and present structural injusti.:e

Personal-individual ethics, addressing the *normative* question of human rights, obligations, and respect for the freedom of others and striving to improve the quality of life in cases where basic goods are lacking, must work in reference to the different contexts of disrespect of others. Especially with the right to health care and development, positive rights are open for debate, determining how much assistance is needed by exactly whom, to enable individuals to lead a decent life.[11] Social ethics addressing the normative question of justice is linked to policies and international strategies of global health care. On this level, political and economic theories are included in the overall reflection.

The task of ethics in this multidisciplinary enterprise is to address and analyze the personal values and social norms underlying different claims and their interrelation, and to work on the normative claims enabling us to identify and prioritize rights and obligations. For individual decision-making, the task of ethics is to address the ethical dimension of the choices within the limits of moral pluralism and diversity, and to help others make responsible decisions.

Considering HIV/AIDS from the perspective of the individual person, we may see how much the idea of a decent quality of life is connected to self-respect, the capacity to care for oneself, and to make sense of life. We can see, too, how power relations play into these concepts. While Christian theology stresses that autonomy and self-determination must be seen against the backdrop of respect and human dignity, the common good supports the necessity of relations with other beings—in reciprocal friendships, asymmetric care-relations, and so forth. Far from irrelevant to ethical analysis, listening to or exchanging experiences with others about coping with one's life under the daily experiences of living with HIV is of immense importance.

The pandemic shows how vulnerable women are. In so many parts of the world, women cannot speak for themselves, their autonomy is defined as a biography others write for them, which writers expect (and get) their consent from these women to whatever the biographers say. In many contexts, women's sexuality does not count except as it may be valued by another. Women's striving for a happier life is hindered by the lack of education, financial means, and prospects to care for themselves. Particularly when the care-giving for the larger family unit is overwhelming and cannot be shared with others, HIV/AIDS becomes another obstacle to women's development. HIV/AIDS touches upon women's basic rights, plays into social concepts and the idea of the common good, and can only be improved by the correction of unjust practices and structures that will achieve more justice for everyone. If we listen, we can hear the shattering stories of women's annihilated dreams, of heartbreaking violence, and of love for partners, for children, and for others. We also hear stories of women who do not have the strength to care for their families, who leave their partners, who survive in the sex market, or who even commit suicide. The ethics of life and the gospel of life are here with these women—caring or not caring, loving or not loving their children, their husbands, and their families.

In short, Christian ethics must respond on several levels. Unconditional affirmation and dignity, the core principle of Christian ethics, means to turn to someone, to acknowledge that person with dignity, and to respond appropriately and voluntarily, without demanding a change of practice or attitude as a condition for caritas. On a societal level, care is transformed into solidarity, either reciprocal or voluntary, as unconditioned benevolence. The means and infrastructure necessary for leading a decent life belong to a communitarian nature. Social visions and a social imagination are needed, and they are strongest when, putting the principle of subsidiarity into practice, they embrace local as much as global conditions. Christian ethics can offer reasons and motivation for home-based or community-based care and charity work as an effort of global solidarity translated into local practices, as the global Catholic community has shown so often in most regions of the world. Yet we must not stop our ethical reasoning there, lest we fail to address injustice and structural sin and the Church's chances to advocate for better international policies.[12]

Human Rights

Human rights are understood by Christian ethics as acknowledging human beings without qualification or judgment. In a human rights approach, the principle of dignity (acknowledged in concrete human rights) enters into social ethics as a primary principle justified philosophically and theologically; individual dignity takes priority over the common good. This priority keeps the common good in check so that it does not override individual rights. Ethics in this sense goes further than the care-and-charity approach suggests: it *demands* from us the need to acknowledge, respect, and protect the other's dignity, while sharing the means necessary to lead a decent life. From here, the distance between indecent conditions, disrespectful encounters, and unjust structures and institutional constraints to the claims of Christian ethics becomes obvious.

Further, though the individual takes priority, questions of the individual's life cannot be separated from the social conditions and/or norms or the overall institutional frameworks that structure health care and development policies. There, justice enters into the analysis. Justice does not work without the concept of human rights, the criterion for justice's content. Fair distribution, correction in favor of those who are discriminated against, exchange on the basis of equality and proportionality, and equal chance to have access to social goods including social and political participation—all these aspects of justice make sense only on the basis of a human rights approach.

This ethical framework reveals the interconnection between concepts of the good life (far from mere egoistic or egocentric "lifestyles") with claims to human rights and justice(respect, recognition, tolerance, and nondiscrimination) along with a guarantee of just means and an infrastructure that is necessary for personal self-care. Sexual ethics does not play a major role in this approach. Sexual expression is only one part of human interaction; other pressing issues must be resolved.[13]

The different dimensions of the framework are interconnected practically, and are required also by ethical theory. Much work is needed before we have a solid reflective basis—even though at first sight it seems so easy to determine what to do, especially with respect to women's rights. While correcting the ethical course, we must continue the struggle against HIV/AIDS—with preventive measures, with the care work for and together with those who are infected and their families who are affected, and with the advocacy for justice in international policies and treaties regulating the health care sector in ways that, at present, fail the common good.[14] Christian ethics can contextualize these practices in drawing attention to countless biblical stories of despair, defeat, lament, and mourning, comparing our attitudes with biblical indifference, complacency, or corruption, and gaining strength from the blessing of "all human beings" that may result in the solidarity and hope that social justice is possible—without which the kingdom of God will not come.

Gillian Paterson

Whose Truth?

Discourses of AIDS in Britain

When tests for HIV became available in Britain in the mid-eighties, three main risk groups were identified: men who have sex with men, IV drug users (IDU), and people who receive treatment with blood products.[1] Until 1998, the majority of infections occurred among men who had had sex with men. In 1999, heterosexually acquired HIV became the largest category, and has remained so since. Around 80 percent of those infected in Britain contracted the virus in countries with high HIV prevalence. Between 1998 and 2007, however, the number acquired within the UK increased threefold. The proportion of diagnoses among women also rose from 20 percent in 1992 to around 70 percent in 2007; the sharp increase is possibly attributable to the routine testing of pregnant women that is now the norm. The availability of antiretroviral therapies (ART) has increased the incentive to be tested by reducing the burden of sickness and of AIDS-related death. Nevertheless, the government estimates that around 30 percent of those with HIV are unaware of their infection, with many NGOs in the field suggesting a higher figure.[2] Meanwhile, widespread high-risk behavior is suggested by the fact that Britain has the highest rates of sexually transmitted diseases and teenage pregnancy in Europe.

Every epidemic is the product of its history. AIDS in the UK has, from the beginning, been culturally defined in relation to men who have sex with men. This link has contributed to the "othering" of the epidemic generally. When AIDS first appeared, it seemed a heaven-sent opportunity for the new, politically right-wing governments of the 1980s to make moral and political capital of the epidemic. From the beginning, AIDS was associated in the public (and particularly the religious) mind with sin, especially sexual sin; the "gay plague" reaction of the popular press reinforced the view that HIV affected only those who "deserved" it. The link with gay sexuality seemed to justify the sluggishness of government reactions, which gained momentum only when it became clear that AIDS also posed a threat to the heterosexual population.

The link between HIV and stigmatized groups such as gays remains. National reporting shows that many new infections today were acquired either in Africa, or among partners of people who acquired them in Africa, Africans being another group that is all too easy for the majority population in Britain to construct as "the other."[3] AIDS, accordingly, has become an issue in our highly politicized national dialogue on asylum, which is where I encounter it in my own work with refugees and asylum seekers. The popular press has contributed to the dialogue by ratcheting up the antiasylum argument with the specter of "hordes" of HIV-positive asylum seekers thronging our shores in search of free treatment "at our expense," leading to new regulations, such as that the National Health Service will provide ART only for those who have lived in the country legally for at least one year. Three brief case studies follow to introduce people from two contexts with which I am closely associated: a theological faculty of London University and a refugee and asylum center in central London.[4]

Three Stories

Becky became infected with HIV during a period in her life when she engaged regularly in binge drinking, used ecstasy and cocaine, and had unprotected sex with a large number of men, some of whom she met through the internet. Being told she had HIV was the worst moment of her life, she says. Until then it had all been a game, but this was for real. She knew two things about AIDS: it was a disease of gay men, and new treatments meant it was no longer life threatening. Following her diagnosis, she was not much wiser. The information she was given was in the form of leaflets that all seemed to be aimed at gay men and clubbing. As a woman with HIV, she felt lost and alone. She told nobody, and was tempted to take refuge in more drink, drugs, and general self-destructive behavior. Then a friend told her about a local network for HIV-positive women. Here she discovered people she could talk to openly and without shame. Today she teaches English to foreign students and is working on a degree in theology. She does not disclose her HIV status at work or at college; it would make others uncomfortable, and she is afraid of losing work if her employers know. She is a volunteer for the same women's network, where she helps other women come to terms with their status by a less agonizing route than the one she took herself.

Aged 28, Jean-Paul is a refugee from Côte d'Ivoire. A former journalist, he is well-read and well-spoken. Diagnosed with HIV in 2004, Jean-Paul bears a triple burden of stigma: he is African, he is gay, and he is HIV-positive. In his culture, Jean-Paul is not a "real man" unless he is sexually active with women. In reality, he says, you cannot be both gay and "a man" in his culture. For Jean-Paul, this reality raises key questions about his identity. Although he feels sexually comfortable in the white gay community, where he can be open about his status, they are not his people. He longs to be back with his own, but with them, he cannot disclose his HIV status, and homosexuality is totally taboo. Gay African men say that it is difficult even to find an appropriate word for homosexuality. "Gay" is okay, but it means something else in Africa.[5] "Men who have sex with men" is overly explicit, and he hates having his whole identity reduced to a sexual function, especially one that brands him as an outsider.[6]

Céleste was born in Rwanda. In 1994, she watched three of her children murdered and was repeatedly raped by men she had known all her life, who then left her for dead. Returning to consciousness, she grabbed the baby from the bushes where she had hidden him, then fled, terrified that her attackers would come back and kill her too. She had been in the UK for two years when she was diagnosed with HIV. She received no counseling either before or after the test; the nurse who told her spoke only English, and the interpreter was absent that day. She is undergoing ART, although she finds it difficult to take so many pills without other people noticing and asking why. She has told nobody in her own community that she has HIV. The stigma attached to AIDS among her own people is too extreme for her to contemplate risking disclosure. She has not even told the man who is her regular sexual partner. "He would beat me or even kill me," she says. "He would surely leave me. He will never use a condom. But I feel so bad when we do that thing together, and he doesn't understand why I say no so often. But what can I do?" If she disclosed her status, she would not be able to show her face at the refugee center, her son would be shunned at school, and she would be denounced as a sinner or "accursed" in her church. "I am a good mother," she says. "But I am not a good *African* mother if I have this bad thing that kills people." She wants to live, if only for the sake of the teenage son she rescued from the carnage of the Rwandan genocide. She thinks they would be happier today in Rwanda, where they still have family. But there would be no free medical care, as in the UK. If she goes back, the next opportunistic infection (or the next, or the next) will kill her.

Truth and Discourse

The ethical issues highlighted by these stories are familiar: stigma and discrimination, silence and denial, sexuality and sexual behavior, gender and sin, ignorance and the need for education, poverty and the disparity of resources between rich and poor worlds, ethical issues of testing, the need for appropriate language, and the stranglehold of culture and gender that makes disclosure so difficult but that has, nevertheless, to be balanced against the moral responsibility not to infect others. The ethical issue I discuss here, briefly, is the complex, multifaceted problem of truth: (1) the way in which AIDS has been socially and morally constructed in the British context, (2) the discourses that have contributed to that construction or been excluded from it, and (3) the way the identities of those who are living with HIV are impacted. Finally, it is important that public education and practical interventions are based on what is *really* the case *now*, not on ignorance, or anachronistic categorization of risk, or politically motivated constructions that seek to conceal truths or to demonize particular social, ethnic, or sexual groups.

Here the discourse theory of Paul Ricoeur is useful.[7] Discourse shapes reality and gives direction and language to the "narrative" within which we are living and the characters in it. Discourse, says Ricoeur, has a tendency to be self-universalizing: to present a subjectively projected world as if it were objectively constructed (and therefore universally true). The aim of discourse-analysis is to bring these subjective projections into the cognitive domain so they can be recognized, critiqued, and challenged. Paul Bové goes further and says that discourse actually "produces" knowledge that makes possible the "disciplines and institutions which, in turn, sustain and distribute these discourses."[8] For Bové, the purpose of discourse-analysis is to map the linkages, in terms of power and control, between institutional power and powerful discourses. If this seems to present an impossibly fragmented view of truth, consider Augustine of Hippo. Augustine claimed that we can no more contain the full truth in words than we can contain the sea in a seashell: "Whoever thinks that in this mortal life one may so disperse the mists of imagination as to possess the unclouded light of unchangeable truth . . . understands neither what he seeks nor who he is that seeks it."[9] On this cautionary note, I will attempt a tentative analysis of the discourses currently influencing the AIDS scene in Britain.

I suggest that the dominant discourses within the dialogue on AIDS in Britain are biomedical, conservative-moral, and liberal–human rights. The reality, though, is that for many people living with HIV, these discourses operate as further endorsement of the stigmatization and marginalization they already experience. The colonizing effects of powerful discourses invariably become apparent when we attempt a shared, articulated discourse, which gives people living with the virus an identity and enables them to be fully human.

Biomedical discourses, shaped by science and the market, have made a huge contribution in recent years. They have prioritized free ART and other interventions aimed at mitigating the physiological effects of HIV, established an agreed biological underpinning to understandings of risk, and provided an evidence basis for public health initiatives. The unintended effect, as demonstrated by Becky's experience, has been the more relaxed attitudes to unprotected sex and recreational IDU. "AIDS?" a new college student was recently reported as saying. "That's not a problem anymore, is it?" Further, the groups most vulnerable to sexually transmitted infections (including HIV) often have limited access to education or information about their sexual health or to statutory health services. Thus, young men and women, asylum seekers and immigrant communities, sex workers, and trafficked women and children may delay seeking help or taking precautions until there is a crisis.[10]

Science favors the apparently neutral language of "viral load," "risk assessment," and "targeted medication." Conservative-moral discourses, however, favor the language of morality and judgment. Transmission is said to be the result of sin, not a virus. Support for sex workers, men who have sex with men, and IDUs is not identified as trying to help those most at risk; rather, this support is considered to be encouraging of sinful ways of life. Educating young people on prevention does not empower them to protect themselves from infection but encourages adolescent sex, a fear that has underpinned the recent outcry at the introduction of a cervical cancer vaccine for 12-year-old girls. These discourses increase stigma by confusing morality and disease-prevention in people's minds and by failing to take into account the social and political dimensions of morality. They undermine prevention education by suggesting that you get HIV because of what you *are* rather than by what you *do*. The epidemic becomes frozen at the "framing and blaming" stage, where disease-related stigmas are honed and the development of coordinated, epidemiologically educated interventions are sabotaged.

In Britain, liberal–human rights discourses have made a key contribution to our understanding of HIV. For gay discourses, in particular, AIDS has created a powerful, uniting metaphor where social marginalization contributed to an ethos of solidarity and mutual support, and an organized insistence on individual rights resulted in huge benefits for many. Arguably, though, the very success of the gay voice has occasioned the marginalization of other voices: women and children, or hemophiliacs, or drug users living with HIV. There is sometimes a sense of gay "ownership" of HIV that is not always helpful. Furthermore, like other liberation or human rights discourses with their roots in the West, the dominance of the white gay voice has tended to obscure the multilayered oppressions often faced by IDUs, women, people with disabilities, children, and homosexual men living in our midst but in non-Western communities.

Identity in a Time of AIDS

The three individuals in the case studies demonstrate the limitations of these paradigm discourses for understanding the UK epidemic. All are examples of what Erving Goffman, in his seminal study *Stigma*, calls "spoiled identity."[11] When Becky looked for information, what she found were leaflets targeting gay men. Jean-Paul's association with the gay community in London does not touch his longing for the identity denied him as an African man. Céleste has to conceal her status in order to retain her identity as an African, Christian mother within the conservative moral culture of her roots.

Within the liberal–human rights discourse, new voices fight to be heard. These include women with HIV struggling for a voice in the public discourse on AIDS and the framing of policy. This movement has led to the formation of organizations such as the International Community of Women Living with HIV or AIDS, and Positively Women, now twenty years old. Africans too are struggling for inclusion, through organizations such as the African HIV Policy Network and also through the Terrence Higgins Trust, which supports gay rights in relation to HIV and tries (without much obvious success) to address homophobia in African communities and persuade well-known black gay men to "come out." Small NGOs focusing on black and African health issues have been effective in supporting HIV-positive African men and women and educating girls in culturally and linguistically appropriate ways. Cara, the Mildmay Mission Hospital, and the Ecumenical AIDS Trust are examples of the churches' efforts to give nonjudgmental care and training. However, a number of small groups have gone out of business recently because of the government's preference for supporting larger organizations, and *Positive Nation* (the only publication exclusively for HIV-positive people) has closed from a lack of funds. Meanwhile hemophiliac men with HIV and their partners still struggle with chronic ill-health and a lack of adequate government compensation, services for HIV-positive IDUs are extremely limited, and no one knows how many children or teenagers there are with HIV in the UK.

John Paul II said, "The church serves humanity with the *diakonia* of truth; we are partners in humanity's shared struggle to arrive at truth."[12] Is there a role here for Christian ethics in making the hidden visible? Can we, as a Church, contribute to the task of ensuring that the way we "see" HIV or AIDS reflects the realities of the marginalized? In the exercise of arriving at the truth, we should perhaps start with ourselves. I did not use, in the case studies, the examples of HIV-positive ordained or would-be ordained Catholics who have shared their stories with me; I could not do so convincingly without the risk of disclosing their identities. Despite the quiet, supportive work of HIV-positive Catholics and others, these stories remain tales of discrimination and fear, silencing and denial, about which we should as a Church be ashamed. I hope one day they will be told, and for that reason I welcome the setting up of INERELA+ UK, the UK branch of the International Network of Religious Leaders living with or affected by HIV or AIDS. It is the aim of INERELA+ to empower clergy, in particular, to support one another in addressing AIDS-related stigma and to redeem the discourse of denial and judgment that has characterized many religious responses to the epidemic and those affected. This redemption will not enable us, in Augustine's words, to "contain the sea in a seashell." But, in an altogether more modest vein, it might help Christian theology to exercise a healing influence on the warring discourses of AIDS by bringing to bear what John Paul II has called "the *diakonia* of truth."

Suzanne Mulligan

What's Love Got to Do with It?

Sex, Survival, and HIV/AIDS in South Africa

What keeps us alive, what allows us to endure?
I think it is the hope of loving,
or being loved.

—Meister Eckhart, "The Hope of Loving"

We have all heard about the statistics on HIV infection rates and global infection patterns. Globally, there were approximately 33 million people living with HIV/AIDS in 2007,[1] and 90 percent of those individuals reside in the so-called developing world. In terms of sheer numbers, sub-Saharan Africa is experiencing an AIDS epidemic not seen elsewhere in the world; figures for 2007 reveal that 67 percent of all people infected with HIV live in sub-Saharan Africa, while this region accounts for 75 percent of all AIDS deaths in 2007.[2]

Furthermore, statistics confirm that in Africa more women are becoming infected than men; approximately 60 percent of all adults living with HIV/AIDS in sub-Saharan Africa are women.[3] The data also reveals that girls and young women 15 to 24 years of age are more likely to become infected than their male counterparts, perhaps by a factor of as much as three to one. These statistics are borne out in South Africa, where we witness increasing rates of infection among married women.[4]

Statistics, of course, are an essential part of information generation; they can offer invaluable insights into patterns of HIV infection around the world, which can help shape our response to this pandemic. But statistics are cold, detached things, and however much we might learn from them, statistics alone fail to reveal the full human tragedy of AIDS. This essay seeks to examine some of the implications of HIV/AIDS for women in South Africa and consider some challenges for Catholic moral theology.

Why Are Women and Girls So Vulnerable?

The epidemic in South Africa reveals a variety of complex social, cultural, economic, and sexual issues determining the direction and severity of the crisis. One major concern for those working in HIV prevention is the scale of sexual abuse and rape, particularly rape directed against women. Rape and sexual assault is a serious problem within South African society in general, and although men are not exempt from it, I will focus on the rape of women and young girls and consider the implications for HIV transmission.

It is difficult to calculate precisely the annual number of sexual assaults on women and girls. Both the South African Police Service (SAPS) and professional groups working with survivors of sexual attacks, such as Rape Crisis Cape Town, acknowledge that the majority of rapes go unreported. Indeed, it is believed that as few as one in thirty-five assaults are ever reported.[5] The reasons for such low levels of reporting vary. It may be (and usually is) the case that the victim knows her assailant and is fearful of reprisal should she report him, she may be socially and/or economically dependent on her attacker, she may also be suspicious of the police service, and in the case of attacks on young children—a growing problem in South Africa—the child may not be able to identify her attacker. Because of underreporting, and shortcomings in the South African legal system, many rapists go unpunished.[6] Less than one-third of reported rapes ever reach court, and of those cases that do, less than half result in conviction.[7]

A disturbing feature of the rape crisis in South Africa is the increasing number of young girls and infants exposed to this kind of attack. Myths suggesting that sex with a virgin—or more recently, sex with a child or an infant—will "cure" a person of AIDS undoubtedly place children at risk of assault. The rate of infection among children following sexual attacks is particularly high, since internal physical injury is common, which in turn results in greater surface area being exposed to the virus. And if we are to accept that sexual myths are a motivating factor in these attacks, it is reasonable to assume that those who carry out such assaults are HIV-positive (or at least have reason to believe they are HIV-positive). Thus, not only are children exposed to a physical trauma, but the attacks often lead to the further trauma of HIV infection.

The conviction rate for child rape in South Africa is especially low, partly because the victims are so young and unable to testify in court. But most perpetrators are known to the family, which is another reason why cases go unreported. Furthermore, methods of collecting forensic evidence are often inadequate, and vital evidence can be either overlooked or lost during the course of an investigation.[8]

Not everyone is convinced, however, of a link between the virgin myths and attacks on young girls and infants. Rachel Jewkes, Lorna Martin, and Loveday Penn-Kekana dispute such a link. They believe these assaults are grounded in the more widespread problem of sexual violence against women and girls. "Cases have been reported in which this myth was a motivating factor for child rape, but most evidence suggests that this motivation is infrequent."[9] They also disagree with evidence that child rape is on the increase. They believe instead that sexual assaults on children are more likely to be the result of the high levels of sexual violence within South African society. Some assaults, for example, have been linked to Cape Town gang initiation rituals.[10] Jewkes and her fellow writers believe that the problem of child rape is related more closely to poverty, inequality, and violence within society than to sexual myths of different kinds. They argue:

> Many people in South Africa have been extremely brutalized by the political violence in the country's past, the disruption of families and communities, high levels of poverty, and the very high levels of violence of all forms. The direction of much of this violence at women and girls might be explained by sex inequalities, a culture of male sexual entitlement, and the climate of relative impunity for rape.
>
> The root of the problem of infant rape, as for rape of older girls and women, lies mainly at these more mundane doors, and it should be seen as part of the spectrum of sexual violence against women and girls. Infant and child rape will be prevented only if these issues can be ameliorated.[11]

It seems likely that a combination of both sexual myths and the problems mentioned by Jewkes and her fellow writers contributes to child rape in South Africa. In a society where violence, poverty, and inequality abound, the motivation for attacks on children will at times certainly lie at these "more mundane doors." But the influence of sexual myths remains an important factor in the equation.

That notwithstanding there is much truth in what writers like Jewkes, Martin, and Penn-Kekana are saying. Child rape must also be understood within the wider context of sexual violence and exploitation in South Africa. Growing numbers of children are exposed to child sex rings, child prostitution, child pornography, and sexual abuse within the home. Furthermore, poverty can force parents to involve their children in high-risk activities for financial returns. In this context, children may come to be seen as "assets." An example offered by Jewkes, Martin, and Penn-Kekana illustrates all too clearly the vulnerability of many young girls within the home. They cite the case of one mother who allowed an HIV-1-positive man to rape her daughter in exchange for money.[12]

Poverty, Sex, and Survival

Much has been written about the relationship between poverty and AIDS; it is no coincidence that the majority of people infected with and affected by AIDS reside in poorer parts of the world. As the statistics illustrate, the greatest concentration of HIV infection occurs in the poorest region of the world: sub-Saharan Africa. It is reasonable to assume that a direct link exists between poverty and AIDS or, put another way, that poverty creates a certain set of social conditions that facilitates the rapid spread of HIV among a population.

Despite its classification as a middle income country, South Africa remains one of the most unequal societies in the world. The Human Development Index (HDI) maps the level of inequality in society.[13] According to its Gini coefficient of 0.58 (measuring the degree of inequality), South Africa is second in its social inequality only to Brazil (at 0.63, the most unequal society among similar middle-income countries).[14] This inequality, historically determined by past apartheid policies, continues to be the primary source of poverty for millions of South Africans today.[15] Post-apartheid governments have tried to tackle the high levels of poverty and unemployment but with little success. Estimates classify approximately 40 percent of the South African population as poor, with as many as 18 million living below the poverty line.

Among the poor, women emerge as a group that is particularly disadvantaged. They often lack the same economic opportunities and financial independence as men, but their poverty is associated with and exacerbated by their lack of social independence. It is not uncommon for women to find themselves economically, socially, and culturally dependent on their male counterparts. In situations where women have few, if any, employment opportunities, prostitution and casual sexual encounters with men may be their only real means of survival. In South Africa it is not uncommon for women to migrate to locations in the hope of finding a man who is employed; in return for sex, these women may receive food or money. This kind of arrangement is especially evident around mining areas. Squatter camps and temporary shelters are erected, and women are attracted to these areas in the hope of finding "security" of some sort. They may well find a man who is willing to feed them in return for sex, but they often find disease and infection as well.

One of the tragedies here is that women migrate to these areas to find the most basic of human needs: shelter, food, security, and perhaps even a little comfort and companionship—"the hope of loving, or being loved." Yet the instinct to survive, to secure these fundamental necessities, is often the cause of infection for them. Sex becomes a means of survival, in the short-term at least. But it may well be accompanied with violence and exploitation. Love, intimacy, and tenderness are rarely the priority for these women however much they may desire it.

Poverty reduction therefore must be a central part of any long-term HIV prevention efforts. Poverty often forces people to adopt "survival strategies" like prostitution that in turn expose them to infection. Once infected, the poor have few, if any, financial, social, and medical support structures to relieve even slightly the burdens of disease. One of the greatest challenges for all those working in the area of HIV prevention—churches, NGOs, political leaders—is to overcome the limitations that poverty imposes on people and the dangers poverty presents in terms of HIV exposure. These, however, remain long-term goals.

A Church Responding?

Catholic moral theology has tended to confine discussion on HIV/AIDS largely to the question of condom use. Some suggest that the recently established Vatican commission investigating this matter may be about to alter the official stance by the Catholic Church on condom use.[16] Even if it does, the account offered here demonstrates that the problems at the heart of the pandemic extend far beyond the availability or use of condoms. It is unfortunate that debates about condom use as prophylactics are framed so often by reference to contraception. In terms of Catholic teaching, there appears no sound reason why condoms cannot be promoted as a means of protecting sexual partners from infection. In any case, condoms alone are not a credible answer in most cases. Many women living in unequal and abusive relationships are unable to negotiate if, when, and how they have sex with their partners, and are unlikely to be able to suggest condom use in those circumstances. And there are cultural difficulties associated with condoms: some men simply refuse them because they believe sex with a condom is not "real" sex, or that sex is less pleasurable with a condom.

Educational programs that provide accurate information about HIV are an important step in eradicating misunderstandings and misconceptions about AIDS and HIV prevention. In South Africa, where sexual myths and confusion about HIV and AIDS abound, a clear strong message is urgently needed. Unfortunately, the South African government contributed significantly to this confusion, mainly through the views and remarks of President Thabo Mbeki and the minister for health, Manto Tshabalala-Msimang.[17]

Meaningful efforts at poverty reduction are essential also if there is any chance of eradicating the social conditions that assist the spread of AIDS. It is particularly important that women achieve some degree of economic independence and security; without this modicum of relief they will remain dependent on men for basic survival, often leaving them vulnerable to sexual violence and infection with STDs. Although it inherited unenviable financial problems from the outgoing apartheid administrations, South Africa nevertheless has greater resources available to fight HIV infection rates than many other African countries. Strategies promoting abstinence and fidelity are unlikely to succeed in South Africa until women achieve greater economic freedom.

Changes in sexual activity must be part of the prevention picture, and education around meaningful and responsible sexual relationships is essential. But for many women, the Catholic Magisterium's insistence on abstinence and fidelity as the most effective means of avoiding infection offers little hope. For although women may remain faithful to their partner within marriage, men regularly engage in sexual activity that exposes both themselves and later their wives to HIV.

Within this context, gender stereotypes and attitudes toward women must also be addressed. A new approach to the way we think about sexuality is needed, particularly the way gender relations and the roles of women in the social and domestic arenas are perceived. Women are often exposed to HIV infection because of their sexual, social, and economic subordination. Preventative efforts that emphasize change in sexual behavior are not enough; they fail women in abusive relationships. Deeper social change is therefore essential. Indeed, theologians such as Kevin Kelly point to the "double-standard morality" so often evident in many relationships, which consequently adds to women's vulnerability:

> It would seem unrealistic and even harmful to suggest that the only real solution to the HIV/AIDS pandemic lies in the traditional "faithful to one partner" sexual ethic. That offers no help to many women. For them, what is lacking is the very foundation without which such a sexual ethic is virtually meaningless. As long as their full and equal dignity is not accepted in theory and in practice, many of the norms of this traditional sexual ethic are likely to work against the well-being of these women and may even prove to be the occasion of their becoming infected by HIV.[18]

A more person-centered sexual ethic, affirming and protecting the dignity of women, is essential if Catholic sexual and social teaching is to respond effectively to the AIDS pandemic. The justice dimension here is vital. It is not simply a matter of finding a solution that will best tackle the AIDS crisis. Rather, it must also be about finding an approach to sexual ethics that affirms the dignity, equality, and rights of women. And part of a more person-centered sexual ethic includes an understanding of the ways in which social and economic injustices influence sexual choices.

Of course these recommendations may appear straightforward, but their achievement will take a considerable amount of time, resources, and effort. The results may not be seen for years. In the meantime there remains a responsibility to help and care for people according to the situations they find themselves in *here and now*. This may involve the distribution and use of condoms; it may not. But in order for the ideals of abstinence and fidelity to be realized as credible life choices, social and economic conditions must be stable for people to realize their "freedoms."[19] The challenge for the Catholic Church is to respond to the needs of those living with HIV/AIDS, even when their sexual activity appears short of the ethical mark. The challenge is to respond in ways that are both hopeful and reflective of the realities faced by millions of people in the developing world. We must recognize with the late Jonathan Mann that "our responsibility is historic. For when the history of AIDS and the global response is written, our most precious contribution may well be that in a time of plague, we did not flee, we did not hide, we did not separate ourselves."[20] Surely at the heart of the gospel message is the call not to flee, not to hide, and not to separate ourselves from those among us who are most vulnerable and in need.

Part Four

Invisible and Vulnerable

Mary M. Doyle Roche

Children and the Common Good

I write about the HIV/AIDS pandemic from the northeastern region of the United States. I write from a position of socioeconomic and racial (if not gender) privilege. I am the married mother of two young children who both enjoy overall good health and who have access to some of the finest medical facilities in the world.

The focus of this essay is the pandemic's impact on children, though as with other demographic groups, the impact is most severe in the developing world. Children's vulnerability in the pandemic arises for both physical and socially constructed reasons. This vulnerability is constitutive of childhood itself and occurs across cultures. Socially constructed vulnerability, often exploiting natural vulnerability, can be challenged using resources from the Catholic tradition. Focusing on children must also incorporate gender analysis, as children's well-being is inextricably linked to the well-being of their mothers. Moreover, in the context of HIV/AIDS, girls are among the poorest of the poor.

The United Nations has embarked on an ambitious program, "Unite for Children, Unite against AIDS," in order to address many of the issues children face. The platforms of the campaign are preventing mother-to-child transmission, developing pediatric treatment protocols, preventing new infections among children and young people, and protecting and supporting children affected by HIV/AIDS.

Even as efforts are made to garner widespread support for children from the world community, contentious debates have arisen as to how best to help them. The pandemic challenges many notions about children and childhood. Competing images of children emerge: willful and in need of discipline from authoritative adults, and pure, innocent, and in need of protection. The tradition of the common good within Catholicism can speak prophetically to this tension as it calls for the full human dignity of children who need justice, care, protection, and meaningful participation in society. The emphasis on children's purity and innocence, which influences cultures worldwide, may undermine concrete attempts to secure their well-being in the age of AIDS. It is the *humanity* of children, shaped by their particular vulnerabilities, not their *innocence*, that demands compassion and solidarity on the part of adults. Themes in Catholic social teaching, the commitment to the common good and the option for the poor in particular, can pave the way to more adequate responses to the complex needs of children everywhere.

Children in the Age of AIDS

The statistics for 2006 from UNAIDS are not promising. Consider: the number of deaths due to AIDS among children under the age of 15 is approximately 380,000 (290,000–500,000). The number of new HIV infections per year among them is approximately 530,000 (410,000–660,000).[1] Among young people aged 15 to 24, new infections reach 6,000 each day. And 2.3 million children have AIDS.[2] Millions of children in the hardest hit regions, most notably sub-Saharan Africa, are affected in many ways: they care for ill parents and siblings, and they are orphaned by the millions, losing not only parents and caregivers but also vital networks of support as teachers, health care workers, and other community members also sometimes become ill and die.[3] Children's vulnerability is dramatically increased in contexts of poverty, political instability, violent conflict, exploitation, and gender inequality, where they lack power and resources to resist these comorbid conditions.

Children's natural vulnerabilities, including their basic developmental needs, impose claims on adults in their communities to nourish, nurture, and educate them. Sadly, these very same characteristics are exploited by individual adults and other larger forces of globalization. The children of the poor and powerless become easy prey for dangerous forms of work (domestic service, sex work, factory labor, soldiering, and mining). Those entrusted with the care of children are often forced by unjust social circumstances to sacrifice their concrete well-being for the economic good of the family or community. Before we vilify the parents of poor children, however, we must recognize the root causes and unjust circumstances constraining their ability to meet their children's needs, causes often traced to consumer choices among the privileged.

These are "the signs of the times" for poor children. Reflecting on these realities in light of the common good in Catholic social teaching and international human rights reveals several important challenges that must be faced in order to respond adequately to children in need. Children need justice every bit as much as they need care. Children's participation in efforts to turn the tide on the pandemic must be enhanced. In order to empower children, the Church and the global community must also challenge the rhetoric that emphasizes children's innocence as the quality that compels action on their behalf. It is instead their humanity and particular physical and social vulnerabilities, which all too easily are controlled by others and exploited by some, that prompt us to bring their needs and voices center stage.

Unite for Children, Unite against AIDS

In October 2005, UNICEF and UNAIDS launched the five-year global campaign "Unite for Children, Unite against AIDS."[4] This campaign introduced the "Four P" approach to stemming the devastation of the pandemic: preventing vertical transmission, developing pediatric treatment protocols, preventing new infections among adolescents, and protecting vulnerable children. First among its goals is to prevent mother-to-child transmission of the virus. While vertical transmission has virtually been eliminated in wealthier nations, it remains a leading cause of infection among children globally. "In high prevalence countries . . . AIDS is responsible for an increasing share of under-five mortality."[5] Without scaled-up antiretroviral treatment and prevention measures, UNAIDS estimates that 35 percent of children born to HIV-positive mothers will seroconvert.

The second goal is pediatric treatment regimens and products. As UNAIDS and UNICEF report, the "course of HIV/AIDS is particularly aggressive in children."[6] Medications need to be tailored to their needs. Improved diagnostics for infants are also required. With successful reduction of mother-to-child transmission, many fear that pharmaceutical companies may not invest in the development of products to treat pediatric occurrence worldwide.[7]

Third, the campaign seeks to prevent new infections among adolescents and young people. How best to do this is controversial, especially in face of the reality of sexual activity and intravenous drug use. Adolescents, no less than adults, need developmentally appropriate comprehensive prevention strategies that reflect the real transmission-likely situations that even as children they face. Behavior change strategies, perhaps more readily achieved among young people, must be realistic and also age, gender, and culturally attentive. Yet we must also be cautious about framing our efforts in terms of individual behavior change.[8] Some prevention efforts, not wanting to encourage immoral behavior among youth, ironically assume that children (and women) have much more control over their sexual activity than is actually the case. A "just say no" approach to sexual activity is disingenuous when children and young people for the most part lack power over what happens to them for ill or for good. Attention must also be paid to the dynamics of the global sex trade, often the only available means of support for women and their children. Abstinence-only programs must wrestle with this complexity, but even programs around condom use face a dilemma: simply advocating condom use as a responsible prevention measure in many circumstances may fall short where women and young girls cannot insist on their use.

The fourth "P" in the campaign's platform is to protect and support children affected by AIDS. Accordingly, the program will "put the missing face of children affected by AIDS at the centre of the agenda and make sure that children and young people are heard on the issues that affect them."[9] Supporting children and young people—those at risk for contracting the virus, those with HIV, those with AIDS-related illnesses, and those orphaned by the pandemic—requires a multifaceted approach that engages real situations and the limited choices available to many of the world's children. Thus, preventing children from being orphaned in the first place should surely be a priority. Yet children are now heads-of-households, and they must be supported with access to resources, education, and training in the skills that will allow them to provide for what remains of their families.

The Common Good

How might the common good tradition engage these efforts?[10] The common good includes the sum total of the conditions of social living whereby persons are able to reach their perfection, their flourishing, more fully and easily.[11] The common good allows for human flourishing and cannot be secured alone but only in community. Resources flow outward to all individual members of a community, and all members in turn bear some share of the responsibility for building those resources. When this commitment is brought to bear on the AIDS pandemic, the common good includes access to education, quality health care, and other basic needs such as food, potable water, sufficient shelter, basic security, and immunity from violence and exploitation. The intersection of the common good with basic human rights is clear. But the common good, because it aims at just living conditions, involves more than the provision of basic needs; it requires the participation of all members of the community, including children. That children have an urgent claim on our resources is a widely supported position, even though we repeatedly fail to respond sufficiently to that claim. The more contentious position is that justice for children requires their participation in issues that affect them; I am hard-pressed to think of an issue that doesn't. If participation is constitutive of the common good for persons, then this must also be true for children. Denying children's participation in the fight against AIDS, in the guise of protection (or "family values"), fails to account for the full, intrinsic human dignity of children and young people.

In the age of AIDS, the common good tradition must be shaped also by a preferential option for the poor. This emphasis keeps common good language from the dangers of collectivism or utilitarianism in which the "common" good sought actually represents the interests of those with power and privilege. The option for the poor demands that the poor and vulnerable have the first claim—that is, their physical, emotional, and health needs are to be met first by all available resources—and that their voices are brought to the fore in decisions on how resources will be best used. The participation of young people must be welcomed, and their experiences of HIV and AIDS must lead in determining the priorities for the world community. The option for the poor also challenges us to be aware of the tendency to equate children's interests with the interests of their families and the adults in their lives.

In the global, cross-cultural debate, the language of the common good and the option for the poor resonates with the language of human rights and children's rights, bringing a robust theological anthropology and account of human flourishing. James Keenan and Jon Fuller, reflecting on their experience at the 2004 International AIDS Conference in Bangkok, noted that human rights language, when used by those in the developed world, often amounted to little more than a rhetorical device aimed at alerting the audience to the urgency of a particular need. Human rights language lost its edge as a tool for the critical analysis of social, political, and economic conditions.[12] Rhetoric around children's rights likewise often falls victim to this tendency. Rights become amorphous, like the "right to an open future" or "happiness" or the "right to a childhood," rather than linked meaningfully to specific responsibilities or relationships.[13] This failure to make rights-language concrete and relevant to specific contexts leads to the charge that organizations like the UN have "abandoned" children to their "rights," failing to provide adequate protection for them and autonomy for their parents.[14] A position on children's rights that respects the developmental needs of children and envisions them as profoundly relational and interdependent can withstand these charges.

The UN Convention on the Rights of the Child envisioned the child as a person whose flourishing is most readily achieved in a family or kinship network that has access to adequate resources.[15] In this network, children grow as individual members of families and communities increasingly able to participate in society and meaningfully exercise their rights. We can use the economic and political rights articulated in the Convention as a benchmark against which to measure the concrete well-being of children and demand that the many institutions of civil society secure that well-being.

A 2002 follow-up to the Convention, the Special Session on Children, assessed the achievements and remaining challenges since the ratification of the Convention.[16] Remarkably, children and young people themselves shared their experiences of poverty, war, unjust working conditions, and diseases like AIDS, as well as their efforts in community activism and work for social justice. Images of these children and young people provide a helpful bridge to my final point—the need to challenge the rhetoric that emphasizes childhood innocence.[17]

I do not mean to suggest that children are somehow responsible for their HIV status or for poverty, sexism, and violence (though children are often caught up in systems that perpetuate these injustices). I do want to caution against the presumptions of innocence as the precondition for a compassionate response on the part of adults. Wishing to avoid the subject, many adults fail to provide important information about HIV prevention and issues of sexual health to children and young people. We may hesitate in our response on behalf of children who complicate our notions about childhood: children in the global sex industry, bandits, child soldiers, or gang members.[18] As we in the United States wring our hands about eliminating child labor entirely, millions of children work to support their families in dangerous and inhumane conditions. Adult insistence on the innocence or purity of childhood can lead to the exclusion of real children in our communities, or the claim that some children are not really children at all. Finally, this focus on innocence plays into the disturbing tendency to set the innocent victims of AIDS against its "guilty" victims.[19] In the United States, because HIV/AIDS was first associated with gay men, a compassionate response from the Christian community was slow in coming, to say the least. Religious rhetoric focused on homosexual relationships rather than on the gospel call to solidarity and healing. It was not until parents insisted that the face of HIV/AIDS expand to include, for example, the images of Ryan White, a white, male child who became HIV-positive through a blood transfusion, that US communities began to think differently about HIV. Pediatric AIDS became a compelling cause for a dominant group, whose power to sway public opinion effectively brought the discourse on HIV/AIDS into people's homes and around even "polite" table conversation.[20] Appealing to the sensitivities of many, in light of an almost amoral vulnerability, Ryan's innocence demanded this response, not his humanity. Yet if we are to follow Catholic social teaching, it is humanity that compels justice. So as interested as we may be in helping children, we may ignore the needs of their parents (often their mothers) and other adults who are subject to the injustice of someone else's complacence and whose well-being is inextricably linked to the well-being of their children.[21]

The children and young people already involved in the fight against AIDS are not asking for a return to innocence. They are asking to be accepted as full and much-needed partners in the struggle. Several examples provided by UNICEF and the "Unite for Children, Unite against AIDS" programs illustrate this claim.

In Gujarat, India, "a formidable force of 14,000-plus peer educators" in the three districts of Vadodara, Surat, and Valsad spread messages about HIV prevention and strive to "shatter prevailing social myths about HIV and AIDS." Young women outnumber young men in the program, and according to one participant, "We were locked behind the four walls of our house. Because of this programme, we can not only do something useful for society—in the process, we are also making a name for ourselves."[22] Recognizing that HIV/AIDS is one important piece of a very complex global public health agenda, these young people have also mobilized to support a polio vaccination program.

In South Africa, "Isibindi—Circles of Care" is a community-based initiative that trains volunteers in communities otherwise overwhelmed by the AIDS orphan crisis to visit families headed by children, allowing them to remain together in their homes. Children and young people are taught life skills and encouraged to stay in school. Isibindi, which means "courage," serves more than 13,000 children in forty different project sites. It provides a vital, community network for these struggling families.[23]

At the Chiang Mai University in Thailand, a group of HIV-positive children participated in a theatrical production, *Who Am I? Why Am I Here?* In the play the children wear masks, visual reminders of the vulnerability created by stigma and of "the missing faces of AIDS." "Do we dare take off our masks?" one of the characters asks. "Don't you know what people will do to us if they know who we are—what we have? We are not living with a terrible illness, but we are living in a terrible world."[24] One of the coordinators of the production has noticed changes in the children who participate in the program. With their confidence and self-worth growing, some of the children now remove their masks at the end of the play and face the audience to answer questions.

We would rather that children not have to face a world ravaged by HIV/AIDS. Scandalously, today this option is not available. Neither, however, should the Christian community drawn together in pursuit of the common good desire that children and young people remain excluded and marginalized. Children should share in the fruits of our common life together, and they should be invited to share in the responsibility for building that life in ways respecting their age and ability.

Conclusion

Ann Sheehy, a colleague of mine in the biology department, urges our students to practice "clock watching." According to UNICEF, a child dies every minute of every day due to AIDS-related illnesses. How many children have died in the time it takes to read this essay, or the time it took to write it? We face a race against time. We must unite for children, and unite with children, welcoming them as full, interdependent members of our communities, whose participation in the fight against AIDS is crucial if we are ever to know a world free of the pandemic. The tradition of the common good, shaped by an option for the poor and vulnerable, provides theological grounding for supporting this claim: children are created in God's image and likeness, they are bearers of intrinsic human dignity, and they remind us of the vulnerability we all share. Interdependence is not only a necessity—it is a gift of human community.

Mary Jo Iozzio

The Vulnerability of People with Disabilities and the Elderly

The most recent population totals from the U.S. Census Bureau counts over 303 million people.[1] Of this number, 56 million have a disability,[2] and as many as 60 million are aged 50 and older.[3] Sadly, like people in just about every other identifiable population, people in both of these populations—people with disabilities and elders—are vulnerable to HIV/AIDS. Together, these groups represent nearly 25 percent of all U.S. cases of HIV/AIDS. These numbers demand the attention of the nondisabled and the young and robust; to the extent that people with disabilities and elders have often unmet needs that require our care, as they are sisters and brothers of our national community and human family, as they may be part of our Christian and Catholic faith communities, or as they may be us, a call for justice on their behalf is required. I am considering both of these populations not as having equal experiences or equal needs;[4] people with disabilities and elders are distinct groups, although both disability and age can, and often do, coexist. I consider these distinct communities to raise consciousness where little now exists in the matter of their vulnerability and risk.

I am concerned about these groups because I am a woman with the privileges of education, employment, and reasonable access to health care, who witnesses and works to reduce the injustices that accompany vulnerability. I am a woman without children and the wife of a man who is in age my senior by almost nineteen years and whose vulnerability increases with each year, whose mother is a reasonably strong octogenarian, whose father died in 2005 as a result of the disabling conditions and bodily-systems failure associated with Alzheimer's disease, and whose brother died in 1993 from AIDS-related infections. And I am a cousin and friend to elders and people with disabilities who, because of their age or disability, are particularly vulnerable to HIV and other communicable diseases.

The statistics on HIV and AIDS for the United States and its dependencies remain alarming and on the rise. The exact statistical information for people with disabilities and HIV or AIDS is not available. This population has yet to be recognized as a distinct class of persons for the gathering and monitoring of statistics. However, the Centers for Disease Control and Prevention

(CDC) reckons that the prevalence of HIV/AIDS in the population of people with disabilities is comparable to the rate of incidence in the general population (15 percent of the select population characteristic).[5] The total number of persons with disabilities (who were so before infection[6]) who are sero-positive may be as high as 140,000. Unlike the estimates of HIV/AIDS for people with disabilities, age is a characteristic that the CDC uses to organize and monitor statistics. The statistics for older persons (50 or older at the time of diagnosis) indicate a 10 percent rate of incidence.[7] The total number of older persons diagnosed and living with HIV/AIDS is greater than 115,000, with as many as 15,000 older than 65.[8] The incidence of HIV transmission, the onset of AIDS, and death from AIDS and AIDS-related causes signals the need to address education and prevention programs for these often neglected populations and to include these populations in discussions of the moral obligations to care.

People with disabilities and the elderly remain two populations in the United States whose concerns are often minimized if not denied outright. For example, people with disabilities often remark that, as noted above in reference to the lack of statistics, they are invisible in the public arena except in efforts to raise research and/or treatment money, in discussions surrounding the reasons to abort or not to abort a pregnancy where a disabling condition has been detected, and in the enlisting of physician-assisted suicide or euthanasia when disabling conditions present. And while the American Association of Retired People (AARP) has lobbied Congress successfully for a number of elder programs and services, older elders often sense that they are targeted as a burden on or waste of scarce resources, undervalued in capitalist economies for their their real or perceived reduced productivity potential, or summarily dismissed for their perceived ignorance of the way the world works these days.

The CDC provides detailed information regarding HIV, AIDS, and older elders, although details on the mode of transmission by age identifiers is left to anecdotal evidence. The CDC is significantly more circumspect with information regarding persons with disabilities; it does not compile statistics relative to this characteristic. What's more, the concerns of these two vulnerable groups stand as a parallel experience to the concerns of people who are oppressed and/or marginalized. Sadly, too many remain invisible for many to care.

Whether you accept or reject the thesis that these populations are marginalized by denials of access either from full participation in society or from serious consideration by the general population and the medical community, people in these populations are both contracting HIV and dying prematurely from AIDS; their deaths are cause for concern. Of the 550,394 deaths in the United States of persons with AIDS (from the beginning of the epidemic through 2005), 92,505 occurred in the population of adults older than 50. Of these deaths 13,500 occurred in elders older than 65.[9] Unfortunately, and again outside the statistics, the number of deaths in the population of people with disabilities is impossible to calculate. However, generalized statistical projections suggest that as many as 80,000 deaths may have occurred in the population of people with disabilities since the start of the epidemic.

Now let us look at the methods of transmission in these populations and what is to be done to reduce the risk factors contributing to their experience of increased vulnerability.

Routes of Infection

First, sexual activity is as prevalent in these populations as it is in the adult population at large. Older people and people with disabilities—developmental and physical—are sexually active. Among people with disabilities, studies show an eight-year disconnect on the level of knowledge of HIV/AIDS and transmission risks between those who are deaf and hard of hearing and their hearing counterparts.[10] Among those with developmental disabilities, deficiencies in cognitive, social, and analytic skills, in conjunction with impulsive behaviors, place these individuals at great risk from unsafe sexual activity, sexual abuse, and exploitation.[11] Among the elderly, studies show many older people lack awareness of HIV transmission and prevention. They are unlikely to discuss sexual activity with their physicians and have little to no training in safe sex practices. Moreover, without fear of pregnancy, postmenopausal women do not request that their partners use condoms.[12] Among the elderly, an AARP study shows that as many as 38–46 percent of people older than 60 report engaging in sexual intercourse once a week or more.[13] Although the level of sexual activity has not been formally investigated in the population of people with disabilities, there is no reason to think that they are not interested and not engaging in sex as well.

Second, members in both of these populations succumb easily to substance abuse. Both populations are subject to unsubstantiated myths about their lifestyles, misunderstanding of their needs, and isolation. Some of the myths regarding people with disabilities insinuate (1) innocence, especially on the part of people with developmental disabilities, (2) a lack of interest in intimacy, and (3) perhaps most disturbing, a presumption that people with disabilities are incapable of adult relationships. These myths effectively isolate people with disabilities from the main. Some of the myths regarding older elders imply (1) that they spend their days leisurely engaged in golf, knitting, and cards, (2) that they have an age-acquired lack of interest in or need for intimacy, and (3) that they prefer the company of their calmer peers over more agitated children, youth, and young adults. Each of these myths contributes to the sense of isolation experienced by members of these populations. In order to relieve the discomfort of exclusion, many turn to drugs and alcohol. People with developmental disabilities are especially vulnerable to substance abuse, either from a failure on their part to recognize limits, or from exploitation. People with physical disabilities and the deaf and hard of hearing may have an incidence rate of substance abuse as high as one in seven.[14] Among the elderly, alcohol abuse may be the the most common form of substance abuse, yet IV drug use is not unknown: as much as 17 percent of the HIV infections among this population are attributable to needle sharing for both illicit and prescribed medications.[15]

Third, members of these populations often misinterpret the symptoms of HIV or AIDS for the aches and pains that ordinarily accompany both the aging process and non–life-threatening health conditions and disabilities. Consider, for example, the general symptoms of HIV infection:

> rapid weight loss
> dry cough
> recurring fever or night sweats
> profound and unexplained fatigue
> swollen lymph glands in the armpits, groin, or neck
> diarrhea that lasts for more than a week
> white spots or unusual blemishes on the tongue, in the mouth,
>   or in the throat
> pneumonia
> red, brown, pink, or purplish blotches on or under the skin
>   or inside the mouth, nose, or eyelids
> memory loss, depression, and other neurological disorders.[16]

Compare those symptoms to the aging process in general and its concomitant symptoms of aches and pains, or compare them to chronic fatigue syndrome, colds, and the flu; regardless of disability or age, these symptoms mimic ordinary inconveniences. It is evident that many HIV/AIDS symptoms will be easily disguised in comorbid conditions experienced by members of both of these populations.[17]

What Can Be Done?

Given the experience of marginalization, the incredulity of mainstream society, and the dearth of sustained attention to these populations even by professionals working in HIV/AIDS programs, the likelihood of further exposure to HIV is all but assured.[18] Prevention education is the key to reducing the incidence of transmission for them just as it is the key for reduction in all other populations; regardless of social location, everyone can be at risk. In order to be successful in preventing disease among people with disabilities and older elders, education must be tailored to meet them where they are.

Both populations—people with disabilities and older elders—negotiate their lives somewhat out of the main. People with disabilities are often corralled in groups with similarly defining characteristics or in a one-size-fits-all large group. Both of these effectively isolate people with disabilities from the nondisabled as well as provide opportunities for group self-identification, such as in deaf culture, L'Arche communities, group homes, and work projects. Older elders may create their own communities through local senior housing communities and retirement enclaves; while these communities are often set apart, they are to a large extent self-sustaining and provide ready access to age-related peers.

Prevention education programs for both of these populations can take advantage of communities where they have already been formed. Professionals working with people with disabilities and older elders must put aside preconceived notions and myths about these populations and recognize that HIV prevention programs epitomize educational challenges for everyone. Many people, from parents to teachers and from service professionals to health care providers, are reluctant to talk with persons in their care about sex or substance abuse. People in these vulnerable populations are being infected and are dying for lack of population-specific prevention education programs. The reluctance to talk and educate about HIV/AIDS and its routes of transmission must be overcome.

For people with development disabilities, education programs must respond to their level of understanding. Teaching materials should include both narrative and visual illustrations about the virus. Persons in this group must understand that their risk for infection is a personal threat, that they need accurate information regarding safe sex practices, and that they must comprehend the dangers associated with substance use.[19] For people who are deaf and hard of hearing, programs depend on advocacy training. Sadly, interpreters for this population are often not available; materials for this population must be designed with graphics, photographs, and diagrams illustrating typical transmission routes.[20] For people with physically limiting disabilities, programs must both empower the participants and explore the mechanics of sexual activity. Materials for this population should address sexual abuse and exploitation as well as adaptations for sexual stimulation.[21]

Prevention and education programs for older elders must be explicit: HIV/AIDS does not discriminate on the basis of age! Older elders are complacent if not aware of their risk for infection; the pandemic began long after their first sexual encounters and monogamous relationships. However, as heterosexual sex is the dominant risk factor for older elders, the newly widowed or divorced are especially vulnerable.[22] Discussion of this vulnerability must recognize also that postmenopausal women and widows, who no longer worry about pregnancy, often participate in unprotected sexual acts that put them at risk for HIV or other STDs. Prevention and education programs must recognize the discomfort that many older elders may experience in a public forum on HIV/AIDS or in the privacy of a health care provider's office. Materials for this population must include a unit on the double stigma of ageism and a disease heavily laden with moral taboo.[23] Like all other populations, older elders must be informed of the routes of transmission. They must be asked by their health care providers to talk about both their sex lives and drug use, and they must be cautioned about the comorbid symptoms of fatigue, weight loss, dementia, skin rashes, and depression. Finally, older elders must be empowered to take precautions against transmission. Nevertheless, once infected, they must resist assuming cultural attitudes surrounding the dual stigmatization of ageism and taboo, the distribution of scarce resources to an already declining population, and the belief that the cause of death is of no consequence for people who have already lived their lives.

Conclusion

Why be concerned with these populations? We may be a parent of a child with disabilities, a sibling or friend of an adult with disabilities, a child of a parent or parents with disabilities; likewise, we may ourselves have disabilities. We may yet have parents, grandparents, elder relatives, friends, and colleagues older than 65; likewise, we may ourselves now qualify for Medicare. Unless death comes unexpectedly, most people will become members of one or both of these populations. Both disability and age complicate the vulnerability everyone has to exposure and the likelihood of becoming infected with this and other communicable diseases. As we claim to be followers of Christ, we recognize that our sisters and brothers are suffering the indignities of apathy where compassion should flow in abundance. We recognize that the compassion of Christ is solidarity with those who suffer and that compassionate justice demands welcoming presence, relief of conditions that cause suffering, and supportive provisions for critical needs. To do anything less is contrary to the gospel, detrimental to the common good, and insulting to the most marginal, for whom Jesus had an especially strong liking.

When God's people with disabilities and with advanced age have HIV/AIDS, God's people are challenged to bring love and care, to be the heralds of justice and the bearers of mercy to a people brought low by suffering and disease.[24] God's vulnerable people require protections from ignorance of HIV, from exploitation, and from indifference. God's vulnerable people need to know, as much as any other, that compassionate care is available. Finally, God's vulnerable people call for mercy. They wait for our "grief for another's distress,"[25] they wait for healing words, access to care, welcome in reply, and justice. "The sum total of the Christian religion consists in mercy . . . which likens us to God" as imitators of God and followers of Jesus.[26] If this insight from Thomas Aquinas is correct, to the extent that we are moved to provide succor when a neighbor is distressed as a result of disability, of age, and of HIV/AIDS, only then can we rightly be called Christian. When God's people have HIV and AIDS, God's people must respond.[27]

Emily Reimer-Barry

Church Communities and HIV-Affected Persons

Toward Abundant Life

A central message of the Bible and Christian tradition is that God loves us and desires our full flourishing. The Gospels contain many stories in which Jesus calls his followers to live in justice. Jesus welcomed the outcast and offered both physical and spiritual healing to the sick, including the man with the withered hand, the blind, the deaf, and the crippled woman. In the Good Shepherd discourse, Jesus proclaims, "I came so that they might have life, and have it more abundantly" (John 10:10). It is evident that Jesus wanted his followers to live whole, healthy, and flourishing lives. But for many women who are HIV-positive, some of whom struggle just to get through each day, abundant life is a distant hope, not a lived reality.

Church communities face a challenge in HIV/AIDS as they seek to follow the example of Jesus. In advocating for justice and healing in the lives of persons infected with and affected by HIV/AIDS, Church communities will need to address the social injustices that continue to negatively impact the lives of those within as well as outside the Church community itself, especially the lives of women with HIV. I have listened with humility to the experiences of those directly affected by HIV and AIDS, and I share in this essay some of what I have learned from conversations with eight HIV-positive women in my community.[1] Their stories confirm that we have a long way to go.

As a student of Christian ethics, I have been interested in HIV/AIDS, public health, and Christian theology for some time. However, I am not HIV-positive, nor are (to my knowledge) any of my family members or intimate friends. I am aware of privilege in my life experience: I am a U.S. citizen, white, upper middle class, and educated; I am in many ways an outsider among these women. For Christian ethicists, ethnographic research can help open the complexity of real women's lives and show that simplistic answers to their struggles are insulting.[2] We must see how a woman's life story is embedded in multiple networks of relationships, and she can tell us what she fears, how she struggles, and what her faith means to her; we might learn how

140

broad social forces, including racism, sexism, and poverty, have impacted particular women's lives. Wanting to know, I sought women with experience of HIV or AIDS to tell me their stories.

I recruited interview participants through social service agencies in Chicago where case managers alerted me to some women who might be willing to speak with me about their lives. The women who have helped me to better understand the larger impact of HIV/AIDS on their lives—Sue, Diva, Crystal, Cheryl, Grace, Carmen, Lettie, and Keesha—shared with me their complex and courageous stories.[3] All are married or widowed and all self-described as Catholic. Their stories challenged me to reconsider my previously held assumptions about living with HIV and AIDS and to reconsider ways in which the church can work to alleviate their suffering.[4]

Seven of these women live in Chicago, and one travels to Chicago regularly from her rural town in order to access health care and support services.

One Urban American City

Since 2002 I have called Chicago my home. Chicagoland is the third-largest urban area in the United States and the largest center in the Midwest. The city has a population of 2.8 million people, and 9.5 million live in the metropolitan area.[5] In a vibrant and diverse city with an active and faithful Catholic community, the Archdiocese of Chicago serves 2.3 million Catholics in Cook and Lake Counties. There are 364 Catholic parishes, 257 Catholic elementary and secondary schools, twelve Catholic hospitals, and five Catholic colleges and universities in the archdiocese.[6] Chicago is also home to 21,038 people living with HIV or AIDS (PLWHA), including a rising number of women.[7] For women in Chicago, heterosexual transmission and injection drug use remain the most common modes of HIV transmission.[8]

The women in my study experienced important benefits by living in a city with extensive educational and public health resources. The AIDS Foundation of Chicago, in collaboration with community organizations throughout the metropolitan area, assists residents in accessing prevention, care, and treatment services through their case management network, and provides emergency financial assistance for utilities, housing, food vouchers, and transit. Additionally, multiple research centers throughout metropolitan Chicago offer PLWHA many different kinds of opportunities to participate in clinical drug trials and other research.[9] Test Positive Awareness Network maintains an online directory of the many support services available for people in Chicago affected by HIV.

We could do better. Like most metropolitan areas, Chicago struggles with myriad urban problems: crime, poverty, deteriorating public health infrastructure, homelessness, and an underfunded school system. An estimated 19.6 percent of Chicago residents live below the poverty line.[10] Many women from marginalized communities are unable to access the same treatments and social supports that other women can. HIV infection in Chicago is increasing among poor, minority women already marginalized in other ways. Despite living in the USA, with its strong industrial and technologically driven economy, many of these women do not have access to regular health care or affordable medications and can fall through the cracks of government assistance programs.

Learning by Listening

Within this complex social fabric, what can be learned from women with HIV? How can church communities understand their experiences, raise awareness within the wider community, and begin to promote the integral flourishing of all? In interviews with these women, I discovered a number of social conditions that frustrate the full flourishing of them and others in my community who are HIV-positive. By understanding these conditions, church communities can begin to see the complexity of the epidemic in Chicago.

Ranging in age from 37 to 59 years, the eight women in my study—self-described as African-American, Hispanic, and white—were exposed to HIV through tainted blood products during surgery, unprotected sexual intercourse while in dating and casual relationships, and IV drug use; some of them are survivors of intimate partner violence. All named financial burdens as a daily stress in their lives. Seven are currently on antiretroviral therapy and under the care of physicians in Chicago.[11]

When I first began interviews with these women, I thought my analysis would focus on their intimate relationships and the risk factors contributing to their HIV infection. I quickly learned that my description of "the problem" did not match theirs. For some of these women, their HIV diagnosis was just one more layer of an already complicated and difficult life. For others, their HIV diagnosis became a "wake-up call," and social supports enabled them to access treatment that gave them hope. Most of the women did not perceive themselves to be at risk for HIV and knew little of HIV or AIDS before their own diagnosis. This perception contributed to their difficulty in accepting the diagnosis when it was first confirmed. In our conversations, I was struck over and over again by the courage and resilience they have shown since discovering their HIV status, no matter what risk factors led to their infection in the first place.

A pervasive theme in these women's stories was the strength and perseverance they exert to get through a typical day. Some have participated in experimental trials for new HIV drugs, and all have challenged themselves to learn more about HIV and how it affects their bodies. They have had to become familiar with the medical terminology, from CD4 counts to viral loads to opportunistic infections to names of antiretroviral medicines and other pharmaceutical controls. They have had to become familiar with many different types of governmental programs in order to understand the assistance available, from programs that focus on prescriptions (such as AIDS Drug Assistance Program, ADAP), to programs that assist HIV-positive persons with housing (such as Housing Opportunities for People with AIDS, HOPWA), to the Ryan White CARE Act and its programs, to more comprehensive medical plans such as Medicare, Medicaid, and other insurance plans.[12] Additionally, for the Hispanic women, who immigrated to the United States from Mexico and Honduras, language has been a barrier to accessing health care and support. (Both are now active in Spanish-speaking support groups for HIV-positive women, particularly safe spaces for sharing their concerns.)

While bogged down by large numbers of pills and schedules of doses, calendars full of appointments and meetings, and the limitations of health care in a free market economy, it would be easy for these women to get lost in paperwork, frustrated by the complexity of the bureaucracy, and overwhelmed by many other concerns that an HIV diagnosis brings. Indeed, they have experienced a spectrum of frustrations: "getting by" on insurance plans and paying out-of-pocket but with a great deal of anxiety, experiencing total dependence on governmental assistance programs. Other women likely experience similar frustrations; I wonder about those who have fallen through the cracks of our health care system, especially those without the support of a partner, a helpful social worker, a support group, fluency in English, or translation assistance. For women in Chicago who are HIV-positive, an enormous amount of personal determination and social support are needed for self-care in a typical day.

Social Ills and Individual Illness

Human health depends on biological factors and on the social, economic, and environmental conditions in which people live.[13] Deteriorating inner-city neighborhoods provide the context for a range of traumatic experiences for urban American women, including sexual violence, gang violence, exposure to drug use and drug deals, unstable housing resulting from development and gentrification projects, and unemployment.[14] While behavior change is certainly necessary to stem the tide of HIV infections, urban communities must address the social factors surrounding self-neglecting behaviors.

Some of the women in my study described trauma rooted in unstable social settings. All of those whose history included drug abuse are African-American and describe growing up amid unstable family networks. Chicago's African-American community struggles with the legacy of slavery and segregation, which persists in overt and covert racism whose impact remains widely felt. Even today, predominantly African-American neighborhoods have, in comparison to white neighborhoods, less homeownership, increased street violence, more transitional housing units, more unemployment, fewer businesses, fewer public parks, lower performing public schools, and a decaying infrastructure.[15]

The Project on Human Development in Chicago Neighborhoods (PHDCN) reports that a typical African-American resident lives in a neighborhood that is 78 percent black, while a typical white or Mexican-American resident lives in a neighborhood that is approximately 85 percent nonblack. Blacks in the study were more likely than whites or Mexican-Americans to live in Chicago neighborhoods with concentrated economic disadvantages and high reported rates of cynicism about law enforcement. According to the PHDCN study, having married parents or a large percentage of professionals in a neighborhood reduces a youth resident's chances of engaging in violence. Community initiatives, like increased economic investment in African-American communities, together with programs that support family stability, could help to decrease neighborhood violence.[16] While many neighborhood revitalization projects are underway, attention to persistent racism and its corresponding social ills is absolutely necessary in order to contextualize people's experiences of epidemic IV-drug use and gender-based violence within the contexts of economic and social distress.

Three women—Diva, Crystal, and Cheryl—described drug use as an escape from the struggles of poverty, including unemployment, paying bills, struggling to feed their children, and keeping their children safe. While their drug use put their children at greater risk, in their minds drugs were a way to escape feelings of fear, responsibility, and despair. As Eileen Stillwaggon cautions, "The epidemic of injecting drug use should also be viewed within this context of economic and social distress. . . . These are not happy, optimistic young people injecting drugs."[17]

Additionally, violence against women remains widespread, and too often unnoticed, unmentioned, and neglected in church communities. Three women experienced gender-based violence. Keesha and Crystal are rape survivors; Lettie and Crystal reported marital violence, both physical and emotional. They are not alone. Worldwide, an estimated one in five women will be a victim of rape or attempted rape in her lifetime,[18] and one in three will have been beaten, coerced into sex or otherwise abused, usually by a family member or acquaintance.[19] More often than not, perpetrators go unpunished. Eliminating violence and empowering women lies at the heart of addressing HIV risk for women.

Toward Abundant Life

When asked to describe what constitutes abundant life for them, all of the women included descriptions of feeling well; emotional support from family, friends, and loved ones; the ability to care for their children and provide for their families; respect from medical workers; freedom from violence; the ability to access affordable, comprehensive health care; employment; safe and affordable housing; educational opportunities; and freedom from discrimination. Their descriptions help to elaborate the work of theologians who describe human flourishing as integral and interdependent. Cristina L. H. Traina argues that human flourishing encompasses "bodily, relational, emotional, and spiritual health; existential, social, and political freedom; and intellectual and moral maturity."[20] The conditions for this integral flourishing include many of the descriptions offered by the women interviewed in my study.[21] Additionally, they described frustration over those aspects of their lives where they perceived limited agency or control (over affordable medical care, safe housing, freedom from violence, and opportunities for meaningful work).

While poverty, drug use, and gender-based violence are clearly contrary to full human flourishing, AIDS-related public debate too often focuses on controversial topics like condom use or needle exchange instead of the other social justice concerns that the Catholic tradition addresses with profound clarity. Catholic social teaching offers a framework for thinking about the moral dimensions of public policies. If more Catholics would advocate public spending for HIV-specific programs like HOPWA, Ryan White, ADAP, and related programs on poverty reduction, housing assistance, and comprehensive/universal medical care, Catholic social teaching could give public voice to affect their success and contribute to the relief of further HIV infection.

In addition to public advocacy, Catholic parishes can offer concrete support to those affected by HIV through the formation of church-based support groups and educational outreach initiatives. Support groups frequently run from social service agencies, hospitals, or clinics; if churches began to host these groups, participants would have a place to discuss the inevitable theological and spiritual questions that arise from the reality of suffering with terminal illness and to express fear, anger, pain, and joy. In addition to support groups and through voluntary networks, parishes could offer assistance with meals and rides for those affected by HIV, as well as HIV educational outreach (adult education, teen education, and age-appropriate material for CCD [Confraternity of Christian Doctrine] classes). While educating parishioners about the fundamental aspects of HIV and AIDS would include descriptions of the modes of transmission and symptoms of infection, a more comprehensive picture would include also the principles of Catholic social teaching that demand a comprehensive response to the pandemic by considering how social forces like poverty, racism, and sexism complicate HIV infection rates.

Conclusion

By reframing AIDS-related questions in the church as questions of social justice, we can better understand the complexity of the pandemic. But to say that it is complex does not imply that the problem is mysterious or that our situation is hopeless. Indeed, HIV/AIDS is a sadly predictable outcome of inter-related social injustices, including poverty, racism, urban violence, uneven economic development, decaying neighborhoods, and the lack of affordable comprehensive medical care for all. What is needed is determined action on behalf of justice.

In listening to the stories of women, I began to understand how their faith remains very important and gives them strength, comfort, and meaning, yet that faith does not shield them from suffering, fatigue, or financial stress. In order to best serve these women, church communities must listen to their experiences, welcome their participation, and stand in solidarity with them against the social injustices they face. HIV/AIDS is especially pressing for Christians who claim to follow the Jesus who called all to full human flourishing and abundant life.

Shawnee Marie Daniels-Sykes, SSND

Hidden in Plain View

Older African-Americans

Although HIV and AIDS threaten the health and well-being of people residing all over the world, extreme epidemic proportions present in all age groups of African-Americans in the United States.[1] In particular, African-Americans with HIV who are 50 and older, while often hidden, ignored, or invisible with respect to discussions concerning the HIV/AIDS pandemic, make up an estimated 48 to 50 percent of newly diagnosed cases for all members of this age group.[2] This older population is not exempt from engaging in high-risk social and sexual behaviors that make them susceptible to contracting and transmitting HIV, nor are they excluded from HIV-contaminated blood transfusions.

For older African-Americans with HIV, race, ethnicity, and age are not the only risk factors for infection; these factors may mark other socioeconomic conditions, like poverty, unemployment or underemployment, retirement, health illiteracy, institutionalized racism, and a lack of or limited access to quality health care. In many instances, these risk factors are the basis for the avoidance by older African-Americans of HIV screening, diagnosis, and treatment opportunities. The plight of older African-Americans with HIV or AIDS remains a major public health and ethical problem. Concerns about HIV/AIDS in this older population must not remain hidden and unaddressed.[3]

In this essay I will summarize the facts and myths about HIV/AIDS among adult African-Americans and will present a Roman Catholic social bioethics as a way to address the pandemic in this population.[4]

Facts and Myths

In the third decade of the HIV/AIDS pandemic, many in the United States with HIV are living longer and healthier due primarily to the use of highly active antiretroviral therapy (HAART).[5] However, research regarding older African-American adults with HIV does not necessarily yield a positive outlook. According to reporter Makebra Anderson, "Fifty-two percent of older Americans living with HIV/AIDS are either Black or Hispanic, reports the CDC. Among men over 50 living with HIV and AIDS, 49 percent are of color. Among women, 70 percent are of color."[6] Older Americans account for the highest portion of HIV and deaths related to AIDS.[7] Great potential exists for the continual and rapid spread of the virus to others; even greater potential exists for older African-Americans to experience AIDS-related death.[8] The CDC reports that "seniors [i.e., those 60 and older] make up less than 5% of those tested at government-funded sites for HIV; they are much more likely than younger people to have full blown AIDS by the time they discover they're infected."[9] The fact that HIV can remain latent for up to two decades before the onset of AIDS raises major ethical concerns, especially as older Americans engage in high-risk social and sexual behaviors.

Further, the aging process speeds the transformation of HIV to AIDS, and early symptoms of the virus such as fatigue may be confused with signs of aging.[10] Health care providers may neglect to inquire about any at-risk sexual or social behaviors or to test for HIV infection among older African-Americans. Considering that the disease exists in epidemic proportions in African-American communities, educational materials about HIV/AIDS that stress the urgent need for counseling or education, testing, prevention, and treatment seem not well disseminated.[11] The Ninth National Black Catholic Congress (NBCC) gathering in 2002 in Chicago captured the Church's commitment to address the HIV/AIDS crisis in its Pastoral Plan of Action, especially among disproportionately infected African-Americans. The pastoral plan called for "educational opportunities for parish staff, schools, parishioners, and the local community, with emphasis on parenting education and HIV/AIDS awareness for youth."[12] Additionally, given the gravity of HIV and AIDS among older African-Americans, it is imperative that this age group be included in education related to prevention of HIV.

Despite these concerns, some argue that older Americans are immune from contracting HIV; thus, no need exists for HIV screening, diagnosis, or treatment. Further, many argue that given the abounding stigma, prejudices, and suspicion among African-Americans about HIV/AIDS, a proposal for screening, diagnosis, and treatment for the disease would be met with rejection. Some of the reasons that older African-Americans give for this rejection include misinformation, stereotypes, homophobia, denial, bisexuality, and distrust.

The perception among older African-Americans of HIV/AIDS as a white homosexual disease stems from biblical interpretations that denounce male-to-male sexual relationships.[13] Too many clerics, preachers, and religion teachers have used isolated passages from the Old and New Testaments—the Leviticus codes (Lev 18:22; 20:13), the story of Sodom and Gomorrah (Gen 19:1–9), and Paul's Letter to the Romans (1:26–27)—to publicly condemn men who have sex with men as acting against the inspired Word of God. For

Christians, believing and following the Word of God results in being saved; not believing or following this Word—that is, committing sin or doing evil—results in condemnation. For many, HIV/AIDS is God's ultimate punishment for sinful sexual and social behaviors.

As a result of widespread visual images in the media depicting white gay men as the primary carriers and transmitters of HIV,[14] many older African-Americans fear the stigma and prejudices surrounding HIV/AIDS. Homophobic and heterosexist attitudes, fear of rejection or of being targets of gossip by family, friends, church members, and coworkers also stifle them, stopping them from getting tested for HIV or of broaching the subject of HIV/AIDS with health care workers. They fear stigma, especially because HIV/AIDS was believed to be a disease of homosexuals and only passed on to other homosexuals—persons whose sexuality is denied in many African-American communities.

As many in the African-American population tend to be homophobic (biased against gays) and heterosexist (biased toward strictly male and female sexual relationships),[15] their negative attitudes uphold the myth that HIV/AIDS is a white gay men's disease, while denying that HIV/AIDS is a grave problem in African-American communities in general and among older African-Americans in particular.

Despite the rise in HIV among older African-Americans, the myth that they do not engage in heterosexual intercourse, homosexual sex, and/or injection drug use (IDU) remains. The stereotype is that sexual activity becomes infrequent or nonexistent in middle age and late adulthood. However, "in 2005 . . . older African American women were infected as a result of high-risk heterosexual contact (i.e., with a person of the opposite sex at high risk for HIV/AIDS), including MSM, or injection drug users."[16] Older African-American women's high-risk heterosexual contact coincides with a number of anatomical and physiological changes occurring as part of their aging process, including

> a general atrophy of vaginal tissue and lessening in the rate and amount of vaginal lubrication produced during sexual relations. With age, the clitoral, vulvar, and labial tissue shrink; the size of the cervix, uterus, and ovaries decrease, and some loss of elasticity and thinning of the vaginal wall occurs. Due to possible tearing or abrading of vaginal tissue during intercourse, which permits easier penetration of the virus, women's biological vulnerability to HIV infection increases following menopause.[17]

Well into old age, men and women may engage in homosexual, bisexual, and multiple partner relationships, but as this description from Judith Levy indicates, women are more susceptible to HIV.

The high rate of HIV, among African-American women in general and older African-American women in particular, is attributed to African-American men on the "down low" (DL).[18] The DL reality must be brought to consciousness in connection to the homophobic and heterosexist attitudes that foster the denial by African-American men of this gender and sexual identity. DL men claim that, despite the fact that they socially have sex with other men, they are not homosexual because they engage equally in "authentic" heterosexual intercourse. While engaging in such heterosexual activity, African-American men on the DL have infected their women partners; these women represent some of the highest rates of infection over the past decade or more. Unfortunately, older African-American men, whether on the DL or not, have increased the rate of HIV infection in older African-American women. Stacy Tessler Lindau and her fellow writers note that "in 2002, approximately 6% of HIV/AIDS diagnoses among women occurred after age 55; 73% of these occurred in black women, 15% in whites, and 12% in Hispanics. . . . Older women are believed to contract HIV/AIDS via heterosexual transmission."[19] Unfortunately, the infection rate of African-American women in general and older African-American women in particular is "hidden in plain view."

The increase in HIV can be attributed to suspicion about government and medical research conspiracies aimed to annihilate the entire African-American population.[20] An extensive history of medical research, exploitation, and abuse directed at African-Americans continues to heighten this population's distrust toward medical science and research; they fear black genocide.[21] Recently, links have been made between African-Americans' attitudes toward the Tuskegee Syphilis Study, HIV/AIDS, and genocide.[22] The Tuskegee Syphilis Study (1932–1972), sponsored by the United States Public Health Service (USPHS), involved unethical research on poor African-American men in Macon County, Alabama. These human research subjects were denied penicillin when it should have been prescribed them; instead, researchers studied the progression and effects of syphilis, which led to their deaths. This medical research experiment on human beings left an indelible mark of suspicion and mistrust among African-Americans toward research institutions and the U.S. health care system. Even prescription medications used to treat HIV and AIDS, like HAART, are met with suspicions that they are lethal poisons rather than medications for slowing the effects of HIV. Nevertheless, we must be assertive about combating the pandemic, by drawing on the NBCC's Pastoral Plan of Action on HIV/AIDS, making appropriate use of other medical resources and programs for testing, taking control of HIV-positive status, and being astute about religious dogma, including that based on biblical passages relating to homosexual behavior and that affront human dignity and human flourishing.

Through the years of the pandemic, a combination of biblical passages used as proof of sin for the incidence of HIV/AIDS have heavily influenced the perceptions of African-Americans, and older African Americans in particular. Stereotypical images linked to homosexuality are deeply cemented within the minds and hearts of many. Even decades later, many in the African-

American population remain convinced that HIV/AIDS is not a concern for them, because it is connected to illicit homosexual behavior.[23]

The teachings of the Catholic Church on human sexuality add to the difficulty of approaching the subjects of awareness and prevention within the African-American community. These teachings include the context of sexuality in the sacrament of marriage and, within that context, instruct further on the content of that sexuality—namely, monogamous sexual relations that must include both unitive and procreative dimensions in every conjugal act. The Church prohibits premarital sexual relations and views homosexual intercourse as intrinsically evil on the basis of its failure to be procreative. Moreover, since condom use is believed to frustrate the unitive and procreative act, it is prohibited. The Church understands the condom singularly as a contraceptive rather than a medical prophylactic that can prevent HIV infection.

A discussion of the sociocultural, religious, and medical reasons that prevent many older African-Americans from directly addressing the problem of screening, diagnoses, and treatment has begun. Other concerns include economics, poverty, institutionalized racism, health illiteracy, health disparities, a lack of medical insurance, and the pros and cons of promoting the experimental microbicide drug to prevent the spread of HIV to women. Although space does not permit a detailed discussion of these concerns, the employment of Roman Catholic social bioethics methodology can assist us in reflecting on these issues, while addressing the HIV/AIDS epidemic.

Roman Catholic Social Bioethics

As elsewhere, in the Catholic tradition HIV/AIDS had an initial association with homosexual intercourse; then concerns about condoms, contraception, safe sex, and needle exchange as prevention methods followed. Church teaching on sexuality remains strictly focused on the sacrament of heterosexual marriage and commits married couples to unitive and procreative intercourse.[24] Thus, since both homosexual encounters and the use of condoms in heterosexual encounters thwart procreation, any deliberately frustrated encounters violate Church teaching.[25]

The nature of HIV and the ways it is transmitted affect how traditional Roman Catholic bioethics responds.[26] Given the resonance of this bioethics with the mission and ministry of the historical Jesus, who cared for outcasts, sinners, and the downtrodden, the Church that follows him is obligated likewise to intervene and care in ways that illuminate the gospel and the principles of contemporary Catholic social teaching: human dignity, respect for life, the common good, social solidarity, and a preferential option for the poor, vulnerable, and marginalized.[27] When these principles are infused into bioethics they create a distinctly Roman Catholic social bioethics (RCSB). RCSB addresses the concrete social justice concerns that emerge when dealing with a bioethical issue, like HIV/AIDS, from a Catholic perspective.[28] Underscoring and pervading RCSB is the fact that human beings are created in the image and likeness of God and are, therefore, worthy of dignity and respect (Gen 1:26); RCSB is thereby social in nature. No matter the ethical issue, God's love of everyone is unconditional, and RCSB must embody what it means to love God with all of our hearts and minds, and to love our neighbors as we love ourselves (see Luke 10:25–28). In turn, we live out the principles of Catholic social teaching as they relate to the epidemic of HIV/AIDS and older African-Americans.

1. *Human dignity.* Because human beings are created in the image and likeness of God, they are of incomparable worth and to be guaranteed dignity. Those with HIV, whether homosexual or heterosexual, older or younger, deserve to have their dignity upheld. Moreover, regardless of the distinct differences of our races, cultures, religions, sexual orientations, or gender, all of us are God's children.

2. *Respect for life* extends from conception to natural death. Although HIV does not discriminate among nations, ages, groups, genders, professions, or sexual orientations, prejudices against people with HIV or AIDS are cemented in the attitudes and perceptions of too many. HIV and AIDS among older African-Americans, in particular, remains hidden in plain view, with their highly disproportionate rate of infection but dearth of reporting in the literature. Their hiddenness or perceived need to be silent is itself both disrespectful and irreverent.

3. *The common good* concerns the interconnections between human beings and the goods of society. RCSB maintains that the goods of society must allow all to flourish by accessing society's institutions of health care, medical research, education, religion, and government, as well as public policy resources to assist in combating the enormous problems surrounding HIV/AIDS. Thus, in terms of the institution of medical research, topical microbicides, which are experimental vaginal drugs used to prevent HIV infection and/or other sexually transmitted diseases, come in a variety of forms (gels, creams, film, sponges, or rings) and provide women with safe, affordable, and cosmetically acceptable protection. Unlike condoms, microbicides are not viewed as a contraceptive device; using them does not violate Catholic teaching and appears to be one good response to HIV prevention efforts for women. Concern for the common good means also that older African-Americans must not be dismissed or overlooked from opportunities for screening, diagnosis, and treatment.

4. *Social solidarity* implies interdependence and interrelatedness. It also calls human beings to be attentive to and understanding of the needs, thoughts, and feelings of others as if they were their own, and to be ready to provide assistance to those with HIV. To be in social solidarity means that stereotypes, attitudes, and prejudices about those with HIV or AIDS, whether homosexual or heterosexual and/or IDU, must be suspended. Relationships of solidarity are sustained by our common humanity.

5. *An option for the poor, vulnerable, and marginalized* acknowledges that we live in a society where the gap between the economically rich and poor is wide. Certain political, social, economic, legal, cultural, religious, and health care structures create and perpetuate this gap. As Catholic Christians and imitators of Jesus, we follow a gospel mandate of social solidarity with one another and especially with those who are on the margins. We are only as strong as our weakest link—only as strong as those who are poor, vulnerable, and marginalized. These poor include those with HIV or AIDS, a stigmatizing and marginalizing disease that complicates vulnerability. Strong resistance persists in acknowledging the dignity and respect of those infected with and affected by HIV or AIDS. This resistance must be overcome.

When these principles of Catholic social teaching are infused into Catholic bioethics, we can acknowledge that HIV occurrence has bioethical and social justice ramifications. The virus disproportionately affects older African-American women and has reached epidemic proportions in this population as a whole, increasing morbidity and mortality rates. African-American women in general and older African-American women in particular have a highly disproportionate rate of HIV infection. We remain morally obligated to eradicate this devastating and opportunistic disease. The Church and its members must dialogue about helpful preventative measures, including education about the meaning of monogamous marital relationships, chastity, celibacy, IDU, DL behavior, and the use of experimental topical microbicides for women.[29] Catholic social teaching obliges intervention regarding HIV/AIDS as the United States Conference of Catholic Bishops confirm in their pastoral letters *The Many Faces of AIDS: A Gospel Response* and *A Call to Compassion and Responsibility: A Response to the HIV/AIDS Crisis.* They acknowledge the existence and devastating effects of HIV/AIDS and take social justice stances that include and incorporate Church teaching, including the principles of Catholic social teaching and Scripture. As the bishops proclaim, "All human beings are created in God's image and are called to the same end, namely eternal life in communion with God and with one another."[30]

Conclusion

Very little has been written on the effects of HIV/AIDS on older African-American women and men. Given that older adults with HIV are living longer due to advances in HAART, attention must be given to the symptomatic progress of HIV to AIDS affecting older African-Americans. HIV/AIDS raises public health concerns, especially when those with HIV are unable to access health care from a lack of medical insurance and/or health illiteracy. Educational materials on HIV/AIDS must be disseminated well. Conspiracy theories and myths must be discussed and debunked, using solid empirical data to further educate and end the negative stereotypes, myths, misinformation, and fear.

The Church has documented HIV/AIDS by addressing the need to actualize the gospel mandate that includes compassion and responsibility for reaching out to those with HIV/AIDS instead of maintaining marginalizing and stigmatizing attitudes toward them. Additionally, the NBCC Pastoral Plan of Action includes the need to address and relieve HIV/AIDS and offers a major avenue for open and public discussion for the institution of religion, namely, the Catholic Church. The Pastoral Plan can dispel the myths and stereotypes surrounding HIV/AIDS, retort popular conspiracy theories, and encourage personal responsibility to prevent HIV infection and its progress to AIDS. Finally, employing the principles of Catholic social teaching and examining the bioethical implications of HIV/AIDS in the context of older African-Americans helps us to see clearly the urgent needs of redressing this epidemic.

Part Five

The Female Face of AIDS

Ma. Christina A. Astorga

The Feminization of AIDS in the Philippines

Culture, Poverty, and Migration

In 2001, the world marked 20 years of AIDS. It was an occasion to lament the fact that the epidemic has turned out to be far worse than predicted, saying, "if we knew then what we know now." But we do know now. We know the epidemic is still in its early stages, that effective responses are possible but only when they are politically backed and full-scale, and that unless more is done today and tomorrow, the epidemic will continue to grow.

—Peter Piot, preface to UNAIDS's *Report
  on the Global HIV/AIDS Epidemic*

To date, the AIDS pandemic has claimed about 25 million lives, up to 3.5 million annually—one death every 15 seconds.[1] What began as a serious health crisis is now a pandemic affecting the foundations of every society.

While the Philippines is a low prevalence country, factors show a hidden and growing[2] HIV epidemic lurking. Factors contributing to difficult detection are problems with monitoring condom use, liberal views on sexual practices and multiple partners, sexual initiation among youth,[3] and the more than eight million Filipinos working abroad under very vulnerable conditions. Ambika Bhushan reports, "Low official rates of HIV infection are belying the extent of the problem and breeding complacency, health officials say. . . . All the ingredients of an explosion are there."[4] The Philippines has 2,200 officially reported HIV and 676 AIDS cases, but the Philippine Department of Health and the World Health Organization estimate that 10,000 Filipinos were HIV-positive by 2003. Extrapolating these figures with nonofficial estimates translates into perhaps 7,000 unreported cases. Dr. Dominic Garcia of the AIDS Society of the Philippines concedes that surveillance systems are inadequate.[5] The officially reported number of HIV-positive women in the Philippines exceeds that of men by almost 50 percent. Where statistics are provided by both age and gender, women have proportionately higher rates of infection in younger ages, nearly surpassing their male counterparts; for those aged 20 to 29, infection of women exceeded that of men three to four times.[6]

Although HIV figures in the Philippines are low in comparison to other countries, the government took a proactive role with the Philippines AIDS Prevention and Control Act of 1998. This law mandates the promulgation of policies and measures for HIV and AIDS in the country, the institutionalization of a nationwide HIV information and education program, the establishment of a comprehensive monitoring system, and the strengthening of the Philippine National AIDS Council.[7]

Government measures are promising: the numbers reported suggest that transmission and infection rates are under control. However, a culture of shame and silence surrounds HIV/AIDS in the Philippines that requires going beyond reports to other realities to thwart an epidemic. Something in the Filipino culture and in the system of close-knit family values locates one person's shame on the family; disgrace then affects the entire community. *Hiya*, or shame, is the driving force creating a collusion of silence—a silence so disempowering that it exacerbates the suffering many endure. The culture of shame and silence is so deeply entrenched that the fight against HIV must break it and liberate people from effects that could claim their lives and destroy their families.[8]

Other cultural factors and religious sensitivities also come into play. In a conservative culture where the Catholic Church is the dominant bearer of values, the use of condoms, about which the Church is vehemently opposed, remains a flashpoint. While religion influences the lives of Filipinos, surveys suggest that contraceptive choice, condom use, and even sexual relations are not significantly informed or influenced by religion. However, because the Catholic hierarchy wields powerful political force in Philippine society, it sways government policies and programs. During the Aquino presidency (1986–1992), the bishops successfully persuaded the government to end all family planning programs.[9] The administration of President Gloria Macapagal-Arroyo has blocked the passage of comprehensive reproductive health legislation that would expand access to condoms. Funds allocated to contraceptive programs were awarded to Couples for Christ to teach natural family planning methods. The government stopped new funding, failed to release local funds earmarked for condom promotion, and enacted local ordinances prohibiting condom distribution from public health facilities.[10]

Given their lack of knowledge, let alone the necessary funds to avail themselves of life-saving HIV prevention technology, the poor, the most deprived, and those at highest risk are affected dramatically by these policies. David Morley states unapologetically that "historians may well be able to show a strong correlation between poverty and the rapid spread of AIDS in communities that follow practices recommended by Rome."[11]

Why are Filipino women at increased risk of HIV? What has made women the more vulnerable victims? These questions relate to the feminization of AIDS in the Philippines, exposed by a cultural approach that links poverty and migration to the epidemic. The cultural approach sees from a perspective larger than and beyond the biomedical perspective in relation to HIV/AIDS. The cultural approach reasons that a "worldwide health crisis such as HIV/AIDS, which is deeply rooted in personal and social issues, is closely linked to culture."[12] This approach interacts with the values, beliefs, traditions, and social structures that constitute the "webs of significance" in which people live.

Understanding HIV/AIDS within the framework of poverty and migration sharpens its female face. I aim to raise consciousness, sharpen awareness, and deepen sensitivity to "the face of HIV/AIDS in the shadows which needs to be recognized and is fast emerging. It is the face of women."[13] Here it is the face of Filipino women.

Why Women?

AIDS is often associated with men. Men's sexual behavior and habits have stimulated its epidemic and pandemic proportions. In the Asia-Pacific region, men constitute the vast majority of HIV infections. So why women? Why has the World AIDS Campaign taken the theme of "Women, Girls, HIV and AIDS"? When men are infected with HIV, it is women who often bear the consequences of meeting financial needs, caring for the sick, and suffering the stigma. And when the women themselves are infected or have AIDS, there is no one left to care for them and no money left for their care.

The increasing number of monogamous women infected by their husbands demonstrates their susceptibility.[14] A report from UN WomenWatch states, "At the end of 2000, women comprised roughly 47% of the more than 36 million adults living with HIV/AIDS. . . . In African countries, HIV infected young women outnumber infected young men by 2 to 1 . . . the most dramatic challenges occurring in countries least able to cope with the epidemic."[15] Women's vulnerability comes from the interplay of biological, economic, and social factors. For biological reasons, the anatomical structure of women's sexual organs provides a larger and more hospitable environment for infection. The lining of the vagina and cervix contain mucous membranes, which, unlike diaphanous membranes, are thin tissues through which HIV and other viruses can pass to the blood vessels. Women's secretions lack immunity from infected seminal fluid, which has a higher viral content. Tearing and bleeding during intercourse, whether from coerced sex or prior genital cutting, exacerbates their risk. Risks are highest among younger women, whose still developing cervical membranes provide a more fragile barrier to infection.[16]

Cultural norms of sexual behavior rooted in social and economic dependence on men increase women's vulnerability. Men often determine when and whether a condom is used in sexual activity, and where a woman is economically dependent, a refusal to have unprotected sex or a request for condom use may arouse suspicions of *her infidelity* or provoke abuse for her lack of trust in *his fidelity*. Sexual molestation and abuse are common. From a lack of self-determination, economic autonomy, and low social status, women cannot negotiate the most basic protection against the disease.[17] Further, some women with HIV are abandoned or forced to leave their homes.

In the Philippines, particularly with the Women's Education, Development, Productivity, Research, and Advocacy Organization (WEDPRO), issues surrounding HIV are related to women's human rights; class, race, and gender inequalities; and culture. Using a woman-centered, gender-sensitive framework, WEDPRO addresses HIV/AIDS from a context larger than immunology and virology.[18]

Gender-sensitive approaches to HIV/AIDS consider the economic, social, and legal factors that fuel the epidemic. Raising women's consciousness of gender equality, these approaches redress widespread power imbalances between women and men. These imbalances are unfortunately disregarded in programs that focus on counseling, partner reduction, male condom promotion, and monogamy; these foci inhibit women's use of these options. Successful programs link HIV prevention to programs that support women's economic independence through training activities, credit programs, saving schemes, and cooperatives.[19]

A Cultural Approach

It is impossible to negotiate any level of human change without confronting culture. "Human beings," writes Tim Gorringe, are "suspended in webs of significance they themselves have spun. Culture is the name for those webs. . . . A failure of modernity . . . has been an inability to grasp how people weave meaning from these webs in order to develop their values, relationships, behavior, social, and political structures."[20] A cultural approach engages the "webs of significance" that people create and negotiate with the patterns, systems, and hierarchies sustaining them. HIV prevention strategies, at global, national, and regional levels, must be determined with a cultural lens. James Wolfenson, former World Bank president, agrees: "We are realizing that building development solutions on local forms of social interchange, values, traditions, and knowledge reinforces the social fabric. . . . Development effectiveness depends in part on 'solutions' that resonate with a community's sense of who it is."[21] Development solutions to AIDS require as much.

An absence of people's cultural references in biomedical approaches to AIDS often leads to mistrust of the global strategy in stemming the pandemic. Cynicism about political and corporate medical-scientific agendas overwhelms human and cultural aspects. Despite limited evidence of the efficacy of cultural approaches to thwart AIDS, more local or cultural approaches are successful. "Where community-level responses have been backed up by HIV/AIDS prevention policy . . . their success has been greater than biomedical approaches or methods introduced from outside," states a report by Healthlink Worldwide. "It represents a 'social vaccine for HIV.'"[22]

Likewise, some communication programs focus on only one level—behavior change. Communication models aimed at behavior change are criticized as Western in orientation for their tendency to influence "attitudes and behavior through telling, rather than by engaging and empowering people. . . . Many communication strategies are culturally inappropriate."[23] Similarly, the Panos Institute concluded the health communication field is "missing the message" by concentrating on "putting out messages [rather than] fostering an environment where the voices of those most affected can be heard."[24]

An effective cultural approach would improve the effectiveness of global HIV/AIDS-reducing strategies and rebuild the trust of communities through culture-sensitive modes of engagement. As prevention and care methods rise from the culture, sociocultural acceptability and community ownership increase. A system of cultural assessments, with data linked to HIV/AIDS-reducing strategies, provides an analysis of the community and a focus on the beliefs and values that impact thinking about HIV.

A study on the training of selected female commercial sex workers (FCSWs) in the Ermita district, Manila, who serve now as peer educators on sexually transmitted diseases (STDs) and HIV, utilized this approach. Its specific objectives were "to generate primary data on the beliefs, attitudes, values, and socialization processes of FCSWs that might contribute to their receptiveness to intervention measures; to design and conduct a culturally appropriate intervention measure to reduce HIV transmission through and among FCSWs; and to recommend areas for future studies and action."[25]

The methodology used case studies through iterative-ethnographic interviews with each of five women to record in-depth data. This approach utilized extensive questioning to gather data, followed by questions that gained access to the fuller context of their lives, with training adapted to their specific needs. The case studies identified messages, symbols, and styles to use as the first component of the intervention to reduce HIV risk. With low levels of education and troubled family backgrounds, the women migrated from rural areas to Manila to escape poverty through employment. Forced into the commercial sex trade to survive and to feed their families, they are not ashamed of their work, though they are aware that society looks askance at them.

Despite their insistence that their work is not wrong, they have very low self-esteem and a weak locus of control. Their male customers determine how services are rendered, even at risk to their own well-being. Their power of negotiation is severely compromised by their lack of self-empowerment. This ethnographic data helped design a more culture- and person-sensitive training program for them. Beyond merely informing them of STDs and AIDS, the seminar-workshop motivated a change of attitudes and behavior, taught them skills in self-protection and customer negotiation, and enabled them to formulate an action plan for information, dissemination, and recruitment among their peers. Core objectives were the strengthening of their locus of control ("your health is your responsibility," "you rely on yourself for protection against STDs," "you can negotiate with customers"), raising their self-esteem (the success of the project, their new knowledge, benefit to peers, friends, neighbors, etc.), and acknowledging their primary role in the design of the action plan.

They learned ways of negotiating with customers and hands-on methods of condom use, as well as techniques to avoid penetrative sex with customers. This interactive, participatory, and self-actualizing workshop created space for self-confidence and self-determination. Since they designed their own action plans, the goals were realistic, the means and techniques informed by their own experience, and the creativity and resourcefulness that flowed from such experience was empowering.[26]

The evaluation of this workshop shows its effectiveness in improving knowledge of HIV and AIDS, motivating attitude changes, and forming skills for protection. The strategies were culture-changing through group participation and involvement. Now, Filipino NGOs are moving from a technical, biomedical approach toward highly personalized workshops that help with psychosocial support, human rights, community building, and empowerment.[27]

This advocacy focuses on women, particularly FCSWs, and addresses sex and gender hierarchies by creating strategies to balance gender inequities in female-male relationships. While in many contexts women are often more vulnerable than men to HIV, different women are differently situated. As Carolina Austria writes, "HIV/AIDS has highlighted how the characteristically overlapping situations of gender, sex, age, class, race, and marital status all figure into the vulnerability of a population to HIV."[28] The effectiveness of strategies in dealing with HIV depends ultimately upon "sexual rights" as an inclusive frame.[29]

Poverty, Migration, HIV, and AIDS

The feminization of migration has increased recently; women constitute about 50 percent of the estimated 175 million migrants worldwide. In Asia, women have surpassed the number of men working abroad, with 65 percent of Sri Lankan and 70 percent of Philippine migrant workers overseas.[30] Why do women migrate? In the Philippines, about 40 percent live below the poverty line, with 30 percent living on P50.00 (US $0.90) on a daily basis. Women are forced to leave their homes and families to seek jobs beyond their national borders. They often become the primary income earners for their families. The demand in more industrially prosperous countries for cheap labor seems insatiable. This labor falls under the "3Ds" of employment: dirty, dangerous, and demeaning. Women migrants predominantly work these jobs; on the bottom of the occupation hierarchy, they are generally disparaged by local women. These jobs represent women's traditional roles in society and are largely concentrated in the reproductive and household spheres, as domestic, child rearing, and caregiving work. These jobs are not recognized as productive, and abuses and exploitation are common.[31]

At particular risk for HIV are the six million overseas Filipino workers, many of whom are women. The study "Breaking Borders: Bridging the Gap between Migration and AIDS" shows that many migrant workers are less than 30 years old, sexually curious, and sexually active. Young, alone, and isolated, they seek recourse in intimate casual relationships or paid sex. However, they are vulnerable to sexual abuse by their older male employers regardless of their work. Workers without legal status who remain abroad often become FCSWs and are exposed to increasingly viral pathogens.[32]

The relation between HIV, AIDS, and migration arises from the conditions migration produces for migrants. Though sometimes viewed purely as economic resources, migrants are social beings with human needs and will create social networks. The Coordination of Action Research on AIDS and Mobility Asia (CARAM-ASIA) shows that migrant workers feeling lonely and alienated often have increased sexual needs. Males engage the services of sex workers and/or take recourse in casual sex. Females engage in casual sex with little bargaining power, and domestic workers are particularly vulnerable to sexual abuse. Though the majority of migrant workers have heard about HIV or AIDS, they know little of how it is transmitted or how to protect themselves from infection; even if they know the need for protection and the risky behaviors to avoid, female migrant workers have little or no negotiating power. The decision to practice safe sex belongs to the dominant male partner.[33]

The CARAM research shows that migrant movement to foreign countries also brings changes in behavior. Anonymous and beyond the control of their cultural and social conditioning, migrants experience unfamiliar freedoms, which often results in risk taking. Bangladeshi women report that they wear clothes of their choice, relate with men without inhibitions, and engage in casual sex without fear of cultural or social repercussions.[34]

Most migrant workers lack access to health information and services. For women particularly, this lack of services surrounds the needs of reproductive and sexual health. Existing social taboos on sexuality pose obstacles to women seeking information about sexuality and health, including HIV. In some countries, seeking this information may lead others to suspect they are engaging in immoral activities. Complicating economic and sociocultural factors, migrants have poor health behaviors, a tendency to self-medicate (with medical or homeopathic treatments), and are governed by a fatalistic attitude about health and sickness in the face of actual illness. For women, this fatalism bears on their reproductive condition, but fear of losing their jobs and the high cost of health care prevent them from informing their employers they are not well. They remain silent, since the truth about their health status might be used as reason for dismissal. And losing their jobs frequently translates into a loss of their hope in contributing to a better life for their families; getting sick abroad means spending the money that would otherwise be sent home.

The accounts of women migrant workers capture the pathos of their situations:

> It is like the moon exploded in your face . . . [or] a bomb blew off. . . .
> Your mind is severed from your body, that's how I felt. My God, what
> will I do? It's a good thing my friend was there advising me, helping me.
> . . . I was shocked, I couldn't accept it. I didn't want to go home. I
> wanted to be alone. I wanted to be up in the mountains. I cried. I told
> the doctor I wish that [the result] would change. Because I remembered,
> I would not be able to work if I was sick.
>
> I cried and cried. It did not matter anymore that there were other
> people in the room. How would I tell my husband? What if I transmit-
> ted it to him? How would I tell my family? I thought about my baby.
> How did this happen?[35]

Beyond these intensely personal feelings, the women shared the common concerns of the economic, social, psychological, emotional, and physical impact of HIV in their lives.[36]

The most severe impact of HIV infection among migrant workers is economic. According to some accounts of women migrants who participated in the research of Action for Health Initiatives, Inc./CARAM (ACHIEVE/CARAM), because of mandatory HIV testing, there are no jobs for HIV-positive migrants abroad, nor would they find work at home which suits the skills they learned abroad. The high cost of living and increasing cost of health care exert a severe economic toll. For women migrants, primary breadwinners, HIV signals the shattering of their dreams and those of their families for a better life. Expenses for care deplete whatever money was saved.

The emotional and psychological distress of HIV is as difficult as economic distress; migrant workers with HIV find themselves isolated, marginalized, and discriminated. Looked upon with disgrace by the community and by their families and friends, some make the painful choice of not returning home and isolate themselves from all they have known and loved; others make the ultimate decision to take their own lives. The pressure is greater on women as women; they do not have the same level of tolerance from society for their behavior as men have; what may be considered immoral for women is normal or right for men.

Access to health care, treatment, and support remain limited for people with HIV. In the Philippines, most HIV patients are unable to afford the treatment and medications they need. Most hospitals lack the equipment to treat and care for those with AIDS. For migrant workers, the compendium of economic, social, and psychological can be overwhelming.

A thorough understanding of the issues and conditions of migrant workers, especially women workers, must ground intervention programs addressing their vulnerability. These programs must include participation by migrants and their families and communities who are affected by the pandemic. Successful ACHIEVE/CARAM programs engage institutional advocacy with national and local institutions to generate policies and programs addressing migration, gender, sexuality, and health in light of HIV/AIDS.

ACHIEVE/CARAM also engages in information management through the operation of a resource center, the maintenance of a Web site, and the monitoring of media information. The information is produced with and for migrant workers for policy and program advocacy. The spouses' and partners' empowerment program aims at the capacity development of wives and partners of migrants. This program includes educational opportunities on gender issues, reproductive health, sexuality, migration, HIV and AIDS, life skills, assertive communication, safer sex practices, and home management. Through community-based pre-migration programs on health, sexuality, and HIV/AIDS, in collaboration with the local government and community organizers of those who have returned from migrant work, future migrant workers recognize the risk and vulnerability they may face and learn how to protect themselves.[37]

Conclusion

The feminization of AIDS in the Philippines is contextualized in a conservative Catholic culture and a culture of poverty. In a culture where sexual behavior is governed by gender inequities and where the Catholic Church wields the power to sway government policies, condoms—the most basic protection against HIV—have been rendered inaccessible to the poor and those most vulnerable. In a culture where *hiya* creates a collusion of silence, the risk of infection is invisible and seemingly invincible. A feminist cultural approach to HIV/AIDS in the Philippines confronts these gender hierarchies, systemic powers, and culture of shame, as it fosters an environment where the voices of those most affected can be heard. In contextual and highly personalized workshops, women are empowered to transform their deep-seated attitudes and values through support, self-esteem, and community. Taking a cultural approach, they move from a technical, biomedical approach to HIV/AIDS devoid of the "webs of significance" with which people weave their own sense of meaning, transformation, and empowerment.

In a culture of poverty, women are forced to migrate for dirty, dangerous, and demeaning jobs and are exposed to abuse and exploitation. As primary earners for their family, they bear the hopes and dreams for a better life for those dependent on them, yet they pursue these dreams in places where they may lose them even before they can create them. Poverty, migration, HIV, and AIDS place the dreams and hopes of many at risk. Given the gender inequities compromising safe sex, the lack of information, social taboos limiting access to protection, and their being in a new place beyond their cultural conditionings, they often succumb to a tragic demise. When the worst happens and they become infected with HIV, their lives cave in, their hopes shatter, and, with no family to turn to, they are abandoned at the margins—sick, poor, and disgraced.

The face of the Filipino woman reveals a culture of gender inequality and poverty in which she negotiates her own webs of significance, where the link between poverty, migration, HIV, and AIDS is found.

Maryanne Confoy, RSC

Communities Visible
and Invisible in Oceania

My concern is to address the HIV/AIDS pandemic from the perspective of women who are virtually invisible in a geopolitical and ecclesial region that is itself almost invisible. While HIV/AIDS is no longer seen solely an illness for gay people, women's increasing rate of infection receives little attention; their invisibility within communities themselves marginalized calls for attention. Furthermore, when they are objectified in their cultural and ecclesial communities, they are often invisible to themselves.[1] I propose an inclusive pastoral perspective for these women in order to affirm them as subjects especially in their ecclesial communities. Within the region of Oceania (Australia, New Zealand, and 25,000 islands in an ocean-bound area as large as North America) we recognize our responsibility as Christians to engage in God's saving work, to participate in the process of creating a new humanity in church and society where all are visible to each other as the body of Christ.[2]

HIV/AIDS and Oceania

Considering the moral ramifications of HIV/AIDS, a major concern must be the way in which for many people, particularly many Catholics, the pandemic strikes like a "misery-seeking missile."[3] This misery has categorized many as "other" and rendered them and HIV/AIDS invisible, outside of normative concerns. The capacity for those whose lives are not immediately touched by HIV to dissociate from the pandemic characterizes many Christian communities. Where wealth, health care systems or education enable such disconnectedness, many Christians resort to almsgiving. The consequent sociopolitical and ecclesial isolation can be erosive of authentic and inclusive community concern.[4]

Although HIV/AIDS is an issue of the demise or survival of cultural communities in some developing countries, with whole adult generational cohorts wiped out by AIDS and new generations of children born with the disease, the subject surfaces with stolid regularity rather than alarming frequency or a sense of urgency in the Western media.[5] The media relates new statistics about the expanse of the disease in developing countries, occasionally presenting new treatments and/or changes in incidence rates or deaths. Although details

about the ravaging effects of the disease in non-Western countries are provided, reports are ordinarily so circumscribed that the reader is relieved of
the burden of considering concrete situations or the implications of the
inequalities of treatment opportunities for those with HIV and for their communities. In Western cultures, where the approach to people is commodifying
and intentions are consumerist, it is easy to remain at a distance from details.[6]

While African and Asian nations are common subjects of discussion in
responses to the pandemic from the perspective of Oceania and from a concern for justice, Oceania is virtually nonexistent. Australia and New Zealand
by themselves are relatively well known, but the region of Oceania itself is
rarely referred to.[7] The diversity of the region and the relative sparseness of
the population is part of the reason for this anonymity.

Oceania is politically recognized as a single region within an area of ocean
approximately the size of North America. The countries and territories of
Oceania range from the island continent of Australia and islands of New
Zealand, to 25,000 widely dispersed and very small islands. Many of these
islands are sovereign states, while others are dependencies of countries in
Europe or the USA.[8]

Communication, health care, and education in regard to HIV/AIDS are complicated by the fact that Oceania is the only part of the world named for a
body of water rather than a landmass. Although interisland transport and communication within Oceania is difficult and expensive for islanders, it is affordable and popular for tourists and, with the increasingly lucrative business of sex
tourism, HIV has become an imported problem for women in Oceania. The
region is ranked alongside North America and Western Europe in terms of
wealth, but this rank obscures the poverty of many islanders and of their
indigenous communities; resource inequity and income disparity betray the
statistic. In these demographic contexts, women struggle disproportionately to
sustain their families and communities. High levels of STDs are reported among
pregnant women in the Pacific Islands. Illness and infection affect their lives,
and their access to medicine is much more limited than in Australia and New
Zealand; efforts to support their families are complicated by poverty.[9] Infection
rates grow as husbands with HIV infect their wives. Because the cultural characteristics of Pacific Island women include shyness, inexperience, and respect
for the widespread Melanesian value of seniority in clan and families, the ability of these women to dismantle oppressive sociocultural patterns is limited.[10]

In 2004, the UNAIDS executive director warned the region of Oceania that
a new wave of HIV infections was likely, with Papua New Guinea (PNG) in particular requiring urgent action to avoid rampant outbreaks of HIV: "PNG has
everything that's wrong—lots of migration within the country, family disrup-
tion within towns and villages, a lot of sexually transmitted infections and a sexual culture that makes HIV spread very rapidly, despite the influence of various
churches advocating abstinence."[11] Sadly, says Kelly Brown Douglas, "women
are the main objects of domestic and sexual violence, which is a serious and
growing problem."[12] The impact of HIV/AIDS on women and their families in

Pacific Island cultures is likewise invisible in a male-dominant society and church where, as Lisa Meo describes, "women are regarded as second-class citizens and are almost passive listeners to any decision of the community."[13]

Although the numbers of people with HIV and AIDS in the islands of Oceania are low, the problems faced by the people, especially the poor, present a microcosm of those faced globally. Issues of migration, movement from rural to urban areas, family breakdown, and a culture of machismo generate sexual promiscuity, physical abuse, and random sexual violence. Women and children suffer most from such societal breakdown.

The relative isolation of Papua New Guinea, one of the larger islands, means that access even to diagnosis, let alone to antiretroviral therapy, is problematic at best. These problems and others are repeated in the smaller and even more anonymous and invisible islands. The questions of treatment and prevention are complicated by the problems of culture, distance, and size of the population. "It's widely assumed that HIV continues to spread because prevention isn't effective," says David Serwadda, director of the Institute of Public Health at Makerere University in Uganda. "The problem is that effective prevention isn't reaching the people who need it."[14] Because of their small numbers or political insignificance on the global scene, many nations in the region of Oceania are left without even some of the basic tools of education and prevention that are more widely available in the global community.

HIV and AIDS are present among women and men from all walks of life and all socioeconomic classes. The roles women are expected to play as caregivers and guardians of their families can cause them to be particularly hard hit, financially and emotionally, by the loss of family members or the impact on family income as a consequence of the pandemic's reach into the household. Women, and often older women, take on additional roles as sole heads of household providing for their families or orphaned grandchildren.

In all these activities women are simply living out and fulfilling the cultural expectations of their communities. They do what is expected in their homes and communities, they take care of family members in need: wives will be there for their husbands, mothers for their children, daughters for their parents. Their place in the familial and communal network of relationships is an unexamined "given." That such a response ordinarily renders women invisible to themselves, thereby compounding their invisibility, is confirmed in research on women's issues across cultures.[15] That such a response consistently renders women invisible to their communities perpetuates their invisibility.

Women and the Catholic Church

Many recognize in various ways that HIV/AIDS is an issue for women. In 2004 the United Nations AIDS program (UNAIDS) was dedicated to women and girls because of their greater vulnerability, compared to men, to HIV infection. On World AIDS Day 2004, the Vatican acknowledged that women are infected 2.5 more times than men in this statement by Javier Cardinal Lozano Barragán, president of the Pontifical Council for Health Pastoral Care:

> Indeed, the impact of HIV/AIDS on women aggravates inequality and hinders progress towards the universality of rights. In addition, the more this infection advances amongst women . . . the more the danger of social breakdown increases. The Church has always defended women and their very great dignity with especial vigor and is struggling to fight those examples of discrimination which . . . require greater efforts to secure the elimination of disparities in relation to women in such sectors as education, the defense of health, and work.[16]

The affirmation of women in such statements is honest, but the larger record shows that the Church is ambivalent with regard to women.

The post–Vatican II emphasis on a preferential option toward the poor has had little impact on many women. Many women whose capacity to develop their own voice and self-understanding has been seriously limited by male-dominated sociocultural structures suffer from gender inequities and conflicts generated by the inequality of power.[17] In Oceania, although the Catholic Church is less dominant in numbers than other Christian denominations, the culture of machismo and oppression of women prevails.[18] Meo summarizes the situation: "The structures of Pacific Island societies are relatively patriarchal and this has been encouraged and strengthened through Christianity."[19] Catholic women recognize the conflictual consequences of their affirmation in some Vatican documents and their negation and subordination in others. This cognitive dissonance characterizes also their experience of church and their efforts to find their voices and become visible.

The ideal of women is recognized, but the reality of their presence is not affirmed when they look for participation in decision making. Still, according to Meo, change is occurring: "[Pacific] women are beginning to take action to bring forth conscientization. This involves the full realization of women's rights, the organizing of women's groups, the education of men and women, and the opposition of all forms of oppression that enhance the suppression of women."[20] These efforts are present in varied ways throughout Oceania, yet the problems with communication result in diffusion rather than cohesion of energies and efforts. Women's services to family, church, and communities are acceptable as long as their presence is subordinate to the male leaders and structures that maintain the status quo.

Inclusive Pastoral Response

Throughout Oceania there are committed Christians working toward the integration of women into all aspects of society; their activities influence pastoral practice, ecclesial relationships, and institutional structures. As Heather Walton explains, "Feminist practical theology is beginning to emerge as women cease to remain complicit in networks of institutional power that work against our wellbeing."[21] That this inclusivity is fundamental to authentic gospel witness is without question. African-American theologian Shawn Copeland considers the marginalization and the rejection of some in church and society:

> At the center of Jesus' *praxis* were the bodies of common people, peasants, the poor and destitute. They were the subjects of his compassionate care: Children, women, and men who were materially impoverished as well as those who were socially and religiously outcast or were physically disabled (the blind, paralyzed, palsied, deaf, lepers); those who had lost land to indebtedness, who were displaced through imperial occupation or religious corruption; those who were possessed and broken in spirit from ostracism and persecution (Lk 4:18, 6:20–22, 7:22, 14:13, 21; Mt 5:3–6, 11, 11:5). Jesus did not shun or despise these women and men; he put his body where they were.[22]

Authentic pastoral concern for women in the region of Oceania invites the recognition of those whose communities have lost land or identity and authority, or those exploited in the tourist or sex trades. That Jesus put his body where the common people were means that, where the body of Christ calls out for recognition and inclusion, this "putting" is with those affected by HIV today and with the women of Oceania in particular. Their invisibility runs deep, says Kelly Brown Douglas:

> Across the region women are largely excluded from meaningful participation in political and national arenas and public affairs, except in domains such as women's affairs, health and education. They are excluded by virtue of male prejudice, lack of education and opportunity, and to some extent by choice: notoriously, women rarely vote for female candidates and most women, especially uneducated rural dwellers, agree with men that politics is men's business.[23]

Though acknowledged by those in governance, Pacific Island women do not see their own potential for power to exercise moral and practical authority and responsibility in their communities.[24] This failure is an issue for women and men in the region. A long-term commitment to work with and on behalf of them is essential for the transformation of Pacific women's self-understanding.

A primary means for this transformation is the establishment of opportunities for authentic conversation enabling women to engage in dialogue and recognize their own subjectivity in place of the monologue characteristic of church and societal discourse. Opportunities to participate in research on their own experiences of faith and faithfulness and of ways of coming to know their own life narratives have been positive; in these experiences women have recognized the transforming potential such opportunities can provide for their empowerment and growth.[25] As Nicola Slee explains, "Conversation with an attentive other [brings an] epiphany and discernment, revealing something of the larger meaning of a woman's life as she tells her story and listens for its shapes and patterns to be worked out in the flow and pattern of the conversation."[26] Opportunities for women to discover their own voices, of their inner and outer selves, in intrapersonal or interpersonal contexts, are essential. Faith communities can provide such opportunities to nurture the connectedness of women's experience of self in relationship to God, others, and themselves.

That Oceania contains a small fraction of the world's population and the Australia–New Zealand nexus contains most of this fraction requires that a pastoral concern for women be initiated by local women and men familiar with the realities of Oceania. As they are prepared and able to open the conversation with women from the entire region, they will be more attentive to hear the voices that have been silenced. Consciousness-raising is important locally and in the global context for the task of women's communal visibility. That my concern is with HIV/AIDS refers this urgent task to those living in the outlying and smaller islands. The contribution of Christianity to such consciousness-raising activities is likewise politically critical. Douglas notes that while churches have led "the international 'good governance' agenda . . . in every Melanesian country . . . together with women's groups . . . Christian spirituality has been mobilized in parts of the Papua New Guinea Highlands to limit tribal fighting."[27] In their pastoral concern for women, many Western churches, seminaries, and theological colleges have opened their institutions to people from Asia and Africa; now is surely time for the women of the Pacific Islands to participate in and benefit from these same educational resources.

To enable women, who are invisible to the discourse on HIV/AIDS and who over time have become invisible to themselves, to find their voices and their places is a matter of urgency for the pastoral work of ecclesial communities and for the identity of the Church today. As women in Oceania suffer increasingly from the pandemic, it is essential they become visible as the body of Christ. Enda McDonagh writes:

> The crucial and cruciform revelation of God's cosuffering (compassion) with human beings in Jesus manifests a new aspect of the mystery we also call love. It is not simply comprehensible to us, but it does reassure us about the presence. "Where are you God as I am overcome by the pain and desperation?" "Right here with you just as I was on Calvary." And the power, the omnipotence as we used to say? No more absent or frustrated than on Calvary but taking its mysterious ways through creaturely and bodily fragility to a healing in love and life that may or may not issue in renewed bodily life and health. The inexhaustible loving which endured through Calvary does not abandon those for whom Calvary was undertaken in the first place.[28]

The healing in love that humankind works in relation to HIV and AIDS is found in many communal activities undertaken by women and men throughout the world. The AIDS Memorial Quilt Project begun in 1987 in the United States now has over 44,000 individual panels commemorating those who have died of AIDS. What began as a local project expanded into the largest community art project in the world, with people from forty countries and all fifty U.S. states contributing to the quilt. Nominated for the Nobel Peace Prize in 1989, the collaborative and communal activities surrounding the Quilt are surely a symbol of the unifying presence of the spirit of love in the healing of the broken body of Christ.

What is ever growing in the global context is echoed in local faith communities. The efforts of Christian women to integrate human suffering into the healing work of God become their prayer and are here offered through a South Pacific women's group. Women envisage a web of relationships that God weaves throughout the universe, a tapestry in which all people are visible to themselves and each other as they share in the reweaving of this tapestry, a creation of God's Spirit alive and working in and through the faith of all:

> God sits weeping,
> the beautiful creation tapestry
> She wove with such joy
> is mutilated, torn into shreds,
> reduced to rags
> its beauty fragmented by force.
> God sits weeping,
> But look!
> She is gathering up the shreds
> to weave something new. . . .
> She is weaving them all
> with golden threads of Jubilation
> into a new tapestry. . . .
> And She invites us
> not only to keep offering her the
> shreds and rags of our suffering
> and our work
> But even more—
> to take our place beside her
> at the Jubilee loom
> and weave with Her
> the Tapestry of the New Creation.[29]

Metti Amirtham, SCC

Women Confronting Stigma in Tamil Nadu

Arockia Mary, HIV-positive, mother of two children, lives in Namakkal, a district in Tamil Nadu, in southern India. Originally from a nearby village, upon learning of her sero-positive status, she moved into town to hide her condition. She has studied up to third grade, was married to a truck driver at the age of 16, and was infected after her marriage. Her husband passed away two years ago and his family broke relationship with her. She believes these circumstances are God's wish for her.

Kavitha, 25, from the remote village of Chibichakaram in Namakkal, was married when she was 19 years old. She did not have a child for three years. During those years of waiting she went to the hospital and received injections and blood transfusions for her poor health. After the birth of a child, she became very weak. When the doctors tested her blood, she was found to have HIV. Though infected through injections and transfusions, her husband and in-laws beat her badly. Her husband divorced her. She says, "Two children were born to me and they died soon after birth. As a woman I have come to a low state because of marriage. I feel like committing suicide."

These realities from Namakkal expose the impact of the HIV/AIDS pandemic on the bodies and lives of women in terms of social stigma, isolation, rejection, secrecy, stress and coping, social support, communication and disclosure, responses to illness, and other factors. In this essay I will look at the impact of HIV on women and point to some of the ethical issues, concerns, and preventive care to which the local and global community must attend.

Epidemiological Facts

UN Secretary General Kofi Annan has called the HIV/AIDS pandemic "the most formidable development challenge of our time."[1] And even though awareness is global, the problems of HIV/AIDS continue to grow in magnitude worldwide, costing many human lives. HIV causes chronic infection and immune-suppression; infection courses vary, though once infected, symptomatic HIV progresses to AIDS within ten to fifteen years.[2] First reported in

174

women in 1981 and affecting women and men, gender inequalities world-wide encourage infection. More men than women live with AIDS; however, biologically more vulnerable to transmission than men, women progress to AIDS at a faster rate.

Since the first case was discovered in India in 1985, AIDS has spread so rapidly that India now has the second-largest AIDS epidemic in the world (after Africa). Tamil Nadu soon became a high prevalence area with more than 52,000 cases, with prevalence in the district of Namakkal higher than the national average.

Given prevailing gender norms in Tamil society, the reality to which this prevalence points is grim: the majority of women infected are married, and their husbands or primary sexual partners of those who are unmarried engage in high-risk sexual behavior, then bring the virus home.

Gender and HIV/AIDS

The impact of HIV on the lives of women presents reproductive health concerns for the future. In sub-Saharan Africa, women make up 59 percent of adults with HIV, and young women of 15 to 24 years are two to six times more likely to be infected with HIV as young men.[3] Additionally, because most infected women are of childbearing age, they risk infecting their children and face difficult choices about pregnancies. As caregivers in their immediate and extended families, women usually attend to dying family members and to AIDS-orphaned children. These factors make the empowerment of women a critical component of programs aimed to curb the epidemic and mitigate its consequences.[4]

The stigma surrounding HIV is scandalous. People fear revealing their sero-status. For women, the effects of stigma are so severe that often relatives force women to leave their marital homes after the AIDS-related death of their husbands. Furthermore, the effects of HIV/AIDS on demographics produce a "population chimney" that causes young people, including women, to die or become infertile, resulting in fewer births, and one-third of the infants born to HIV-positive mothers succumb themselves to infection—in ten years, they have AIDS. The number of women and men who would be parents is compromised, and there is negative population growth in especially hard-hit regions. In India and elsewhere, the association between HIV and promiscuous sexual behavior has created a belief that people with HIV deserve their fate. Paradoxically, studies of attitudes show that regardless of their sero-status, women are suspect when their husbands die of AIDS. While they themselves are often monogamous, they can still be infected by their spouses.

On average, men have more male or female sex partners than women and have more opportunities both to contract and transmit the disease. Moreover, men have more influence over whether or not to have safer or protected sex. In Tamil society, since women have little access to health care, education, and employment, their unequal status relative to men is reinforced by the double standards of sexual morality. When women are subjected to violence or sexual abuse, they "get what they deserve"—yet another belief that further stigmatizes and exploits the bodies of women.

Complicating these beliefs, Tamil society upholds the expectation that women are to preserve their virginity before and to remain faithful after marriage. Conversely, young men are encouraged to gain sexual experience; indeed, sexual relationships may make young men popular with their peers. In some societies, sex with a young girl is believed to increase virility, and sex with a virgin or a young woman is believed to minimize the risk of contracting AIDS, or to even to cure it. Yet older, sexually promiscuous men put young girls at risk of HIV, other STDs, and unwanted pregnancies, thereby continuing the cycle of exploitation and stigma. Many women with HIV face the twin prospects of coping with their diagnosis and finding a way of informing their husbands or male partners. Men and their families may accuse these women of bringing HIV home, though it is more likely that the men are responsible. In most cases, infection in women, including those who are pregnant, comes from their husbands, many of whom travel extensively in their work as long-haul truck drivers and become infected by commercial sex workers.

Worldwide, women are increasingly infected and are at parity with men. Equally disturbing, more than 13.2 million children have been orphaned from AIDS. The National AIDS Control Organization of India (NACO) estimates that 3.6 million people in India are living with HIV/AIDS. By July 2005, the total number of AIDS cases reported to NACO was 111,608. Of this number, 32,567 were women, and 37 percent were under the age of 30. These figures do not reflect the actual situation; large numbers of AIDS cases go unreported.[5]

Biologically, socially, and economically disadvantaged, women are vulnerable, and safe sex is often not an option for them. They are often primary caregivers who, even when themselves HIV-positive, take care of infected family members. When their children die, grandmothers take care of their orphaned grandchildren. Women will only be economically, legally, and socially empowered if their vulnerability to HIV is addressed.

Correlatively, HIV/AIDS must be regarded as core business for everyone, not just for those who are HIV-positive. Information about HIV/AIDS must be integrated into every women's rights program. Even those who are HIV-positive question free and fair global trade when women can no longer offer their goods and services in the marketplace but are sick or busy caring for the sick. It does not make sense to fight for girls' equal right to education when they have to stay home from school to take care of their siblings orphaned by AIDS.

Impact on Women

Many of these gender issues are found in the context of Tamil Nadu. In Tamil society a double standard of sexual morality ensures that women are viewed as creatures who lead men astray. Unfortunately, even dressing well and looking attractive can earn a woman the label of sexually promiscuous. And when women are beaten or sexually abused, it is sometimes believed that they got what they deserved.

Women continue to have less access to health care, education, and employment. They are likely to have less formal education, less knowledge of HIV, language barriers, and fewer financial resources. Many are dependent economically and socially on men. They are at increased risk of HIV from this dependency. The interplay of many factors—powerlessness, dependence, and poverty—diminishes women's abilities to protect themselves from unsafe sex, their ability to negotiate when or with whom to have sex and whether or not to use a condom. Moreover, society's acceptance of men's questionable behavior multiplies women's infection risk.[6]

Another complication for women is their desire to have a child. Decisions about motherhood are not made in a vacuum. Every society, more or less, accords status and respectability to women as child-bearers. A childless woman in Tamil Nadu faces a cultural stigma.[7] In Tamil society, motherhood is more important than any other role for women. Hence, early pregnancy is common, at an age when the girl is neither mentally nor physically prepared for motherhood. This ideology limits her potential to develop the talents she possesses to do otherwise.

The culture of silence surrounding sex prevents women from openly discussing sexual matters, and access to information about reproductive health and sex is limited. Cultural barriers inhibit discussions of sexuality, preventing better understandings of the human body, sex, and sexuality, and discouraging women from initiatives on sexual matters. Moreover, society entrusts complete control of female sexuality to men. Under the jurisdiction of men, most if not all decisions related to sexual activity, including a woman's right to exercise control over her own body, belong to him.

Additionally, from a lack of sex education at the right time, women are ignorant or ill-informed about sex and sexuality. In Tamil society, knowing or talking about sex is immoral, and "good women" should be ignorant and silent about sex. Without formal and accurate education on sexuality, myths abound to women's ruin.

Cumulative evidence indicates that women are about four times more susceptible to HIV infection than heterosexual men, and they are more likely to be infected with HIV from men than vice versa. Many women progress to AIDS and die faster than men. This progress results from unequal access to care and treatment. When husbands are infected, wives remain loyal to their marital commitment and care for them in their need; when a woman has

AIDS, rarely does her husband come forward to look after her. More likely, he will look for another woman to meet his sexual needs, as well as the needs of the household. This behavior is accepted as normal. This lack of care and treatment hastens women's demise. These forces render all women ever more vulnerable to HIV and its progression to AIDS.

In Tamil as elsewhere, women lack the social structures, religious support, and psychological self-understanding to refuse risky sexual relations. In turn, the epidemic deepens poverty, destitution, and homelessness. Contrary to Europe, where women instigate three-quarters of all divorces, in India, divorce is a remote reality for ordinary women who discover their husbands have HIV or AIDS.[8] While the epidemic has increased women's share in the labor force, so has it increased the proportion of women and women-headed households below the poverty line. Poverty accelerates the spread of the pandemic, particularly for women when commercial sex work is often the only available survival strategy.

Regardless of this poverty, in face of their powerlessness to influence their husbands' or male sexual partners' behaviors, women are vulnerable. And marriage itself contributes to risk for those lacking decision-making power about sex and the use of condoms as protection against HIV or for contraceptive purposes.[9] This subordinate position of women exacerbates their vulnerability to HIV.

Implications for Women's Survival

After more than two decades, our understanding of the pandemic and its implications for human survival and human development remains immature. Searching for ways to empower women with HIV or AIDS, who thirst deeply for justice, I offer solidarity with them and others affected by the pandemic. Social structures, laws, practices, values, and attitudes must change if the status of women and other vulnerable persons is to improve.

HIV prevention is not a one-time intervention. It must be accepted as a continuous, multigenerational effort extending into human communities from childhood to old age. The primary way of thwarting HIV is to avoid and to prevent certain risky behaviors. Toward that end, the following must be done.

1. *Sex education must be available to provide information that could delay first sexual encounters and decrease risky behavior by men and women.* Young women and men should have sex education as part of their formation, and especially before they become sexually active. Well-planned and well-taught sex education reduces the risk of STDs, HIV, and unwanted pregnancies. School curricula must include HIV-related life skills and extend peer education to vulnerable populations in or out of school as well as in-service programs for those employed out of the household and those working at home.

Comprehensive efforts must address the complex issues surrounding HIV and injection drug use.

2. *Steps must be taken to prevent mother-to-child transmission,* the most significant source of HIV infection in children under ten. Children will be protected if their parents are protected, especially their mothers, and if child rape and other abuses are brought to an end. Toward these ends, women must have access to information and testing, follow-up clinical care, and support that includes family planning and nutritional support.

3. *More women-centered preventive programs must be developed.* Effective methods empowering women to protect themselves and their families should come with their education, health care, and economic security.

4. *Women and parents must be encouraged to discuss sex, sexuality, and gender roles with each other and their children.*

5. *AIDS prevention and care programs must become widespread.* Many current programs fail to address the particular contexts of women and men. These contexts must be engaged if programs are to be successful.

6. *Education must reflect real situations.* While abstinence and mutual fidelity are effective in preventing HIV infection, not everyone can, or wants to, adopt these options. Even the consistent use of condoms is difficult for many. Messages must reflect and respond to actual realities. Women and men should be addressed separately, and messages should be delivered to young, old, rich, poor, urban, and rural dwellers throughout the land.

7. *Women who engage in sex for money must be empowered to make their own decisions.* These women must be taught life skills that will lead to safe employment and be empowered to reject sexual advances from men, or at least to negotiate condom use, which will reduce their risk and vulnerability.

Given that young people, especially women, bear the brunt of the economic transitions in the Tamil region, socioeconomic programs that reduce their vulnerability are vital. HIV/AIDS must be on the agenda of every organization and institution working for the humanitarian causes of global justice.

Future Guidelines

The most important long-term goal involves prevention. In addition to behavior change, strategies include the use of vaccines and microbicides. Female condoms, marketed for several years, are too expensive for most women. Vaginal microbicides are still under research and, while promising, are not yet effective; presumed advantages include nondelectability (the lack of smell and taste), safety and efficacy, antimicrobial properties against HIV and other STDs, and spermicidal properties.

As the primary route of HIV transmission is sexual contact, HIV prevention must be closely linked to women's and men's sexual behaviors and reproductive health. Effective prevention programs include promoting abstinence from sex, delaying the onset of sexual activity, maintaining fidelity to one mutually faithful partner, limiting the number of sexual partners, using condoms consistently and correctly, and undergoing counseling and tests for HIV status.

The most effective mix of these interventions depends on the characteristics of the people with HIV. Effective programs consider the social, economic, and cultural factors influencing people's behavior. Preventing transmission from mothers to their infants is also critical. Women with HIV need contraceptive choices and counseling for decisions regarding pregnancy. Increasing contraceptive use to prevent mother-to-child transmission is at least as cost-effective as providing antiretroviral drug therapy during delivery and to the newborns of HIV-positive mothers.

Key challenges for the future include controlling infection of infants and young adults, treating and supporting the millions of people with HIV and AIDS, and mitigating the impact of the pandemic in poor countries. To meet these challenges, the Church must be culturally sensitive to issues of extra-marital sex, and the use of condoms must be tackled head on—with a view to incorporating their prophylactic, not contraceptive, properties. The promotion of responsible reproductive behavior among youth is important. Adolescent ignorance about sex and sexuality is compounded by the reluctance among parents and teachers to impart information about sex and STDs. Mothers expect their adolescent children, particularly their daughters, to remain uninformed about sex and reproduction; sex and puberty are still considered embarrassing and taboo subjects, and parents are not free to discuss sex and sexuality in the presence of their adolescent children. The Church can be more proactive in empowering parents in this regard.

The present education system has not paid sufficient attention to these issues either. Teachers too find the subject embarrassing, and they avoid this discussion. As a result of this avoidance, adolescents gain much of their information (much of it problematic) on sexuality from their peers and a sex-commercialized mass media. Their education becomes critically important for reproductive health and prevention of STDs and HIV, as well as for the morality and principles to be adopted in life. This education includes prevention strategies that are pro-life prevention and includes hard data about the pandemic.[10] This education recognizes also that the statistics represent people like ourselves, and, while we may practice safe(r) sex and think that the epidemic is not our problem, people are still dying.

Concluding Strategy: Six Principles

Women-centered preventive programs must be implemented now. This imperative arises from the contexts of women's lives and livelihoods. Compared to men, they account for a higher proportion of marginalized people with HIV and constitute a large part of the homeless population in India. The following principles are offered as a countermeasure to what is otherwise the inevitable spread of HIV and its toll on the human community in India and worldwide.

1. The Principle of Being Informed

Each person engaged in a part of the response to the epidemic needs actively and in an ongoing manner to continue the quest to understand this pandemic in all its complexity as it unfolds and changes its own dynamic. Information is a prerequisite for the conceptual and programmatic flexibility demanded by the pandemic.

2. The Principle of Association and Representation

To educate people about HIV/AIDS, denial must be overcome. Almost every community in the world reacted initially by denying the existence of any problem. Sometimes denial takes the form of perceptions of personal invulnerability to AIDS.[11] Responses to this pandemic require collaboration and partnership with those who are living with HIV. Denial will be overcome by speaking for and about those who, having been silenced, cannot speak; by attending conferences on these subjects; and by rejecting myths and telling the truth.

3. The Principle of Engagement

Without a "them" and "us," each of us must be engaged as actors and must be active in seeking our own interests and the interests of those we love and those for whom we care. This engagement flows from the principle of compassion, acknowledging that each person is linked by relations of kinship, love, neighborliness, empathy, dependency, respect, and solidarity. To bring about a change of perception of the pandemic demands the presence, care, and support of others. As Elizabeth Reid recalls, "Compassion is the ethical reflection of this inter-dependence."[12]

4. The Principle of Empowerment

The principle of empowerment marks the manner of work: as equals, in partnership, each bringing experiences and skills in a process respecting mutual capacity and capacity building. The development of effective responses to the pandemic requires, above all, the active participation of people affected and infected by HIV and AIDS, and the building of partnerships among communities, governments, and the legal, health, and other professions.[13]

5. The Principle of Protection

People living with HIV and AIDS must be provided with opportunities to protect themselves from opportunistic infections, and those who are sero-negative must be provided with methods of effective prevention.

6. The Principle of Inclusion

Those most directly affected by the pandemic must be recognized as an integral part of their communities, with access to the benefits available to others: education, training, employment, health and legal services, social support and benefits, sports, marriage, and so forth. The principle of inclusion is constitutive of the principle of nondiscrimination and its behavioral imperatives against rejection, neglect, repudiation, and stigmatization.

Therese Tinkasiimire, DST

Responses to HIV/AIDS in Hoima Diocese, Uganda

The Roman Catholic Church was established in Uganda over a hundred years ago. Since then, the Church has offered the message of Christian faith and morality. Today the Church is faced with the challenge of HIV/AIDS, which has ravaged this country since 1982. The main mode of HIV transmission in Uganda is heterosexual intercourse, accounting for 85 percent of infections.[1] This mode of transmission is due to economic, social, cultural, and gender relations that encourage people to engage in unprotected sex.[2] In "The Church in Africa in the Face of the HIV/AIDS Pandemic" (2003) the Catholic Bishops of Africa committed to work tirelessly to eradicate stigma and discrimination and to challenge any social, religious, cultural, and political norms and practices perpetuating them.[3] In response to this message the Church faithful are called to go a step further: to work to prevent the spread of HIV, to accompany and care for those who are already ill, and to develop a discourse on sexuality suitable for the local culture.

I present in this essay research findings carried out in the parishes of Kitoba and Nyamigisa, in Hoima Diocese, on the messages given by Catholic priests, nuns, and lay ecclesial workers to parishioners seeking counseling regarding HIV prevention and/or treatment.[4] The main objective was to identify the messages Catholic women and men hear from their Church representatives and to assess how these messages influence the gender roles and relationships in their daily lives. The research focused on to what extent these messages hinder or assist HIV prevention strategies. Related to these aims is the question of whether the Church was willing to venture into the new area of addressing the root cause of cultural sexual taboos and whether it could facilitate people's ability to discuss them openly in order to learn how to protect themselves against HIV, and for the Church, with its people, to develop a new African sexual ethics suitable for the era of HIV/AIDS.

Theoretical Framework

I have used a conceptual framework for gender analysis and planning developed by Caroline Moser, a gender specialist,[5] that analyzes gender equity using two concepts: women's practical and strategic gender needs.[6] Moser's framework explores gender roles, control of resources, decision making within households, and community roles, with a view to balancing these roles. I analyzed gender roles at household and community levels by looking at Church leaders' messages and how they address women's and men's gender roles. Do the messages equip the most vulnerable people with strategies that safeguard them against HIV?

Here women have a voice. They talk freely about Church leaders' messages and (1) whether these messages address harmful sexual practices in their communities and (2) whether the women will be empowered on how to use protective strategies. The men too are empowered to go beyond cultural practices and with women together walk a new path paved by a new understanding of their sexuality. Hopefully, Church leaders' messages will change, empower the powerless, and create a new African Christian ethics enabling health and protection against HIV.

Background

Hoima Diocese is in a rural area about 150 miles from Kampala, the capital of Uganda. No single paved roadway runs across all three of the diocese's districts; travel is very difficult. Most people walk, and a few use bicycles. Health care facilities are few and limited in their medical capabilities. There is a government hospital in each of the three districts, but it is difficult to get to these hospitals; some people must walk fifteen miles to reach them. There is a missionary health clinic in Nyamigisa Parish, but no facility in Kitoba Parish (both locales under study). The only option for many people is to walk, but when they reach a hospital, medicines are often not available. If they are lucky and find that supplies have just come from Kampala, they still must spend many hours waiting.

Rural areas like Hoima Diocese present a huge challenge to the Church's efforts in response to AIDS in western Uganda. Hoima is also very poor and is home for many internally displaced people from war-torn northern Uganda and refugees from Sudan and Rwanda. The people have all kinds of physical and spiritual needs. Hoima offers one example of how priests, nuns, and lay workers deal with HIV and what strategies are in place for prevention and care.

The Epidemic in Uganda

In order to understand the magnitude of the problems of HIV among the Banyoro people of Hoima Diocese, it is imperative first to consider the whole country, the continent of Africa, and the world at large. After more than twenty years since the first clinical evidence of AIDS, worldwide estimates show that over 60 million people have been infected with HIV. Every day 16,000 are infected, and 46 million people live with HIV or AIDS today.[7] Of these, 28.5 million live in sub-Saharan Africa. The majority of new infections occur among young adults, with young women among the most vulnerable, accounting for about one-third of the HIV infections among those 15 to 24 years old.

Uganda has a population of approximately 26 million. It was the first country to experience heavy mortality and morbidity due to AIDS. The first cases of AIDS in Uganda were reported at two of Lake Victoria's fish landing sites in 1982. From these cases developed one of the deadliest epidemics in Ugandan history. At first, Ugandans, like many Africans, looked at AIDS as an illness that one did not acquire through natural means. In African conceptual thinking, nothing happens by "accident" or by "chance"; some agent, either human or spiritual, is responsible.[8] AIDS was therefore thought to have been caused by some supernatural or supranatural power, and remedies would need to address this power. Although some prevention programs were launched, behavioral change did not follow.[9] However, Uganda has gone from an average prevalence in the mid-1990s of 18 percent, with about 30 percent in the worst-hit areas, to estimated rates of 6.2 percent and 7–8 percent, respectively, today.[10] This success is the result of the government's commitment to HIV prevention and care.[11] A combination of same-day results for HIV tests, social marketing of condoms, and self-aid kits for STDs, backed by sex education programs, has reduced the highest infection rates, especially in urban areas.

Recent statistics indicate that over 1.5 million people in Uganda have HIV, and over 800,000 had died from AIDS by 2004.[12] About 110,000 people have AIDS and are in need of antiretroviral therapy (ART). Despite a UNAIDS report of a decrease of infections in Uganda, the people needing ART will increase every year. Only 10 percent of those needing ART, mostly urban residents, actually use them; their costs are out of pocket. People in rural areas lack access to ART because of the lack of availability in most rural clinics, high costs, untrustworthy time-keeping with watches or clocks, and unreliable refrigeration.

Government's Response to Prevention and Care

The National Committee for Prevention of AIDS (NCPA) was formed in 1985. In 1986, the AIDS control program was established in the Ministry of Health with support from the World Health Organization (WHO) and charged with the responsibility of tracking the AIDS pandemic. With WHO, substantial progress was made in HIV/AIDS epidemiological surveillance, safe blood supply, care and counseling, and provision of HIV information and education. In 1992, the Uganda AIDS Commission and its Secretariat were established by statute and charged with coordinating the National Action Plan, resulting in a multisector approach on prevention, care, and management. The government embarked on a sensitization plan known as ABC (A = abstinence, B = be faithful in marriage or "zero grazing," and C = condom use). Education became a major weapon against infection.

Faith-Based Responses
to Prevention and Care

The Church is renowned worldwide for its stringent position against the use of contraceptives. The rationale reckons that people should only engage in sex within marriage and with the dual dimensions of union and procreation. Thus, many Church leaders argue that as long as a person restricts sex to marriage, there is no need for condoms. "No one has ever died of abstinence," explained a Catholic community organization coordinator.[13] Among its arguments against condom use, the Church in Uganda emphasizes that condoms are not 100 percent effective in preventing HIV transmission, and the Church considers condom promotion analogous to promoting promiscuity and other sexually immoral activities. "In Africa, people try to go with many sex partners," explained the Kampala Archdiocese's medical coordinator, "so if they think they're protected, they'll follow the urge to go with many."[14] In the eyes of the Church, the ideal way to protect oneself from HIV is abstinence or "zero grazing" (faithfulness in marriage). Some change is hinted with consideration that discordant couples may use condoms at the discretion of their pastors through the internal forum; I hope the Church will allow all couples to use a condom as a preemptive measure against HIV and other STDs.

Nevertheless, the Church has established counseling centers in some dioceses in Uganda. In the Central region, there are HIV/AIDS counseling centers at Nsambya and Rubaga Hospitals; these centers deliver ART and support people with AIDS. Nsambya Hospital and Kitovu Hospital in Masaka district have mobile AIDS home care programs reaching homebound people with HIV or AIDS (PLWHA).[15]

Moreover, PLWHA live longer and better lives when they receive spiritual care. With spiritual care, emotions and feelings are comforted, PLWHA are strengthened and empowered, and they feel they are in control of their lives. They experience a sense of support and belonging, and their personal relationship with God creates a significant support system. The acceptance of illness is facilitated and self-blame is reduced, dignity is restored, and fears and uncertainties of death are relieved. This kind of care is indeed the work of the Church.

Besides spiritual care, the Church must address silence and denial. Some people in rural areas look at AIDS as something "out there." But laypeople, religious women and men, and priests who have HIV/AIDS are living among them; some have died from AIDS. Denial and stigma abound, unfortunately, even among some Christian communities, because AIDS is considered God's punishment. AIDS is a cause for shame and disgrace, for those infected and for their families; to speak openly about having AIDS is virtually unthinkable.[16] Yet Christian theology does not support this belief. What messages, on the other side of these mistaken beliefs and harmful traditional customs and practices, are given to the people in regard to HIV?

Nyamigisa and Kitoba Parishes

The parishioners of Nyamigisa, regular Church attendees, said that their Church leaders spoke occasionally about HIV prevention and AIDS but that abstinence before and faithfulness in marriage dominate. One person with HIV said that his great desire was that the Church leaders would speak about prevention every Sunday in their homilies but that this message was rare. He was happy that government representatives spoke about HIV whenever they went to the different villages. However, the words of Church leaders are more carefully heeded; people feel that God is speaking to them and will, perhaps, heal them. The messages given by Church leaders differ from those of the government with its insistence on condoms (they are not readily available in the villages). People feel they should stick to the advice of their pastors, since this advice has helped them thus far.

On the whole, Christians in Hoima Diocese appreciate what the Church is doing. The diocese has established a center called "Meeting Point" in Hoima Town and employs counselors for those infected and affected on Tuesdays and Thursdays. I visited Meeting Point and met both counselors and patients, who come for medicine, food, and guidance. I talked to patients who told me they are still alive because of the support of Meeting Point. When they first came to Meeting Point they were received well and treated like people who are still useful in the world. They were advised to be tested and, if positive, were given support. Comorbid conditions such as skin rashes, fever, and tuberculosis were treated, and some of the patients now live positively with HIV. Many of them, especially those newly arrived, are still bad off because medicine is very scarce. This scarcity is attributed to the former minister of health, who embezzled the global fund earmarked to buy medicine for tuberculosis, malaria, and ART. Nevertheless, these people are better off than those living in rural areas.

When I visited Kitoba Parish, located in a more remote area than Nyamigisa Parish, the scenario changed. I found that while many people have heard about HIV/AIDS, they do not have sufficient information regarding prevention. The people I talked to were very grateful and wanted to hear more. They too wished that priests would talk about it every Sunday. The priests visit to administer the sacrament of the sick near the end of their lives, and the parish has a team of catechists who visited the sick regularly and reported to the priests. Besides this team, a charismatic group visited, counseled, and advised the villagers about religious matters; the methods of HIV prevention they provided were abstinence and faithfulness in marriage. As some of the people I talked to say their priests tell them the condom is not 100 percent safe, they do not trust condoms to protect them. Government agents promote condom use, but villagers suspect that the government agents are liars. They have promised many things in campaigns, but nothing has been implemented; the people do not trust them or their advice. The people expressed the desire to have a health unit at their parish to help meet their needs, and especially the needs of PLWHA. More than others, PLWHA often fall sick, the government hospital is far away, and there is limited transport in the rural areas. If this health unit were run by religious people, the villagers would be sure of getting good care and treatment. Unfortunately, the parish is too poor to fulfill this desire.

Non-Christians and nominal Christians, especially those in towns, said that the government representatives give them useful information about HIV prevention strategies. Many of them have received free condoms, and they feel safe. The young people in this category feel glad that, since they do not attend religious services, at least someone comes and talks to them about life issues. Some of them grew up without parents; they died either from war or AIDS. PLWHA there said they receive treatment from the government hospital and Church-run clinics. They said they are not discriminated against and that every time they visit such clinics they receive counseling and food. Two counseling centers have been established by churches: Meeting Point by the Catholic Church in Hoima Town, and the Duhaga Counseling Center by the Anglican Church of Uganda. These two centers are visited by all people. Those who live far from the towns are disadvantaged by the long walk to and from these centers. Many lives would be saved if some of these services were brought to people in these rural villages.

Women's Vulnerability:
Cultural Customs and Practices

Since the principal mode of HIV transmission is heterosexual intercourse,[17] sexual care is very important in combating the disease. However, Uganda is a patriarchal society where women are regarded as inferior to men and cultural practices favor men over women. The Banyoro practice of "bridewealth" in marriage exemplifies this unequal regard. The family of the man pays the family of the woman. Symbolically, this payment deprives the woman of the ownership of her sexuality; the man owns her sexuality and has unlimited access to her for sexual relations. She cannot deny him anything. She is expected, per the payment, to make herself available on his demand. She is culturally powerless to defend or protect herself, and any request on her part for a condom creates suspicion that she has been unfaithful. She fears to raise the request, since it can easily end in divorce or violence. The implications of this vulnerability are mortal.

This cultural practice of ownership increases a woman's risk of contracting HIV. Such a practice is an instrument that oppresses and may even kill women.[18] Kathleen Cravero argues, "The prevention strategies now in place are missing the point when it comes to women and girls. Women, particularly young women, are not in a position to abstain. They are not in a position to demand faithfulness of their partners. In many cases they are in fact faithful, but are being infected partners."[19] Social and cultural change plus greater access to health care are the only ways to check the pandemic in countries where women, like the Banyoro, have no status or power. The Church, members of the elite class, and the government must expose the consequences of patriarchal cultural practices like bride-wealth. Perhaps these oppressive practices could be replaced by nonviolent and nonvictimizing practices: giving simple gifts instead of money as the bride-wealth payment, or giving the money to the new couple, rather than the woman's family, for a good start of life together.

Polygamy is another cultural practice oppressing women. Among the Banyoro, the man is free to marry more than one wife, but a woman can marry only one man at a time. Polygamy is found in other communities in Uganda, such as among the Banyankore, where 27 to 30 percent of married men are polygamous, and the Madi community, where about 20 percent of married men and 33 percent of married women are in polygamous unions.[20] Polygamy brings inequality between the sexes. One of the claims for polygamy is children: a man with a barren wife must find a fertile woman to perpetuate the clan. The Church advises people to let go of the practice. Women parliamentarians have taken the Church's advice to Parliament for debate. There the advice to eradicate polygamy has developed into the "Domestic Bill." Some men are adamant; they do not want to let go. Nevertheless, these women parliamentarians and the Church hope that similarly positive initiatives will come about and one day this "Domestic Bill" will become law.

Additionally, UNAIDS urges governments to reform inheritance laws and pass legislation protecting women from some customary laws, so that a woman may keep her house, land, and furniture when her partner dies. With education and economic power, women will control their lives and be able to negotiate sex, but right now they do not have the right.[21] Empowerment of women in Uganda is the way forward and will lead to a better life for women, children, and men.

The Church's Teaching on Sexuality

Many ethicists have looked at the different messages given to Christians on sexuality and the pandemic in Africa. Their work suggests that understandings concerning sexuality have been imported from another culture and do not address the concerns of Africans.[22] The Church wants to address sexuality for Africans but has trouble making its address contextually appropriate. Honest discourse on sexuality must take the local culture into account. The Church must address those cultural practices generating and facilitating the spread of HIV. This need applies to polygamy, bride-wealth, inheritance laws, and other practices oppressive to women. The situation is worse in rural areas, where patriarchy is strongest. Moreover, in terms of illness, a man will receive treatment because he has monetary control, whereas a woman is at the mercy of her husband, who may or may not find the expense for her treatment necessary.

John Mary Waliggo from Uganda speaks to Christians in Uganda of their responsibilities: "We have an obligation to journey to our final destiny without abandoning anyone on the wayside."[23] If the Church journeys with all infected and affected people, there will be hope for everyone that God cares for them. Waliggo recognizes also that discrimination against women in Africa has rendered them voiceless and helpless.[24] As the Church struggles with the AIDS pandemic, it must make plans to accept the mothers with HIV and to ensure life and consolation to their orphaned children.

Another priest involved in pastoral work in Africa identifies the dilemma of condom use by young girls. African tradition reinforces the gravity of the situation by perpetuating certain taboos. When at puberty parents stop looking after their female children in some African communities, girls become responsible for meeting their own needs. They fall prey to "sugar daddies," who give them money in exchange for sex. The overzealous promotion of condoms makes the situation disastrous.[25] Letters "D" and "E" must be added to the familiar "ABC" for HIV/AIDS awareness and prevention campaigns: A = abstinence, B = be faithful, C = condom use, D = detection, and E = education. The polemics surrounding the condom is a tree hiding the forest. The Church must move from the phenomenology of evil located partially in condom use to fighting the root of evil. In Africa, the root is none other than profound poverty. From my perspective, only radical change in sexual behavior will bring about real protection against HIV in Africa. Real behavioral change requires that the Church reexamine the ethics it presents. The Church in Africa must address harmful traditional customs and practices connected with HIV, such as wife sharing/ménage à trios/group sex and the sexual and economic subordination of women. Additionally, vigorous efforts establishing an African person-centered sexual ethics that motivates change in high-risk sexual behavior will begin to reduce the primary routes of infection.[26]

Sadly, the experience of women shows that the Church does not care. When women are forced into high-risk behavior and the Church does not come to their rescue, it colludes with the cultural norms of widow inheritance by a male in-law, leviratic unions following the custom to provide an heir for a brother, and bride-wealth.[27] Two examples of these cultural norms illustrate: a young girl was asked by her parents to go and replace her sister who had died of AIDS, which she contracted from her husband. The girl was to marry him and look after her sister's children. She too became infected and died. After a man passed HIV to his wife who then died, he asked her parents to give him their young daughter. They did so, because they reckoned he paid the bride-wealth for their first daughter but she had hardly lived with him and therefore needed to be replaced. These cases, involving practices committed in the name of culture, illustrate both danger and injustice to women. The Church did nothing to address the practices or to advocate justice for the women; instead, the priests used the funerals to preach against sin.

Conclusion

In responding to the challenges of HIV in Uganda, the Church stands as witness to cultural practices that both help and harm. For the help, many are grateful and live full lives. For the harm, a critique here only exposes the silence and collusion. The Church must do more. My hope is that this work will contribute to knowledge about the messages Church leaders give to their parishioners and will lead to an ethics of transformation for healthier and better lives for the people of Hoima Diocese and beyond.

Pushpa Joseph, FMM

Retrieving Spirituality as a Resource for Coping with HIV/AIDS

Perspectives from South India

Mary: Spirituality is like a surging force within me. It gives me the drive to be fully human and alive even in the face of impending death. Despite the knowledge that I will be fading away soon, I experience a power swelling from within. This disease, though it steals life from me, paradoxically has given me a reason to think deeply about my life. It has clearly shown me my life's purpose.[1]

Remani: Spirituality is an experience of a deep-seated sense of meaning and purpose in my life, together with a sense of belonging. When I was told that I had HIV, I was initially angry, sad, and frightened. I wanted to be alone always. I was mad at the world and above all at my husband, who gave me the virus. When I started the meditation exercises I found a new kind of strength dawning on me. I slowly started accepting my situation. I started feeling a new power within me. I began to feel that the universal energy has a purpose in my life. Then I started looking at myself and my disease differently. What helps me most is the thought that I can give others power to live life more meaningfully.[2]

Rita: The spiritual dimension helps me to be in harmony with the universe. This is important for me because when I am really low I draw lots of energy from the trees and from nature. It helps me find answers in my search for the meaning of my illness. Spirituality comes especially into focus in times of emotional stress, physical and mental illness, loss, bereavement, and death. For people like me, with HIV, this desire for wholeness of being is not an intellectual attainment; it lies in the essence of what it means to be human.[3]

These testimonies reveal the power of the divine in fractured lives and broken bodies.[4] Evoking faith, they have supernatural power. "Faith comes from hearing and hearing through the Word of Christ" (Rom 10:17). They impart faith, signal awareness of God's purposes, and bring intellectual encouragement and assurance to the hearer of the Word. The soul-stirring witnesses of Mary, Remani, and Rita are examples of how spirituality becomes a resource for coping with HIV.

The HIV/AIDS pandemic has complex concerns that call for multidimensional responses. Different approaches attempt to reduce transmission and minimize negative effects on individuals, families, and society. However, no simple formula works everywhere. Research with reference to South Asia, particularly India, shows infection risk is dependent on heterogeneous factors related to cultural, social, economic, and religious particularities. These factors call for multipronged approaches that include the cultural and spiritual repositories of the land.

Based on my interaction with women and men with HIV in South India, themselves using different spiritually empowering approaches, I consider spirituality and related indigenous resources by persons with HIV.[5] Spirituality, freed of its patriarchal and often institutional trappings, can be an important resource for people with HIV.

Spirituality

Spirituality is wide-ranging and may include religion in its support of human urges to reach the greater whole of which we are part. Broader than religion and more inclusive, spirituality provides meaning and transcendent stimulus that includes prayer, meditation, interaction with others or nature, and relationship with God (or Atman).[6] And spirituality supports religion where institutional forms offer a specific set of beliefs and structures attuned to the transcendent.

However, like other systems and structures, religion can be manipulated to justify what is right and positive, or harmful and negative. With regard to HIV/AIDS, some religious concepts on sin and sexuality contribute to a stigma that, in South India as elsewhere, has direct negative repercussions. Since the beginning of the epidemic, powerful religious images have reinforced and legitimized stigmatization. Some of these images have presented AIDS as punishment from God, some have presented people with HIV as afflicted, and others have presented a divine power with malicious intent. Associated with guilt, death, punishment, crime, horror, and worse, these metaphors have compounded stigma through religious sanction.[7]

Spirituality has the capacity to free individuals from the constraints of or indictments from religious institutions. As the white-robed monks of St. Benedict understand, with spirituality "the person is free to know. The person no longer has to be told how to know God and what to know about God."[8] While religion and its institutions may discriminate against and control those infected with and affected by HIV/AIDS, spirituality has awakened them to their dignity and to the responsibility they have for themselves.[9]

Most definitions of spirituality evolved from traditional religions to broader constructions of individual perspectives finding spiritual meaning beyond them. Many definitions incorporate ideas about sacredness and faith, as does Ronald Rolheiser's: "Spirituality is more about whether or not we can sleep at night than about . . . church. It is about being integrated or falling apart, about being within community or being lonely, about being in harmony with Mother Earth or being alienated from her. . . . What shapes our actions is our spirituality."[10] This approach focuses on meaning and purpose in life, connectedness with self, others, and the cosmos, and empowerment—aspects that are foundational to the empowered existence that people with HIV desire and deserve.

The nexus between spirituality and HIV/AIDS meets in theological anthropology rather than religion.[11] Spirituality from an interdisciplinary perspective reveals an anthropologically transformative search for the sacred.[12] While the sacred refers to a divine being, ultimate truth, or reality, for those with HIV, spirituality is their search for identity, belonging, and meaning with others who are striving similarly.[13]

As Mary, Remani, and Rita testify, spirituality is a pervasive life force leading to realization of a higher self—that is, their source of will and self-determination—and gives meaning, purpose, and connectedness to the contexts of their lives. They recognize spirituality emerging from their experiences of brokenness, pain, and struggle to live and endure with dignity. Though some challenge this life force as secular, meaningless, even emaciated of its mysterious, sacred, and supernatural content,[14] discussions of spirituality highlight a life-generating force invigorating human beings and providing impetus to live a sublime and meaningful life.

Spirituality, Resourcefulness, and HIV/AIDS

Resourcefulness provides the ability to cope. Someone who copes well has great resources for dealing with unusual problems. A source of strength in adversity, this inner resource resides at the core of our being. Deep within, it can be identified by a visceral feeling and a source of knowing on which to draw when faced with difficulties. A form of positive energy, this resource acts as a center of strength.

An empowering spirituality creates synergistic patterns by using centripetal, centrifugal, and unifying gravity forces—universal sources of energy available beyond and within our embodied space. The centripetal force controls inward movement, allowing us to observe and connect with our inner world, where what is natural for us is known. The centrifugal force controls outward movement, allowing interaction between ourselves and others. Gravity regulates the centripetal and centrifugal forces to ensure universal balance.

Spirituality, "linking the deeply personal with the universal," encompasses these inclusive and unifying forces. Consequently, spirituality is as much about the body and material reality as it is about the spirit and transcendent; it includes all areas of human, cosmic, and divine life.[15]

People with HIV often experience isolation as a result of AIDS-related stigma. When linked to a perverted understanding of sexuality, especially of female sexuality, religious concepts such as sin in Christian theology and papa/karma in Indian religions support the notion of HIV/AIDS as disgraceful and the person with HIV a victim of divine wrath. But spirituality can overcome this perversion and allow people with HIV to face the struggles of life with dignity, to affirm meaning and identity, and to lead a joyful life.

Regarding people with HIV, spirituality provides a different way of seeing our own lives, the lives of others, and all life in a different light and from a different perspective. The discovery of new light and wisdom reshapes the ability to reflect on the presence and help of God. Moreover, spiritual growth signals an inner awakening, a discovery and transformation of understanding. Responding to this growth, we answer to the dance of the spirit across the struggles, the depths, and the heights of human life. As Kenneth South notes, the spirituality of those with HIV emphasizes a "lived experience, an experience linked to our broken bodies and spirits, to nature, to relationships with others and society. It . . . seeks the fullness of life, a life that touches the hem of the spirit . . . [that] often resemble[s] the whirls of a dance."[16]

Spiritual resources require building a framework for strategies and planning to undergird ways of life, value systems, traditions and beliefs, and fundamental human rights. These references serve as the bases for appropriate responses to and sustainable actions for HIV prevention and care. These resources are central to the coping processes of women and men with HIV across cultural and religious boundaries; to ignore them denies crucial dimensions of embodied spirits. These resources improve the quality of life of patients and their families, who together face the problems associated with life-threatening illness. Spirituality provides positive resources for coping by locating and empowering the strength that ensures well-being for those with HIV and others despite the onset of AIDS, or death as it approaches.

Spirituality as Empowering

Consider four perspectives of power for spirituality: power over, power to, power with, and power within. "Power over" creates relationships of domination and subjugation. Power as dominion includes cultural and social systems of functioning and institutions that sustain and maintain it. The power of domination is not static; as Michel Foucault rightly points out, it circulates in the capillaries of the social body.[17] Domination and subjugation of "power over" is embedded in the everyday social and cultural practices in the entire society.

In the second conception of power, "power to," a person or a group can act without coercion. This power has positive connotations, enabling autonomy, choice, and the achievement of goals freely chosen. This power is necessary for realizing the inherent potentialities within and human flourishing of one and all.

The third conception, "power with," highlights the collective dimensions of power. Power is not what an individual possesses or loses; rather, this power derives from being together. Perhaps solidarity best expresses it. Insofar as subordinates and other weaker parties do not possess power individually, by exercising their "power with," collectively they could exert power equal to or greater than those holding "power over."

The fourth understanding, "power within," refers to what someone has within, no matter the external circumstances. Power within is connected with the subjectivity and moral agency belonging to everyone and fortifies self-confidence in the face of internal or external threats. This form of power is particularly significant for people with HIV.

Among those with HIV, these kinds of power, whether dormant or latent, endure. Nevertheless, all power valorizes subjectivity and the moral agency of even those people ostracized by society. Many women and men with fatal diseases claim their inner spiritual resources to empower themselves. Interactions with people with HIV confirm that the techniques of spirituality enhancing the power within enable them to transform adversity into occasions of spiritual fulfillment for themselves, for those with whom they live, and for society. In solidarity with persons with HIV, an empowering spirituality—relational, indigenous, and corporeal-centered—gives meaning despite viral load.

A Relationship-Based Framework

A study conducted in Chennai, South India, among people with HIV underscores that a relationship with a higher power, a renewed engagement with life, and a new relationship with oneself and the cosmos are qualitative ingredients in their spirituality practices.[18]

In connecting to God, touching the transcendent within, spirituality empowers. This connection (in Catholic terms, "communion") signals for people with HIV transcendence from the fatalistic notions of karma or sinfulness dominating some worldviews. Communion reaffirms intrinsic worth and confirms that we are created in God's likeness despite sickness or health. The Chennai study showed that 75 percent connected positively with the divine power; this experience challenges society's constructions of shame and

stigma imposed on those with HIV. Remarkably, 85 percent of the participants had the strength to cope and achieve acceptance of their condition,
despite the mental and emotional tensions wielded by negative social and religious constructions of the disease.

Spirituality focused their lives in line with the higher or sublime self.[19] An
in-depth focus on the sublime self enables those with HIV to face diagnosis
with equanimity. Sheena, a woman with HIV, reports that "our higher self is
the greater part of us from which we sometimes draw in times of deep inner
focus, exhilaration or extreme crisis. . . . We tap into our intuition, our wisdom and those abilities that seem to be beyond what we think of as normal."[20]
As we read in the testimonies of Mary, Remani, and Rita, their lives positively
affirm that they really are something greater than their diagnosis.

When HIV strikes, many begin to examine their lives so as to understand
their diagnosis. However curiously, HIV provides an opportunity to review the
past, consider the present, and contemplate where life will lead after the diagnosis. F. P. Lamendola and M.A. Newman observed that as patients came to
grips with the disease, a change in their lives "included a deepening of their
spirituality. They were facing the profound issues of living and dying in a
meaningful way."[21]

Mark Cichocki agrees: "An HIV diagnosis is often the stimulus needed for
a person to get in touch with the spiritual part of their life."[22] Neetu, HIV-positive through injecting drug use, presently works at a community drop-in center and outreach program for drug users. She has devoted her life after HIV
to helping people kick their drug habit. Says Neetu, "If not for my HIV diagnosis, I would still be 'shooting up' each night."[23]

Consciously or unconsciously, people use HIV as a way to better understand their spirituality and themselves. Spirituality helps them incorporate
HIV into their lives: the changes that result with diagnosis and the eventual
onset of AIDS. They reconcile themselves with the "new" person they have
become. They find significant meaning to life after diagnosis; spirituality helps
them let go of those things that were once important but that no longer fit.

The modern view of the human being as potentially all-powerful can pit the
individual against nature, against other human beings, and against the humane,
emotional, intuitive, and spiritual parts of the self. Drawn by the power of the
extraordinary faith that many ordinary people with HIV witness, I understand
that deeper growth and genuine spiritual empowerment come from accepting
the potential within and the relationship between the self and the cosmos;
though one, together we stand with all. Deepti Priya Mehrotra observes, "The
wave is small if it sees itself as an isolated wave, but large if it knows itself as
part of the limitless ocean—is able to become that ocean."[24] As Mehrota came
to understand this potential in her work with the New Delhi–based Forum for
Women and Religion, "it is important to understand and know oneself both
as wave and as ocean. This points first of all to the significance of examining
and deepening our own concerns, values, and identities."[25]

In many centers for people with HIV, the awareness of this intrinsic identification with the cosmos is facilitated and nurtured through the healing
forces of nature, stewardship relationships, and cosmos-centered meditation,
confirming universal harmony. These practices reclaim embodied relational
agency as the necessary theological anthropology in this age of AIDS.[26]

Indigenous Framework:
Integrating Therapies

Many centers use traditional, low-cost, and integrated therapies that include
nutrition, yoga, and individual-specific homeopathic and Ayurvedic medicines. These therapies are effective in delaying for up to fifteen years the
onset of AIDS.[27] The use of these therapies is based on an integrated and
holistic spirituality.

Traditional medicine recognizes that energy flows within, around, and
through all things. Energy cannot be destroyed, but when affected negatively
it leads to flow imbalances or disease. When affected positively, it leads to
equilibrium and health. Traditional medicine views disease not as an invasion
or poisoning of the body by a foreign organism but as an imbalance. Healing, therefore, is the art of manipulating the energy flows to reestablish balance in the whole, not just the area of complaint. Spirituality, unlike
allopathic medicine, is an integral part of traditional medicine and, individ-
ualized, no two people receive the same treatment, despite similar complaints
or the same condition.

Many factors, such as health status, beliefs, attitudes, and motivation
underlie decisions to use alternative therapies; at present, no clear or comprehensive theoretical model accounts for the increased use of these alternatives. In the case of HIV treatment in India, three assumptions prevail for their
use: technology, autonomy, and worldview.

Social workers involved with therapies for persons with HIV confirm this
dissatisfaction. Allopathic medicine is ineffective, produces adverse side effects,
especially in the case of antiretrovirals, and is impersonal, too technologically
oriented, and often too expensive.[28] Indigenous or traditional therapies have
fewer adverse side effects and offer nonaddictive and naturally occurring anal-
gesic relief.

Traditional medicines and alternative indigenous therapies allow for more
personal autonomy and subjective control over decisions relating to health
care. Unlike "Western medicine," which often involves treating specific symptoms, traditional healing practices see many dimensions to health and aim at
restoring balance between the body's *chakras* (energy centers) of mind, body,
emotion, and spirit. Alternative therapies are more compatible with patients'
values, worldviews, spiritual and/or religious philosophies and beliefs regarding the nature and meaning of health and illness. As many as 80 percent of

users of these complementary medicines are satisfied with the treatment. Interestingly, this satisfaction is not always dependent on a simultaneous improvement of health.

Devan Nambiar, an HIV-positive person of South Indian descent living in Canada, notes, "I've incorporated some of the Ayurvedic immune boosters into my health regimen. They are bio-available tonics prepared according to ancient Ayurvedic texts for boosting immunity, increasing muscle mass and energy, and reducing stress."[29]

Native therapies can increase immune function, lower viral load, and prevent infection. Holistic approaches further help as antidotes to the side effects of conventional medicine; they also relieve stress, depression, and fatigue, and improve general well-being. Taking a more holistic approach, many people with HIV report more positive experiences in contrast to their experience with allopathic medicine. One study that looked at the attitudes of people with HIV toward alternate medicines highlighted women's additional reasons for using them: they kept them healthier to look after family, conventional medicine neglected their needs, and indigenous medicines were "more natural/less toxic."[30] Alternative medicines offer more than physical and mental health care—they utilize spirituality. Through the patient's participation with nature, vital forces, and a "human" science, the quest for health assumes sacred proportions, revealing ultimate meaning and profound connections with the universe.

Corporeal-Centered Framework of Spiritual Coping

Nambiar affirms the body-centered nature of his spirituality and the reasons for abstaining from the allopathic medications and routine blood work prescribed for HIV patients. "I just listen to what my body needs. This is an innate skill that one must cultivate over time: an eastern cultural belief, a knowing—not something one can easily explain to persons steeped in highly technocratic cultures."[31] The body has the power to heal itself, and spirituality and therapy help this healing process. The body is inextricably linked with the self and personal identity, and to ignore the body, the spirit too may fail— all the more evident to persons with HIV, as Kenneth South explains: "AIDS is about life and death, about living life into death, about death of the body and healing of the spirit, about joy in the midst of suffering, about knowing the love of the spirit in the midst of bigotry, hatred, abandonment and fear."[32] A corporeal spirituality affirms that the body is not merely biological but that an elemental agency inheres—an agency that gains power especially in the fractured corpus of persons with HIV.

A reappraisal of the body and its affirmation in spirituality is helpful in reducing excessive fears and anxiety and in building inner strength through self-body awareness and relaxation. Thus, the aim of yoga is to help the individual balance *chakras*, relieve stress, and restore well-being; it supports detoxification, strengthens particular organs, improves stamina, and alleviates chronic fatigue. Two centers in South India utilize *asanas* (postures) and yoga philosophy to reduce the stress associated with HIV. They combine meditation and group sharing to deal with latent emotions, causing or accelerating progress to AIDS. Many practitioners in India have claimed positive results using Ayurveda and herbal medicine along with yoga meditation to treat AIDS.[33]

Conclusion

The acid test is not whether spirituality makes more sense of the human condition in the age of AIDS than fear. The poignant questions to a world that faces HIV/AIDS are "How have or will our lives change?" and "How may our world be transformed by grace and by our work for justice and the common good?" The inherent possibilities of a relational, indigenous, and body-centered spirituality provide one holistic response to the brokenness that AIDS reveals.

There is a brokenness
Out of which comes the unbroken,
A shatteredness out of which blooms the unshatterable.
There is a sorrow
Beyond all grief which leads to joy
And a fragility
Out of which depth emerges strength.
There is a hollow space
Too vast for words
Through which we pass with each loss,
Out of whose darkness we are sanctified into being.
There is a cry deeper than all sound
Whose serrated edges cut the heart
As we break open
To the place inside which is unbreakable
And whole, while learning to sing.[34]

Conclusion

Maria Clara Lucchetti Bingemer

Translated by Wanda Sily
with assistance from Mary Jo Iozzio

Kissing the Leprous

A Theological Praxis for AIDS

HIV/AIDS cries out for a theological response and pastoral action—a theological praxis. In this essay I will look at biblical presentations of leprosy to compare the treatment of people with leprosy there to people with AIDS today. Since Jesus approached rather than shunned people with leprosy, Christians must do likewise for people with HIV and AIDS. Theological praxis for HIV—the leprosy of our times—moves us toward dispositions in accord with God's heart.

HIV, Leprosy, and Scripture

If world statistics are shocking, they should guide reflection on the Word of God about the way disease is perceived in the Bible. Theology and pastoral praxis can define Christian dispositions in face of the loss of health by contagious diseases that endanger the community and raise difficult questions about God's justice and our response.

Lamenting with the prophet Jeremiah, "we wait for peace, but find no good; for a time of healing, but there is terror instead" (Jer 14:19). The New Testament likewise calls attention to epidemics that, among other catastrophes, devastate the earth and humankind: "There will be great earthquakes, and in various places famines and plagues; and there will be dreadful portents and great signs from heaven" (Luke 21:11).

Our scriptures refer often to a disease that, in many aspects, is similar to AIDS: leprosy. Leprosy, in fact, refers to many different infirmities. According to the purity laws of Leviticus (Lev 13:1–2, 44–46), leprosy encompasses, besides Hansen's disease,[1] a variety of superficial or deep skin infections, stained clothing and objects (13:47–59), and conditions found in houses (14:34–53). The Levitical Code concerns priestly functions, guarantees purity by distinctions among impurities (13:44), and dictates the attitudes of the impure in relation to the (pure) community, and vice-versa; sadly, that rule requires total distance of one from the other (13:45–46). This code prescriptively and proscriptively stigmatized: leprosy was a mortal disease resulting in the isolation of those with the disease (or its correlative expression) from community life—a curse and a penalty for sin.

The Levitical Code named the leper dirty and ritually unclean (13:2–3). Often considered plague-like, leprosy was thought to have been sent by God to punish the insurgence of the people (14:34).[2] The instructions against leprosy are rigorous: have no interaction with others, ring a bell calling attention to your leprous presence, remain otherwise apart from others. These rules limited contagion even centuries before physicians understood disease transmission.

Additionally, this teaching reckoned God's sovereignty over physical realities, including diseases, questions of hygiene, or the differences among animals, and sanctioned the Levitical Code as divinely inspired. There are, at least, two spiritual lessons about these instructions: obedience and distinctions of clean/unclean. Among the last instructions given by Moses, the people hear, "Guard against an outbreak of a leprous skin disease by being very careful; you shall carefully observe whatever the Levitical priests instruct you, just as I have commanded them" (Deut 24:8). Distinguishing between the clean and the unclean, the effect is underscored with ritual: "for an itch, for leprous diseases on clothing and houses, and for a swelling or an eruption or a spot, to determine when it is unclean and when it is clean. This is the ritual for leprous diseases" (Lev 14:54–57).[3]

Once the leprosy was discovered and the spiritual curse weighed, the biblical people sought every effort to rid the community of the leprosy among them and to protect the clean from becoming unclean. Lepers were publicly identified and removed from the community. When attempts to purify houses failed, they were razed to thwart the spread of the plague (14:43–45).

Scripture often identifies dishonorable living and sin with leprosy as just punishment. Leviticus 13 and 14 reveal the gravity of leprosy as both a physical and spiritual disease. Other texts dictate measures to be taken when suffering from leprosy or encountering someone with leprosy and include matters of sanctified food or food prepared in accordance with the Torah (see 22:4–6). The people are enjoined to obey everything the priests tell them, following instructions with the utmost care (Deut 24:8).

Second Kings exemplifies this obedience or suffer motif. The Syrian Naaman looked to Israel for a cure, and the prophet Elisha healed him of his leprosy. Healed of the disease, Naaman wished to recognize the God of Israel as true God; he offered gifts to the prophet, though Elisha refused them. Elisha's slave Gehazi went, unknown by Elisha, to Naaman to accept the silver and other gifts. When Elisha learned of Gehazi's ruse, he angrily appealed for God to intervene, and Gehazi was covered by leprosy (2 Kgs 5:8–27).

More than a terrible disease, leprosy is a sign from God with spiritual and religious consequences. King Azariah, chief priest Azariah, and Job, among those with leprosy, thought themselves struck by the Lord. This understanding affected them deeply, forcing reflection, rightly or wrongly, about theodicy, culpability, and changes in their lives (2 Kgs 15:5; 2 Chr 26:19; Job 2:7). A disease in which the physical reflects the spiritual, leprosy was increasingly a factor in the discrimination and isolation of those infected.

Jesus and Inclusive Practices

Even with careful reading and reflection on the New Testament, it is difficult to affirm that Jesus talked about himself as the Son of God and difficult to prove that the New Testament witnesses to this revelation. Nevertheless, the early Church acknowledged the divine nature of Jesus of Nazareth and lived in communities that grew from this witness. They understood that a different and unique relationship had existed between that man Jesus and God, that he had been different from other human beings.[4]

Jesus' attitude toward sinners and those excluded from social and religious communities is instructive. Jesus eats with sinners and publicans, those kept apart from the community—and from God (Matt 11:19). In the Middle East then as well as now, table sharing reflected a communal shared life and anticipated the eschatological feast between God and the people in the long-awaited consummation of time. Jesus' meal with sinners and publicans is inserted into this referential position; his action welcomes even sinners in communion with God.

In Luke 15, Jesus clearly demonstrates this intention, and finds his action condemned. The religious authorities directed that no one was to eat knowingly with this kind of people—that is, publicans and sinners. But Jesus answers them with parables: the lost lamb, the lost coin, and the prodigal son, where divine love and forgiveness are realized. Sinners, as wrongly ordered as they may be, join the eschatological feast with the Lord, receiving full citizenship in communion with God.

Among these "sinners" were women, children, and the sick. According to the law, to a greater or lesser degree, all of them belonged to the category excluded from salvation and friendship to God. And among the sick, the leprous were most excluded of all; the gravity of leprosy, risk of contamination, and curse weighed heavily upon them.

Jesus met the leprous many times. Often the lepers approach him and ask for cure. Jesus never runs nor sends them away. On the contrary, he approaches or lets them approach, and expresses his desire to heal (see Matt 8:1–3; Mark 1:40–48; 8:22–26; and Luke 5:12–14). Here as elsewhere, the

Gospels refer to Jesus' proximity to those rejected by society and religious law. His corporeal healthiness and holiness eclipses the corporeal sickness and sinfulness imposed on others; in perilous proximity to disease and impurity, he moves toward and touches the diseased and impure despite the threat of contagion. Whoever touches one of them becomes untouchable, but Jesus does not let this thinking deter him; his touching challenges the law. Jesus recognizes the power of touch for corporeal health and, by touch, the leper is relieved of infirmity, the twelve-year hemorrhage ceases, and sins are forgiven (Luke 7:36–50; 8:42–48).

To understand Jesus, consider his behavior. A faithful Jew actively participating in the synagogue and temple, he was not passive. His piety and mercy had a revolutionary characteristic that, for his religious contemporaries, was scandalous and sacrilegious.[5] The healed leper was "dead," but was now resurrected. The only existence lepers knew was apart from the community; any contact with lepers would contaminate others in the "holy" community, making them as impure and unclean as if they had gotten near a corpse.[6] For this exclusion, Jesus pities the marginalized leper, who, humiliated, falls on his knees, imploring Jesus to heal him. Jesus' mercy is not measured by the law but by the favor of those who pray for salvation. With a corresponding restoration of liberty, Jesus removes barriers, heals social wounds, accepts infirmities, and carries them in his person (see Mark 8:31–38).

Jesus' praxis gave room for ambiguous interpretations of his work and his own person, up to rejection on the cross. However, only from his action and his history is it possible to access, interpret, and understand him, opening to all who would believe the treasures of salvation and grace. Guided by compassion, Jesus reveals sympathy and empathy, and bestows benevolent love to those marginalized and those segregated on account of their impurity.

By touching the impure and thereby rejecting the purity laws, Jesus reveals the Incarnation Law, the solidarity of going toward the other, assumed in the strangeness and repugnancy of disease. Besides the scandalous consequences of impurity, Jesus liberates the people from oppressive and marginalizing religious laws, humanizes religious institutions, and founds the Incarnation Law. Standing above the law, he affirms the messianic-divine eschaton.

The leper too violates the law with his approach: "If you choose, you can make me clean" (Mark 1:40). The leper demonstrates a previous knowledge that he will not be rejected, and he knows the healing power of Jesus. Soon after the healing, Jesus sends the leper away, warning him not to say anything to anyone: "Go, show yourself to the priest, and offer for your cleansing what Moses commanded, as a testimony to them" (1:44; cf. Lev 14:1–32). In sending the leper to the priest, Jesus wants the representatives of the law to recognize the power of grace, upon which no other power prevails.[7] A situation ordinarily bringing exclusion becomes the reason for a reintegration in the communitarian life, and for an even greater involvement of people. R. Fabris writes that this is nothing short of the coming of the kingdom of God:

Where the kingdom of God stands, the barriers and exclusions fall. . . .
This is a proof and a testimony of a new time. The cured leper can
become a messenger of the word . . . communicating the new message
enclosed in Jesus' gesture . . . [that] the kingdom has come.[8]

Different Moments in Christianity

Mirroring Jesus of Nazareth, others also encountered people with incurable
and contagious diseases. They exercised compassion, stood with the other,
cured, cared for, and accepted. Consider Francis of Assisi (1181–1226). One
day Francis was riding his horse around Assisi, perhaps to the valley, near a
leprosarium. An ugly figure distracted him suddenly and made him aware of
the place: a leper stood there, dressed in rags and with purulent face. Initially
and with an instinctive gesture, Francis pulled the bridle of the horse to ride
away. However, recovering from his disgust, he reversed course. Francis dis-
mounted and, trembling in face of the decision born in his heart, found some
coins in his pocket and gave them to the leper. He forced himself still more:
taking the leper's hand with fear and compassion, he kissed it.

According to the *Legend of the Three Companions*, "a few days later, taking a huge amount of money with him, Francis went to the leprosarium, sharing the money with all of them, and kissing their hands." Francis reported,
"The event that seemed so bitter to me some days before, turned into something sweet both for the body and the spirit."[9]

In this experience, Francis made an irreversible and passionate step. To
understand the gesture, consider that dispositions toward leprosy had not
changed much from Jesus' time. As recipients of pity, lepers could receive
alms, but they had no rights. They would have had a funeral service in church,
with candles and black fabric, symbolizing their death in preparation for the
social death of the leprosarium.[10] Like the dead, for whom the liturgical
requiem was sung, the leper was mourned; though not entombed, the leper
was institutionalized in the outlying leprosarium. As earlier, they rang a bell
when they went from the leprosarium to announce their proximity and protect others from contagion.

Directed at a group that was almost entirely excluded and marginalized,
Francis' kiss of the lepers is astonishing. As Jesus knew, the little poor one, the
"poverello," of Assisi knew it was not enough to give money and material
things to them. Like Jesus, Francis was moved by God to approach and touch
that embodied infirmity. Without the experience of embracing those marginalized by society, approaching their marginality in ourselves, we will not
understand Francis' impulse and radical option to kiss, to love, to liberate.

Francis Xavier (1506–1552), the patron saint of missions and cofounder
with Ignatius of Loyola of the Society of Jesus, also served the poor and sick.[11]
In Goa, West India, Francis Xavier took care of the sick, the imprisoned, and

the lepers living outside the city. Asking nothing for himself, he cared for them day and night, washing their clothes, begging for alms in their names, feeding them, and administering the sacraments. He gave the testimony of his proximity, reintegrated them with communities and within themselves, and restored their dignity as human beings.

Damien of Molokai (1840–1889) presents a similar account. A Capuchin friar from Belgium, he went to Hawaii as a missionary. Damien responded to the call of the Most Reverend Maigret, Bishop of Hawaii, who was himself concerned with the pain, misery, and seeming abandonment of lepers who were living on the Hawaiian island of Molokai.[12] Lepers were forced to live totally segregated on this Pacific island until their deaths. When Damien arrived on Molokai on May 10, 1873, the people approached him and he did not hesitate to touch them. He was soon recognized as their hope and helped them organize a community. He loved them, identified with them and, though he did not know he too would become infected, he always preached with the words "We, leprous." When he learned of his leprosy, he declared that next Sunday, "Now I can say truly, my leprous brothers." Sharing their lives, he died among them.[13]

With Francis of Assisi, Francis Xavier, and Damien of Molokai, we see that life acquires it greatest significance and has immortal value when it is given over to those in need, poor or not, leprous or hale.

AIDS, a Contemporary Leprosy

Like leprosy, AIDS is a terrible and contagious disease. Like leprosy, it brings the prejudice that connects it to behaviors considered personal transgressions and sinful. As such, HIV/AIDS carries the stigma of immorality. And AIDS, like leprosy, carries the terrible weight of a theodicy that considers disease God's punishment. Associated early with the homosexual community in the Western world, many considered the worldwide spread of AIDS a signal that God was punishing sexual deviance.

However, the presumption of punishment from God is based on two false conceptions: (1) that God causes pain and (2) that God punishes sinners with infirmity. These claims result from a particularly harmful way of understanding and of conceiving guilt or innocence. And, perhaps more problematically, they suggest a distorted consideration of how a loving God works in this world.

The world is filled with people suffering from starvation, disease, misery, and many forms of oppression and injustice. Can these troubles mean that God wants people to suffer? Many suffer without being guilty; the world is an unjust place to live. In reality, AIDS is a tragedy, not the will of God. When God perceives that people are stigmatized and excluded because of AIDS, then even God suffers with them. God does not will tragedy or punish with disease;

God answers suffering with love. On some occasions, God may heal physical infirmity; on others, God sends enough grace to persevere in love in the burden of suffering, or when it is necessary to accept death.[14]

Moreover, there is no sense cloaking prejudice with religious coverings, as if God would reject people with AIDS because of some right or wrong association with sin. As God does not discriminate against or reject people, in the same way the Church, its theology, and its pastoral praxis are obliged to engage every effort to rescue the dignity and self-esteem of those who are sick. Those who have to carry the physical and emotional burdens of HIV and AIDS, with the heavier weight of the prejudice that isolates and excludes them, deserve more.

Infectious diseases, despite the positive effects of prevention programs, medical technologies, and social policies, continue to take numerous lives. This persistence reveals the inevitable limits of the human condition. However, the liberality of the human heart, based upon hard and efficient compromises, should never surrender the search for means and methods of effective intervention and relief of burdens. The examples of Francis of Assisi, Francis Xavier, and Damien witness that outreach.

John Paul II remembered that "many consecrated persons *have given their lives* in service to victims of contagious diseases, confirming the truth that dedication to the point of heroism belongs to the prophetic nature of the consecrated life."[15] These initiatives and generous gestures stand in opposition to many injustices. How can we forget the many people harmed by infectious disease, those obliged to live in segregation and all too often humiliated by stigma? These conditions manifest with ever greater gravity from the economic inequalities between the global north and south.[16] Benedict XVI speaks with clarity and compassion: "Closely following Christ's example, the Church has always considered care of the sick as an integral part of her mission. I therefore encourage the many initiatives promoted especially by the Ecclesial Community to rout this disease, and I feel close to persons with AIDS and their families, invoking for them the help and comfort of the Lord."[17]

The pope exhorts the Church to extend its efforts in "proximity with those who are sick" and afflicted by infectious disease—an aim to which the ecclesial community should be always devoted.[18] Christ's example, opposing the determinations of the temple, allowed the lepers to approach him. He restored their health and dignity as human beings, as have others in Christian witness. This rich tradition must continue and, through the exercise of charity toward the sufferer, make visible the values inspired by the gospel: the dignity of the person, mercy, and identification of Christ with the sick.

The pope recommends that proximity be joined with the evangelization of the "cultural environment" in which we live. Among the prejudices that limit or prevent efficient aid to victims of infectious diseases stands an attitude of indifference, exclusion, and rejection that wrongly supersedes the common good and social welfare. This attitude is reinforced by obsessions with physical appearance, health, and biologic vitality. A perilous cultural tendency reduces the individual to an enclave in our small world, rejecting the mandate to help those in need.[19]

John Paul II recognized "that suffering, which is present under so many different forms in our human world, is also present in order to unleash love in the human person . . . on behalf of other people, especially those who suffer. The world of human suffering unceasingly calls for, so to speak, another world: the world of human love; and in a certain sense man owes to suffering that unselfish love which stirs in his heart and actions."[20] We must find a praxis capable of helping those who are sick to endure their suffering, a way to transform this moment into grace for them and others, through participation in the mystery of Christ's church.

Conclusion: A Praxis of Affection, Friendship, and Mercy

In Brazil, the *General Instruction for the Evangelization of the Church in Brazil* offers directions for Church members toward those infected by HIV: a praxis of respect, restoration of their dignity, and loving proximity. These directions recognize that "the Church assumes this service and, without prejudice, receives, follows and fights for the rights of those infected with and affected by HIV/AIDS. Also, the Church undertakes prevention work, advocating Gospel values, being a merciful presence, and promoting life as the greatest gift."[21]

A theological praxis for HIV/AIDS must be organized as a service of the Church in prevention of the pandemic. The Church's primary mission is the evangelization of women and men, which it carries out today with an awareness of the needs of people living with HIV and AIDS. Following this praxis, Christian women and men collaborated in the search for an answer to HIV/AIDS. Members of organizations, agents of pastoral praxis, and people living with HIV met in a Latin American and Caribbean symposium in 2006, where they presented their concerns over HIV in Latin America, especially among populations poor and marginalized. They lamented that Latin America is not well represented in the global agenda. In every place, silence, indifference, stigma, and discrimination prevail, bringing still more suffering and death where welcome and treatment ought to hold. The Church has been a supportive presence in ensuring and fighting for the human rights of those with HIV and AIDS. The Latin American Bishops' Conference's "Pastoral Letter on HIV/AIDS" attends also to the need for collaboration. Catholic organizations join others to exchange experiences and increase efforts in response to the pandemic.[22]

The Church has the ability to influence public policies and, because of its structure and reach, it also has the conditions to amplify its contributions to prevention and the promotion of life. Thus, the Church must raise prophetic and theological praxis, denounce injustice where the roots of HIV lie, transmit hope, and support women and men infected with and affected by HIV and AIDS. They cry out for vision, which starts by recognizing the complex social problems surrounding HIV and supports an open dialog between science, religion, and society.

The continuing threat of HIV/AIDS demands double action: prevention of infection and assistance to those with HIV and AIDS. Christians and the Christian churches have been sensible, although slow, in response to this pandemic. The Church has several houses of shelter for those with HIV and, mirroring Francis' kiss, many pastoral agents accept those who are rejected by society and see in them the face of a neighbor in Christ.

The Church was not founded to condemn, but to manifest the benevolence of the Lord. Many people with HIV and AIDS carry strong feelings of guilt and bear the stigma of rejection. May the Church and all Christians bring the tenderness and love of God that restores to them their self-esteem, welcomes them into communion, and embraces them with a kiss.

Notes

Mary Jo Iozzio

1. James F. Keenan, SJ, with Jon D. Fuller, SJ, MD, Lisa Sowle Cahill, and Kevin Kelly, eds., *Catholic Ethicists on HIV/AIDS Prevention* (New York: Continuum, 2002), 14.

2. Jonathan Mann founded and directed Project SIDA, an AIDS research project based in Kinshasa, RD Congo (formerly Zaire), resulting in a collaborative effort of Zairian, U.S. (Centers for Disease Control), and Belgian AIDS researchers. In 1986, Mann founded the World Health Organization's Global Program on AIDS, based in Geneva, Switzerland. Mann's message is that "AIDS is a global crisis. . . . Human rights and public health go hand in hand: In each society, those people who before HIV/AIDS arrived were marginalized, stigmatized, and discriminated against become those at highest risk of HIV infection . . . a problem mainly for *les exclus*, the 'excluded ones' living at the margin of society." See Mark Schoofs, "Body and Soul, Remembering AIDS Pioneer Jonathan Mann," September 9, 1998, and http://www.thebody.com/content/art2779.html.

3. "Over 400 theological ethicists from more than 60 nations have travelled great distances. . . . We are accompanied by nearly 50 doctoral students, representing our next generation. We come with significant expectations." James F. Keenan, SJ, chair, "Catholic Theological Ethics in the World Church," program booklet (Casalserugo-Pd: Nuova Grafotecnica, 2006), inside front cover.

4. Catholic News Service, "Theologians Discuss Concerns at First Catholic Ethics Conference," *Morality* 31 (July 10, 2006), Padua, Italy. "I'm reluctant to use the term 'unprecedented.' . . . [Keenan] organized the gathering as an opportunity for the scholars to share the major ethical concerns they face and to exchange ideas on how to deal with the concerns." John L. Allen Jr., "A Truly International Gathering of Catholic Ethicists," *National Catholic Reporter*, July 14, 2006. Follow the link to the Padua Conference at http://www.catholicethics.com.

5. For the plenary papers see James F. Keenan, ed., *Catholic Theological Ethicists in the World Church* (New York: Continuum, 2007); for some of the concurrent applied ethics papers see Linda Hogan, ed., *Traditions in Dialogue: Applied Ethics in a World Church* (Maryknoll, NY: Orbis Press, 2008).

6. Thanks to Esther Daganzo-Canteñs, Maria Lourdes Cuervo, and Wanda Sily for their translation assistance.

7. Benedict XVI, Munich homily, September 10, 2006, http://www.vatican.va/holy_father/benedict_xvi/homilies/2006/documents/hf_ben-xvi_hom_20060910_neue-messe-munich_en.html.

Mary Jo Iozzio with Mary M. Doyle Roche and Elsie M. Miranda

1. "[The] doctrine of the Trinity, properly understood, is the affirmation of God's intimate communion with us through Jesus Christ in the Holy Spirit." Catherine Mowry LaCugna, *God for Us: The Trinity and Christian Life* (New York: Harper-Collins, 1991), 9.

2. Teresa Okure, SHCJ, "A Theological Reflection on 'Globalising Solidarity,'" speech given at Caritas Internationalis's 17th General Assembly, Rome, July 2003, http://www.caritas.org/jumpNews.asp?idChannel=3&idLang=ENG&idUser=0&id News=1522.

3. John Paul II, *Ecclesia in America*, January 22, 1999; John Paul II, *Ecclesia in Europa*, June 28, 2003; and John Paul II, *Novo millenio inuente*, January 6, 2001.

4. Youhanna-Fouad El-Hage, speech given at Caritas Internationalis's 17th General Assembly, July 2003, http://www.caritas.org/jumpNews.asp?idChannel=3&idLang= ENG&idUser=0&idNews=1513.

5. Phyllis Trible, *God and the Rhetoric of Sexuality* (Philadelphia: Fortress Press, 1978), 12–18.

6. See Catherine Mowry La Cugna, *God for Us* (San Francisco: HarperCollins, 1993).

7. Thomas G. Weinandy, "St. Irenaeus and the Importance of Being Human," *Logos: Journal of Catholic Thought* 6, no. 4 (2003): 20.

8. Alejandro Garcia-Rivera, *The Community of the Beautiful: A Theological Aesthetics* (Collegeville, MN: Liturgical Press, 1999), 63.

9. "The infant is brought to consciousness of himself only by love, by the smile of the mother. In that encounter, the horizon of all unlimited being opens itself for him, revealing four things: (1) that he is one in love with the mother, even in being other than the mother, therefore all Being is one; (2) that that love is good, therefore all Being is good; (3) that that love is true, therefore all Being is true; and (4) that that love evokes joy, therefore all Being is beautiful." Hans Urs von Balthasar, *My Work in Retrospect*, trans. Johannes Freiburg (San Francisco: Ignatius Press, 1993), 114.

10. Timothy Radcliffe, OP, homily, National Catholic AIDS Conference, 2004.

11. See Mary Ann Donovan, SC, "Alive to the Glory of God: A Key Insight in St. Irenaeus," *Theological Studies* 49 (1988): 238–97.

12. Weinandy, "St. Irenaeus and the Importance of Being Human," 10.

13. Benedict XVI, "The Human Family: A Community of Peace," message delivered at the 2008 World Day of Peace," http://www.vatican.va/holy_father/benedict_xvi/ messages/peace/documents/hf_ben-xvi_mes_20071208_xli-world-day-peace_en.html.

14. *Gaudium et spes* (1965), paragraph 26

15. See David Hollenbach, SJ, *The Common Good and Christian Ethics* (Cambridge, UK: Cambridge University Press, 2002); and *The Global Face of Public Faith: Politics, Human Rights, and Christian Ethics* (Washington, DC: Georgetown University Press, 2003).

16. See Tracy Kidder, *Mountains beyond Mountains: The Quest of Dr. Paul Farmer, a Man Who Would Cure the World* (New York: Random House, 2003).

17. *Gaudium et spes*, section 26.

18. For the text of the Universal Declaration on Human Rights, see http://www .un.org/Overview/rights.html; for the Millennium Development Goals, see http://www .un.org/millenniumgoals.

19. Marcia Angell, "The Ethics of Clinical Research in the Third World," *New England Journal of Medicine* 337, no. 12 (1997): 847–49.

20. *Gaudium et spes*, sections 1 and 4.

21. "To us, the Pastors of the Church, belongs the duty to educate the Christian conscience, to inspire, stimulate and help orient all of the initiatives that contribute to the formation of man. It is also up to us to denounce everything which, opposing justice, destroys peace." CELAM, "Justice and Peace," Medellín Conference Documents, 1968.

22. See CELAM, *Mensaje a Los Pueblos de América Latina*, Puebla Document (1979) §1134–56.

23. See Paul VI, *Octogesima adveniens* (1968), and Christine E. Gudorf, "Commentary on *Octogesima adveniens*," in *Modern Catholic Social Teaching: Commentaries and Interpretations*, ed. Kenneth R. Himes, OFM, et al. (Washington, DC: Georgetown University Press, 2004), 315–32.

24. See Caritas Internationalis, "Vision Statement," http://www.caritas.org/jump News.asp?idChannel=3&idLang=ENG&idUser=0&idNews=4500.

25. These statistics are from the US Census Bureau, http://www.census.gov/cgi-bin/ipc/idbrank.pl.

26. These statistics are from the UN, http://data.unaids.org/pub/EpiReport/2006/05-Asia_2006_EpiUpdate_eng.pdf. Alternately, Gao Qiang, executive vice minister of health, reported a reconfigured total in 2003 indicating that China has 840,000 people with HIV. See http://www.casy.org/overview.htm.

27. See Deborah Phillips, "Slaying the Dragon," University of Miami Medicine Online, http://www6.miami.edu/ummedicine-magazine/winter2003/dragon.html.

28. Reports on male homosexual transmission are scant. China has no comprehensive data regarding this population; if the incidence of AIDS present in Beijing hospitals indicates a nationwide ratio, 30 percent of HIV transmission is due to unprotected homosexual relations. See http://www.casy.org/overview.htm.

29. "The 'Four Frees and One Care' policy refers to a nationwide policy to provide the following services: 1. Free ARV drugs to AIDS patients who are rural residents or people with financial difficulties living in urban areas; 2. Free Voluntary Counselling and Testing (VCT); 3. Free drugs to HIV infected pregnant women to prevent mother-to-child transmission, and HIV testing of newborn babies; 4. Free schooling for children orphaned by AIDS; and 5. Care and economic assistance to the households of people living with HIV/AIDS. . . . The "Face-to-Face" programs bring educational materials into migrant and rural educational settings to raise awareness especially among China's school-age girls so that they will learn prevention techniques both to protect themselves and to prevent mother-to-child transmission if pregnant." *2005 Update on the HIV/AIDS Epidemic and Response in China*, report produced by the Ministry of Health, People's Republic of China, the Joint United Nations Programme on AIDS, and the World Health Organization, January 24, 2006, http://www.casy .org/engdocs/2005-China%20HIV-AIDS%20Estimation-English.pdf.

30. "Japan Only Now Confronting Rising HIV Rate," The Body: The Complete HIV/AIDS Resource, March 27, 2003, http://www.thebody.com/content/world/art28197.html.

31. "Stigma Associated with AIDS Very Strong in Japan," News-Medical.net, July 5, 2005, http://www.news-medical.net/?id=11497.

32. "Japan put on sex-trade watch list," International Edition, Breaking News, CNN.com, http://www.cnn.com/2004/US/06/14/trafficking.report/index.html.

33. *Japan's Response to the Spread of HIV/AIDS* (Tokyo and New York: Japan Center for International Exchange, 2004), http://www.jcie.or.jp/thinknet/pdfs/hiv.pdf.

34. "In the eyes of the Japanese public, responsibility for deciding the "public good" has long rested on the shoulders of the national government and the bureaucracy." Ibid.

35. "HIV/AIDS hardly stands out as top priority for the ministry [of Health, Labour, and Welfare], which is dealing with many other infectious diseases requiring immediate attention . . . all of which are seen as being in competition with one another." Ibid.

36. "Relationships in Japan . . . rely on Confucian-influenced notions of role and vertical social structure that are tied to a paternalism that is almost maternalistic in nature: nurturing, benevolent, kind and supportive. These sorts of relationships rely . . . on the Japanese concept of *amae.*" Leslie Di Mare and Vincent R. Waldron, "Researching Gendered Communication in Japan and the United States," in *Sex Differences and Similarities in Communication*, ed. Kathryn Dindia and Daniel J. Canary (New York: Routledge, 2006), 207.

37. "An estimated 150,000 people [70,000–290,000] people were newly infected with HIV in 2007 . . . a 150% increase over that time period." UNAIDS, "Aids Eoidemic Update," December 2007, http://data.unaids.org/pub/EPISlides/2007/2007_epiupdate_en.pdf.

38. "Rooted in the socioeconomic and sociopolitical upheavals of the 1990s, Russia's AIDS epidemic is driven mainly by the extraordinarily large numbers of people who inject drugs, many of them young and out of work. . . . Estimates vary, but at least 1% and possibly as much as 2% of the country's population inject drugs, and an estimated 5–8% of all men younger than 30 years have injected drugs." UNAIDS/WHO, "AIDS Epidemic Update," December 2005, http://www.unaids.org/epi/2005/doc/EPIupdate2005_html_en/epi05_07_en.htm. Similar causes are at work in Ukraine and Uzbekistan.

39. Few doubt the connection between joblessness and drug addiction. In the context of post-Marxist Eastern Europe, see Martha Rosler, "If You Lived Here . . . ," in *Marxism in the Postmodern Age: Confronting the New World Order*, ed. Douglas Kellner (New York: Guilford Press, 1995), 154–68.

40. UNAIDS/WHO, "AIDS Epidemic Update," December 2005, http://www.unaids.org/epi/2005/doc/EPIupdate2005_html_en/epi05_07_en.htm.

41. AIDS Foundation East-West, "Second Mass Media Campaign for Solidarity with PLWHA Russian Federation," 2006, http://www.afew.org/english/projects.php#hr.

42. AVERT, "HIV/AIDS in Russia, Eastern Europe, and Central Asia," 2008, http://www.avert.org/ecstatee.htm.

43. The thriving sex trade, IDU, and unprotected sex combine to spread HIV throughout Eastern Europe and Central Asia. Ibid., http://www.avert.org/ecstatee.htm.

44. Human Rights Worldwide, "Illicit Drug Use and Drug Policy in Russia, 2007, http://hrw.org/reports/2007/russia1107/2.htm#_Toc181427641.

45. The World Bank, "Central Asia AIDS Project Launched," May 12, 2005, http://web.worldbank.org/WBSITE/EXTERNAL/COUNTRIES/ECAEXT/EXTECAREGTOPHEANUT/EXTECAREGTOPHIVAIDS/0,,contentMDK:20488295~menuPK:571178~pagePK:34004173~piPK:34003707~theSitePK:571172,00.html.

46. This figure is from the US Census Bureau, http://www.census.gov/cgi-bin/ipc/idbagg.

47. HIV Insite, "Latin America," November 2006, http://hivinsite.ucsf.edu/global?page=cr05-00-00#S1.1X; UNAIDS, "AIDS Epidemic Update," December 2007, http://data.unaids.org/pub/EPISlides/2007/2007_epiupdate_en.pdf.

48. Pan American Health Organization, "What is PAHO?" http://www.paho.org/english/paho/What-PAHO.htm.

49. The World Bank, "HIV/AIDS in Latin America and the Caribbean," April 2007, http://web.worldbank.org/WBSITE/EXTERNAL/COUNTRIES/LACEXT/EXTLACR
EGTOPHEANUTPOP/EXTLACREGTOPHIVAIDS/0,,contentMDK:20560003~menu
PK:841626~pagePK:34004173~piPK:34003707~theSitePK:841609,00.html.

50. "Several factors may put migrants in this region at a high risk of HIV infection: poverty, violence, few available health services, increased risk-taking, rape, loneliness, and contact with large numbers of sex workers. In some cases, migrants themselves are sex workers, or resort to sex work while travelling in order to survive. . . . Since condom use is often low among regular sexual partners, male clients of sex workers may pass on HIV to their wives and girlfriends once infected." Avert, "HIV and AIDS in Latin America, 2008," http://www.avert.org/aidslatinamerica.htm.

51. "Throughout the region, women are becoming increasingly infected." HIV Insite, Latin America," November 2006, http://hivinsite.ucsf.edu/global?page=cr
05-00-00#S1.1X.

52. Inter Press News Agency, "Health: HIV Positive Women Activists in Latin America Stand Tall," May 11, 2007, http://www.ipsnews.net/news.asp?idnews=37705.

53. *Science*, "HIV/AIDS—Latin America and the Caribbean," July 28, 2006, http://www.sciencemag.org/sciext/aidsamericas.

54. "The world's failure to globalize health as a human right stands as a stark indictment to today's era of economic globalization. All too often the health of people living in poverty serves as collateral damage in the pursuit of economic growth and advancing commercial interests at all costs. The stakes of globalization have never been higher than around the crisis of HIV/AIDS due to the lethal relationship between AIDS, inequality, and poverty." Adam Taylor and Paul Farmer, "Liberation, Medicine, and US Policy toward Haiti," in *Let Haiti Live: Unjust US Policies towards Its Oldest Neighbor*, ed. Melinda Mile and Eugenia Charles (Coconut Creek, FL: Educa Vision, 2004), 26.

55. Haiti ranks 89th in world population and 188th in wealth (out of 224 and 229 nations, respectively). See Solcomhouse, "Poverty," 2007, http://www.solcomhouse
.com/poverty.htm and US Census Bureau, "Countries and Areas Ranked by Population," 2008, http://www.census.gov/cgi-bin/ipc/idbrank.pl.

56. UNICEF/UNITE for Children, "Preventing HIV Transmission in Haiti," 2008, http://www.unicef.org.uk/whatwedo/features/feature_detail.asp?feature=10&nodeid=
hivaids.

57. UNAIDS, "AIDS Epidemic Update," December 2007, http://data.unaids.org/pub/EPISlides/2007/2007_epiupdate_en.pdf, 30.

58. UNAIDS, "Uniting the World against AIDS: Haiti," 2008, http://www.unaids
.org/en/CountryResponses/Countries/haiti.asp.

59. National Geographic News, "AIDS Virus Travelled to Haiti, then US, Study Says," October 29, 2007, http://news.nationalgeographic.com/news/2007/10/071029
-aids-haiti.html.

60. AVERT, "The Origin of AIDS and HIV and the First Cases of AIDS," 2008, http://www.avert.org/origins.htm.

61. Haiti Innovation, "Here We Go Again: American Academics, HIV/AIDS, and Haiti," October 30, 2007, http://www.haitiinnovation.org/en/2007/10/30/here-we-go-again-american-academics-hiv-aids-and-haiti.

62. This is a rough estimate based on total population records of the world population clock. US Census Bureau, 2008, http://www.census.gov/cgi-bin/ipc/idbrank.pl.

63. This list was derived from a Columbia University Press survey. See "The Countries and People of Arabia," 2003, http://www.hejleh.com/countries.

64. UNAIDS, "Aids Epidemic Update," December 2007, http://data.unaids.org/pub/EPISlides/2007/2007_epiupdate_en.pdf, and HIV Insite, "Middle East and North Africa," December 2006, http://hivinsite.ucsf.edu/global?page=cr06-00-00.

65. Kaiser Network, "Kaiser Daily HIV/AIDS Report," November 9, 2006, http://www.kaisernetwork.org/daily_reports/rep_index.cfm?DR_ID=40953.

66. "HIV/AIDS cases have increased 300 percent in the Arab world over the past three years. This is against an annual rate of increase of 20 percent in the United States, Japan, Europe, and Australia." The Body Pro, "HIV/AIDS in Arab World up 300 Percent," March 29, 2007, http://www.thebodypro.com/content/world/art40433.html.

67. UNAIDS, "2006 AIDS Epidemic Update/Middle East and North Africa," http://data.unaids.org/pub/EpiReport/2006/10-Middle_East_and_North_Africa_2006_EpiUpdate_eng.pdf.

68. International Lesbian and Gay Association, "State-sponsored Homophobia," April 2007, http://www.ilga.org/statehomophobia/State_sponsored_homophobia_ILGA_07.pdf.

69. "It is 'important' for Arab countries to 'break the silence and denial and start moving in the right path by stopping stigma and discrimination.'" Kaiser Network, "Kaiser Daily HIV/AIDS Report," November 9, 2006, http://www.kaisernetwork.org/daily_reports/rep_index.cfm?DR_ID=40953.

70. Sandy Sufian, "HIV/AIDS in the Middle East and North Africa: A Primer," Middle East Report 233, Winter 2004, http://www.merip.org/mer/mer233/sufian.html.

71. "There are fears that HIV transmission could accelerate and broaden in the aftermath of more than two decades of war, as the lives of former refugees and displaced persons gradually return to normal." UNAIDS, "2006 AIDS Epidemic Update/Middle East and North Africa," http://data.unaids.org/pub/EpiReport/2006/10-Middle_East_and_North_Africa_2006_EpiUpdate_eng.pdf.

72. "The relative youth of Arab societies also puts them at risk. More than a third of Middle Easterners are younger than 25 years old. . . . School curricula include little about sexual health, so young people have scant access to reliable advice." Shereen El Feki, "Middle Eastern Efforts Are Starting to Tackle Taboos," *Lancet* 367 (March 25, 2006): 975–76.

73. Sufian, "HIV/AIDS in the Middle East and North Africa: A Primer," http://www.merip.org/mer/mer233/sufian.html.

74. The region is not absent of Christian, Jewish, and other religious traditions, but the dominance of Islam and the control of governments by a Muslim majority are the largest influences on the status of women throughout the region. The National Bureau of Asian Research, "Behind the Veil of a Public Health Crisis: HIV/AIDS in the Muslim World," June 2005, http://www.aei.org/docLib/20050608_eberstadtNBRreport.pdf.

75. "AIDS threat grows for Arab women," BBC News, February 23, 2005, http://news.bbc.co.uk/1/hi/world/middle_east/4289367.stm.

76. Women Living Under Muslim Laws, "Sexual and Bodily Rights in the Middle East and North Africa," May 14, 2004, http://www.wluml.org/english/newsfulltxt .shtml?cmd[157]=x-157-48946; emphasis added.

77. Women for Women Human Rights, "Gender, Sexuality, and the Criminal Laws in the Middle East and North Africa," http://www.synergyaids.com/documents/ Turkey_GenderSex&CriminalLaws.pdf.

78. The Coalition for Sexual and Bodily Rights in Muslim Societies General Assembly Meeting, April 26–29, 2007, Istanbul, Turkey.

79. Women for Women Human Rights, "The Coalition for Sexual and Bodily Rights in Muslim Societies," 2007, http://www.wwhr.org/musluman_toplumlarda _dayanisma_agi.php.

80. Women for Women Human Rights, "Homepage," http://www.wwhr.org.

81. WHO, "World Health Statistics," 2007, http://www.who.int/whosis/whostat 2007_10highlights.pdf.

M. Bernadette Mbuy Beya, CSU, with Jeanne Bluekens

1. Bernadette explains: In my culture, people address and commit to God all things, since God is the Lord of Life. People believe that if someone is sick, it is because God wants it. Our mission is to lead our people from this fatalist conception of life and of sickness or health. The goal of this prayer is to give to God that which belongs to God without denying our own responsibility to take care of ourselves. The prayers offered by suffering women are born from dire circumstances; they arise from the foundations of the heart in meditation and compassion. Jeanne, my Belgian sister, shared with me this preoccupation with women, whose suffering is helped by these spontaneous prayers. One woman said, "The Church sends us to pray but does not tell us how to pray; but this prayer to God that I see my own face places me directly before the face of God and helps me to speak with him." Even the title of the prayer, *Montre-moi mon visage*, contains resilient hope and faith in God: my true face is the one from my Creator, because I am the image of God, not the image of death or the battered or disfigured face of sickness.

2. Seigneur, montre-moi mon visage, celui que tu m'as donné toi-même le jour où tu m'as appelée à la vie! Laissez-moi toucher la frange de ton manteau car il est temps que je retrouve le goût et la joie de vivre envers et contre tout!

3. Scripture passages in this essay are translations from the French Bible (Louis II).

4. See M. Bernadette Mbuy Beya, "La femme africaine et la sexualité," in *The Will to Arise*, ed. Mercy Amba Oduyoye and R. A. Musimbi Kanyoro (Maryknoll, NY: Orbis Books, 1992), 155–79.

5. See Matt 9:18–26.

6. Littleton is a singer, songwriter, and ambassador of the Negro spiritual in France.

Lisa Sowle Cahill

1. For a more extended theological treatment, see Lisa Sowle Cahill, "AIDS, Global Justice, and Catholic Social Ethics," *Concilium* 2007, no. 3, 91–101; and Cahill, *The-*

ological Bioethics: Participation, Justice, and Change (Washington, DC: Georgetown University Press, 2005).

2. See especially John Paul II, *Sollicitudo rei socialis* (1987), nos. 38–39.

3. Henry J. Kaiser Family Foundation, "HIV/AIDS Policy Fact Sheet: The Global HIV/AIDS Epidemic in Sub-Saharan Africa" (June 2007), http://www.kff.org/content/factsheets.cfm?topic=hivaids.

4. Ibid., 2.

5. Ibid.

6. See "Two Cheers on Global AIDS," editorial, *New York Times*, June 18, 2007, A20.

7. Kaiser Family Foundation, "HIV/AIDS Policy Fact Sheet."

8. See Paul Collier, *The Bottom Billion: Why the Poorest Countries Are Failing and What Can Be Done about It* (Oxford and New York: Oxford University Press, 2007).

9. Laurie Garrett, "The Challenge of Global Health," *Foreign Affairs* 86, no. 1 (January–February 2007): 22.

10. Ibid., 23.

11. Ibid., 36–37.

12. Dashka Slater, "Delivering the Goods," *Santa Clara Magazine*, Summer 2007, 28–30; and the CFWshops Web site, http://www.cfwshops.org, n. 11.

13. Michelle Fertig and Herc Tzaras, *What Works: HealthStore's Franchise Approach to Healthcare*, World Resources Institute (Washington, D.C.), November 2005, available in PDF format at http://www.nextbillion.net/node/1643. The World Resources Institute promotes environmental conservation but is also pro-business. However, the HealthStore Foundation has been the subject of a 2007 PBS documentary (see http://www.pbs.org/now/shows/321/index.html) and gets a positive review from the Bellagio Forum for Sustainable Development, an international network of grant-providing institutions committed to "social progress." See Wayne Farmer and Gina Malloy, "The HealthStore Foundation," *The Forum: Magazine of the Bellagio Forum* 14 (March 2006): 12–15, http://www.bfsd.server.enovum.com/en/components/com_docman/d12.php?archive=0&file=RM9ydW1fTWFnYXppbmUxNC5wZGY=. See also Slater, "Delivering the Goods," 29.

14. See "Model Program Overview: South Africa," on the Harvard Medical School Division of AIDS's Web site, at http://aids.med.harvard.edu/oip.htm.

Y-Lan Tran, CND

1. UNAIDS and WHO, "The Global Coalition on Women and AIDS: 2006 Progress Report," accessible at http://womenandaids.unaids.org/publications.html.

2. See Lisa Sowle Cahill, "AIDS, Justice, and the Common Good," in *Catholic Ethicists on HIV/AIDS Prevention*, ed. James F. Keenan et al. (New York: Continuum, 2000), 282–93.

3. See WHO, "Vietnam: Summary Country Profile for HIV/AIDS Treatment Scale-up," (2005), www.who.int/hiv/HIVCP_VNM.pdf.

4. Lan Nguyen Thi Hoang, Jean Pierre Aboulker et al., "The Resistance of Anti-HIV Drugs in Ho Chi Minh City, Vietnam," *Journal of Practical Medicine: Scientific Research on HIV/AIDS from 2000 to 2005* (Ministry of Health, November 2005): 13–16 (original in Vietnamese).

5. This statistic is from the Joint United Nations Program on HIV/AIDS (UNAIDS), http://www.poverty.com/aids.html.

6. Huan Q. Trinh, "Introduction," *Journal of Practical Medicine* (2005): 5.

7. See the UNAIDS report, "AIDS Epidemic Update: December 2005 Asia 6," http://www.unaids.org/epi/2005/doc/EPIupdate2005_html_en/epi05_06_en.htm.

8. Ibid.

9. Ha Thi Lam et al., "A Number of Dangerous Behaviors at Risk of HIV Infection of Sailors at Thai Binh's Transport and Fishing Services," in *Journal of Practical Medicine* (2005): 78 (original in Vietnamese).

10. The transition of the nation from one with a socialist, planned economy to a market economy at the end of the 1980s included development of and access to worldwide mass media. This media provides helpful means of communication to promote human life, but it also imports certain negative lifestyles, harming the moral life. Vietnamese youth are not prepared to appropriate some lifestyles with moral discernment. Before 1989, the Vietnamese government condemned premarital sex as illicit and immoral and punished the wrongdoers. Today sex outside of wedlock, though not encouraged, is legally permitted.

11. Education programs have been changed many times in recent years and are heavy on theory. They do not help students to develop sufficiently their individual critical thinking skills. See Hung Q. Dang, "Morality is Misconstructed," *Catholics and Nation*, July 8–July 14, 2005, 54 (original in Vietnamese). Tran Tuan Huy, "Instrument to Prevent the HIV/AIDS Epidemic: Communication and Education," in *AIDS and Faith*, by the Pastoral Committee Caring for HIV/AIDS People (Archbishop House in Ho Chi Minh City, internal circulation, 2007), 150–53 (original in Vietnamese).

12. Quoc Ngoc, "AIDS Crisis and Our Opportunity," in Pastoral Committee, *AIDS and Faith*, 212 (original in Vietnamese).

13. WHO, "Vietnam: Summary Country Profile."

14. See Phan D. Nguyen, "Vietnamese Catholics Responding to the HIV/AIDS Pandemic," in Pastoral Committee, *AIDS and Faith*.

15. WHO, "Vietnam: Summary Country Profile"; Vu Ngoc Uyen, "Observation on Clinical Characteristics and Treatment of HIV/AIDS at Nam Dinh Hospital," in *Journal of Practical Medicine* (2005): 167.

16. Nguyen Dang Phan, "Vietnamese Catholic Responding to HIV/AIDS Pandemic," in Pastoral Committee, *AIDS and Faith*, 121.

17. UCA News, "Vietnam: The Local Church Trains Personnel to Serve HIV/AIDS Persons," in Pastoral Committee, *AIDS and Faith*, 65–68.

18. See Hop T. Nguyen, "Introduction," in Pastoral Committee, *AIDS and Faith*.

19. Last year, I submitted an article to the archbishop on condom use in the case of discordant couples; sadly, the bishop still keeps silent.

20. Ian Fisher, "AIDS, Condoms, and the Magisterium," *New York Times*, May 1, 2006, http://www.mirrorofjustice.com/mirrorofjustice/2006/05/aids_condoms_an.html.

21. Body Health Resources Corporation, "Catholics around the Globe Urge Pope Benedict XVI to Lift the Ban on Condoms," November 30, 2006, http://www.thebody.com/content/art38946.html.

22. WHO, "Vietnam: Summary Country Profile."

23. Nguyen Kham, "SIDA," in Pastoral Committee, *AIDS and Faith*, 29–34.

24. Gervas Rozario, "As AIDS Just Emerges in Bangladesh," in *Catholic Ethicists on HIV/AIDS Prevention*, 68.

25. Peter L. Tenore, "Internet Sex and Dating Sites Need Warnings," in *Topics in HIV Medicine* 14, no. 4 (2006): 146–47.

26. UNESCO, "UNESCO's Strategy for Responding to HIV and AIDS" (February 2007), 20, http://unesdoc.unesco.org/images/0014/001419/49998e.pdf.

27. Defined as Australia, Brunei, Cambodia, China, East Timor, Indonesia, Japan, (North and South) Korea, Laos, Malaysia, Mongolia, Myanmar, New Zealand, Philippines, Singapore, Thailand, Vietnam, and the Pacific Islands States.

28. John Paul II, *Familiaris consortio* (1981), section 22.

29. Myriam de Loenzien et al., "HIV/AIDS, Gender and Youth in Rural and Urban Vietnam: Knowledge, Attitudes, Behaviors, and Implications for Prevention," in *Scientific Research on HIV/AIDS from 2000 to 2005*, 90; UCA News, "Vietnam: Rural Women and Women Who Were FSW, Before Are Trained to Have Stable Jobs," in Pastoral Committee, *AIDS and Faith*, 41–42 (original in Vietnamese).

30. UCA News, "Vietnam: Helping Rural Women to Have Jobs in Order to Reduce Immigration and Risk of HIV/AIDS," in Pastoral Committee, *AIDS and Faith*, 73–76 (original in Vietnamese).

31. UCA News, "Vietnam: Building Up Houses for High-Risk Girls," in Pastoral Committee, *AIDS and Faith*, 35–37 (original in Vietnamese).

32. John Paul II, *Laborem exercens* (1981), section 19.

33. John Paul II, *Familiaris consortio*, sections 22–23.

34. John Paul II, *Laborem exercens*, 19.

35. Ngoc Thanh, "Prevention of Youth's Social Evils: Everyone's Responsibility," *Bing Duong Magazine* (July 11, 2006), www.baobinhduong.org.vn/detail.aspx?Item=7731 (original in Vietnamese).

36. Cuong V. Vo et al., "Communication on Knowledge about HIV/AIDS for Street Sex Workers in Ho Chi Minh City," unpublished paper, 1994 (original in Vietnamese).

37. In Hanoi, 70.4 percent of FSWs do not have sufficient knowledge of the methods of HIV transmission, or do not yet understand it correctly. See Nguyen V. Thanh et al., "The HIV Infection Situation HCV, HBV, Syphilis, Gonorrhoea, and Drug Use in FSW in Hanoi," in *Journal of Practical Medicine* (2005): 62.

38. UCA News, "Vietnamese Government Recognizes the Success of Individual Contact Approach in Helping IDU," in Pastoral Committee, *AIDS and Faith*, 38–40 (original in Vietnamese); UCA News, "Vietnam: A Religious Woman's Caring for FSW through 'Street Pastoral Ministry,'" in Pastoral Committee, *AIDS and Faith*, 47–49 (original in Vietnamese); UCA News, "Vietnam: Rural Women and Women Who Were FSW Before," 41–42 (original in Vietnamese).

39. Le Ngoc Thanh, "Catholics' Caring for and Educating Children Living with HIV," in Pastoral Committee, *AIDS and Faith*, 161–64 (original in Vietnamese).

40. UNESCO, "UNESCO's Strategy for Responding to HIV and AIDS."

41. Le Ngoc Thanh, "Catholics' Caring for and Educating Children," 161–73.

42. Interview with Fr. Le Quang Uy, "The Most Effective Therapy for the Century Disease: Love and Spiritual Power," in Pastoral Committee, *AIDS and Faith*, 192–97 (original in Vietnamese).

43. Nhom Tieng Vong (Hoping Voice Group), "Extraordinary Liveliness of a Good Mother Living with HIV," in Pastoral Committee, *AIDS and Faith*, 295–300 (original in Vietnamese).

44. Toan Anh, *Con nguoi Viet-Nam (Vietnamese People)* (HCMC Publisher, 1996), 333–34.

45. Bich Van, "The Caretaker of HIV/AIDS Patients at Home," in Pastoral Committee, *AIDS and Faith*, 109–12 (original in Vietnamese).

46. This was revealed in a private sharing among a Catholic doctors group in Ho Chi Minh City; also see "Sad Night in a Province," in Pastoral Committee, *AIDS and Faith*, 82 (original in Vietnamese).

47. David C. Thomasma, "The Basis of Medicine and Religion: Respect for Persons," in *On Moral Medicine: Theological Perspectives in Medical Ethics*, ed. Stephen E. Lammers and Allen Verhey, 2nd ed. (Grand Rapids: Wm. B. Eerdmans Publishing Co., 1998), 423.

48. Le Huu Trac, or Hai Thuong Lan Ong (pseudonym), (1724–1791) was the great writer and Vietnamese traditional physician. Considered to be the founder of Vietnam traditional medicine, he led a virtuous and devotional life. Hai Thuong's *Summary of Theories and Practices in Traditional Medicine* laid out a solidly foundational theory and practice of traditional medicine and ethics for Vietnamese physicians. See Huong X. Nguyen, "Hai Thuong Lan Ong Le Huu Trac with His Great Medical Cause," *Vietnam Traditional Medicine Journal*, no. 358 (February 2004): 5–9 (original in Vietnamese).

49. "The Hippocratic Oath," in Lammers and Verhey, *On Moral Medicine*, 107.

50. National Conference of Catholic Bishops, "Ethical and Religious Directives for Catholic Health Care Services" (2001), part 1, introduction, http://www.usccb.org/bishops/directives.shtml.

51. Benedict M. Ashley and Kevin D. O'Rourke, *Ethics of Health Care: An Introductory Textbook*, 2nd ed. (Washington, DC: Georgetown University Press, 1994), 76–77.

52. Benedict M. Ashley and Kevin D. O'Rourke, *Health Care Ethics: A Theological Analysis*, 4th ed. (Washington, DC: Georgetown University Press, 1997), 75.

53. *Hai Thuong's Summary of Theories and Practices in Traditional Medicine*, book 1, ed. Mong V. Dinh, Hoa T. Nguyen, Long D. Le, trans. Tiep Quy Ngo and Gian T. Nguyen (Tây Ninh: HCMC Traditional Medicine Association and Tay Ninh Traditional Medicine Association, 1987), 33–35; Edmund D. Pellegrino, and David Thomasma, *For the Patient's Good: The Restoration of Beneficence in Health Care* (New York: Oxford University Press, 1988), 118–19; Pellegrino, *The Christian Virtues in Medical Practice* (Washington, DC: Georgetown University Press, 1996), 1–4.

54. Bernard Häring, "The Physician-Patient Relationship," in Lammers and Verhey, *On Moral Medicine*, 793.

Maria Cimperman, OSU

1. In general, I use "Church" in this essay to refer to the Roman Catholic Church as an institution. Particular groups within the church are specified as needed.

2. Henry J. Kaiser Family Foundation, "HIV/AIDS Policy Fact Sheet: The Global AIDS Epidemic," June 2007, http://www.kff.org/hivaids/upload/3030_09.pdf; UNAIDS, "2006 AIDS Epidemic Update," December 2006, http://www.unaids.org/en/HIV_data/epi2006.

3. Kaiser Family Foundation, "HIV/AIDS Policy Fact Sheet"; UNAIDS, "2006 AIDS Epidemic Update."

4. See, for example, the current statistics posted on the following Web sites: UNAIDS, http://www.unaids.org; and the Henry J. Kaiser Family Foundation, http://kff.org.

5. See, for example, Gillian Paterson, *Women in the Time of AIDS* (Maryknoll, NY: Orbis Books, 1996; the UNAIDS Web site, http://www.unaids.org; and Musa W. Dube and Musimbi Kanyora, eds., *Grant Me Justice: HIV/AIDS and Gender Readings from the Bible* (Maryknoll, NY: Orbis Books, 2005).

6. Commission for Healthcare of the Catholic Bishops' Conference of India, *Commitment to Compassion and Care: HIV/AIDS Policy of the Catholic Church in India* (August 2005), 21.

7. Ibid., 22.

8. Ibid.

9. Ibid., 23. See UNAIDS, "Fact Sheets—Men Make a Difference," 1, http://data.unaids.org/pub/Report/2000/20000622_wac_men_en.pdf.

10. Commission for Healthcare of the CBCI, *Commitment to Compassion and Care*, 23.

11. Ibid., xiii.

12. Ibid., 24.

13. I am grateful to Fr. Robert J. Vitillo for the copy of this one-page statement. He served as the facilitator for the meeting that generated the document. Fr. Vitillo is the special advisor on HIV and AIDS for Caritas Internationalis. The Roman Catholic bishops who signed this statement are the archbishop of Maseru and the bishop of Leribe.

14. "Statement of Commitment by Lesotho's Church Leaders on AIDS," http://data.unaids.org/pub/ExternalDocument/2007/20070718_lesothodeclaration_en.pdf.

15. While the focus is on women and girls here, the benefits extend as well to men and boys. I am convinced that when either women or men (or girls and boys) are treated with less than full human dignity, the dignity of all is diminished. Together we are one human family.

16. I am grateful to Constance FitzGerald, OCD, for the insight about the integration of contemplation and social commitment. See FitzGerald, "Impasse and Dark Night," in *Living with Apocalypse: Spiritual Resources for Social Compassion*, ed. Tilden H. Edwards (San Francisco: Harper & Row, 1984), 93–116.

17. This participation will not exclude men as important conversation and action partners, but it will place women into crucial conversations where they are not equal participants at this time. Egyptian physician Mahmoud Fathalla warns, "Women are not dying because of a disease we cannot treat. They are dying because societies have yet to make the decision that their lives are worth saving." http://72.14.253.104/search?q=cache:lfm3t3hkUgUJ:www.iwhc.org/getinvolved/events/2007gala/rosenfield.cfm+Mahmoud+Fathalla+women+are+not+dying&hl=en&ct=clnk&cd=5&gl=us. Mahmoud Fathalla is professor of obstetrics and gynecology, Assuit University, and is immediate past president of the International Federation of Gynecology and Obstetrics (FIGO).

18. For more on these goals, see http://www.un.org/millenniumgoals. This agenda reflects a global partnership that requires participation of rich and poor countries in specific ways.

19. "Since the advent of combination, anti-retroviral medications that are capable of prolonging the life of people living with AIDS, both the late Pope John Paul II and,

more recently, Pope Benedict XVI, and their personal representatives at various international conferences, tirelessly advocated to make such medications available to all people in the world. Not content with restricting the access of such medications to those in high income countries who could afford the prices imposed by pharmaceutical companies, the late Pope John Paul II has emphasized the Church's consistent teaching that there is a "social mortgage" on all private property, that this concept must be applied, as well, to "intellectual property," and that "the law of profit alone cannot be the norm of that which is essential in the struggle against hunger, sickness, and poverty." *Message to the Jubilee 2000 Debt Campaign*, September 23, 1999, quoted at http://www.caritas.org/jumpNews.asp?idLang=ENG&idUser=0&idChannel=3& idNews=4502.

20. That is, in areas presumed to be in harmony with gospel values.

21. See Richard Eves, *Exploring the Role of Men and Masculinities in Papua New Guinea in the 21st Century: How to Address Violence in Ways That Generate Empowerment for Both Men and Women* (Sydney: Caritas Australia, 2008), http://www.baha.com.pg/downloads/Masculinity%20and%20Violence%20in%20PNG.pdf.

22. United States Conference of Catholic Bishops, "When I Call for Help: A Pastoral Response to Domestic Violence against Women," 10th anniversary ed., November 12, 2002, http://www.usccb.org/laity/help.shtml.

23. In some places, misunderstandings about church teachings are impediments to women trying to make decisions for the safety and care of themselves and also their families. Churches may also need to connect with other groups to officer support to women parishioners leaving abusive relationships.

24. Though all areas of church ministry are important to discuss, here I simply call for the intentional invitation and education of women for all areas of ministry in which the church currently is publicly engaged.

25. David N. Power, OMI, "Eucharistic Justice," *Theological Studies* 67 (2006): 879.

26. For further consideration of grief and lament, see Maria Cimperman, *When God's People Have HIV/AIDS: An Approach to Ethics* (Maryknoll, NY: Orbis Books, 2005).

Margaret A. Farley

1. Joint United Nations Programme on HIV/AIDS and World Health Organization, *2007 AIDS Epidemic Update*, http://www.unaids.org/en/KnowledgeCentre/HIVData/EpiUpdate/EpiUpdArchive/2007/default.asp.

2. According to the *Fact Sheet*, about 50 percent of the difference between previous and current (2007) estimates is explained by reductions in estimates of prevalence in India. Other countries with reduced estimates are Nigeria, Mozambique, Kenya, and Angola.

3. For a detailed history and description of the Women's Initiative and the Circle of Concerned African Women Theologians, see Margaret A. Farley, "Partnership in Hope: Gender, Faith, and Responses to HIV/AIDS in Africa," *Journal of Feminist Studies in Religion* 20 (Spring 2004): 133–48. See also Farley, *Compassionate Respect: A Feminist Approach to Medical Ethics and Other Questions* (New York: Paulist Press, 2002), 6–20.

4. Robert J. Vitillo, *Universal Access to HIV Prevention, Care, Treatment and Support*, Report to Caritas Internationalis (Geneva, Switzerland, 2006). In light of UNAIDS and WHO's *2007 AIDS Epidemic Update*, these numbers may be revised somewhat downward; they will nonetheless remain astonishing.

5. UNAIDS and WHO, *2007 AIDS Epidemic Update*. Despite new sophistication in estimates, the numbers remain unstable; the range within which estimates are calculated are significant in themselves.

6. See Alison Munro, "In Conversation with the Catholic Church: A Response to AIDS," Report from South Africa Bishops Conference AIDS Office, 2006, http://sacbc.org.za/pdfs/aids_office/CONFEREnce,%20mUNRO,%202005.PDF.

7. Isabel Apawo Phiri, "African Women of Faith Speak Out in an HIV/AIDS Era," in *African Women, HIV/AIDS, and Faith Communities*, ed. Isabel Apawo Phiri and Beverly Haddad (Pietermaritzburg, South Africa: Cluster Publications, 2004), 9.

8. For a fuller consideration of these patterns, see Margaret A. Farley, *Just Love: Framework for a Christian Sexual Ethics* (New York: Continuum, 2006), 79–89.

9. I frequently refer in this essay to faith traditions and Christian churches in the plural. I have found similar problems across traditions and across churches. Nonetheless, given the overall focus of this volume, I note examples recognized as more particular to the Roman Catholic Church and tradition than to other Christian churches or world religious traditions.

10. See my treatment of this cross-cultural work in *Just Love*, especially in chapter 3.

11. I turn therefore to a more particular focus on Christian churches and to a concern that has been heightened through my experience of responses to HIV/AIDS by African Roman Catholic women. Nonetheless, there are clear analogies to be drawn, both ecumenical and interfaith.

12. I by no means intend to imply that condoms alone can solve the problems of the AIDS pandemic. Condoms are necessary as a strategy, but they are not sufficient. This issue is both exaggerated and underplayed, to the detriment of many efforts at AIDS prevention.

13. Changes in Catholic social teaching regarding rights to private property and the permissibility of slavery are examples of developments in social ethics. It is difficult to find such examples in sexual ethics, for reasons that have been critiqued by moral theologians for many years. Nonetheless, see John T. Noonan, *A Church That Can and Cannot Change* (Notre Dame, IN: University of Notre Dame Press, 2005), esp. 161–90.

Carolyn Sharp

1. See Lisa Sowle Cahill, *Sex, Gender, and Christian Ethics* (New York: Cambridge University Press, 1996), 109–20; and Dorothee Soelle with Shirley A. Cloyes, *To Work and to Love: A Theology of Creation* (Philadelphia: Fortress Press, 1984), 143–44.

2. Maria Cimperman, *When God's People Have HIV/AIDS: An Approach to Ethics* (Maryknoll, NY: Orbis Books, 2005), 11–13, 38–41, 52–56.

3. Edwin Cameron, foreword to *Waiting to Happen: HIV/AIDS in South Africa— The Bigger Picture*, by Liz Walker, Graeme Reid, and Morna Cornell (Cape Town: Double Storey, 2004), 8.

4. Didier Fassin, *When Bodies Remember: Experiences and Politics of AIDS in South Africa* (Berkeley: University of California Press, 2007), 208–9.

5. Gillian Paterson, *AIDS Related Stigma: Thinking Outside the Box—The Theological Challenge* (Geneva: World Council of Churches), 1.

6. Okwui Enwezor, "The Uses of Afro-Pessimism," in *Snap Judgements: New Positions in Contemporary African Photography* (New York: International Center for Photography, 2006), 10–19. See also Jill Olivier, "Where Does the Christian Stand? Considering a Public Discourse of Hope in the Context of HIV/AIDS in South Africa," *Journal of Theology in Southern Africa* 126, (2006): 81–90.

7. For a discussion of insufficient pastoral care, see Agbonkhianmeghe E. Orobator, *From Crisis to Kairos: The Mission of the Church in the Time of HIV/AIDS, Refugees, and Poverty* (Nairobi: Pauline Publications Africa, 2005), 101–6.

8. For a discussion of racism, see Paul Farmer, *AIDS and Accusation: Haiti and the Geography of Blame* (Berkeley: University of California Press, 1992).

9. See Jonathan Morgan and the Bambanani Women's Group, *Long Life: Positive HIV Stories* (Cape Town: Double Storey Books, 2003).

10. Fassin, *When Bodies Remember*, 148.

11. See Edwin Cameron, *Witness to AIDS* (New York: I. B. Taurus, 2007), 185–88.

12. James R. Cochrane, "Of Bodies, Barriers, Boundaries, and Bridges: Ecclesial Practice in the Face of HIV and AIDS," *Journal of Theology for Southern Africa* 126 (2000): 11.

13. Michael Czerny, "Fighting HIV/AIDS: But Are ARVs Enough?" *Challenge* 8, no. 4 (2006): 30–31.

14. Nomawethu, in Morgan et al., *Long Life*, 24.

15. Babakwa Cekiso, in Morgan et al., *Long Life*, 170.

16. Fassin, *When Bodies Remember*, 204.

17. Paterson, *AIDS Related Stigma*, 9.

18. Soelle with Cloyes, *To Work and to Love*, 134.

19. Fassin, *When Bodies Remember*, 209. Disclosure of infection always carries risks. See Radikobo Ntsimane, "To Disclose or Not to Disclose: An Appraisal of the Memory Box Project as a Safe Space for Disclosure of HIV Positive Status," *Journal of Theology for Southern Africa* 125 (2006): 7–20.

20. Bulelwa Nokwe, in Morgan et al., *Long Life*, 86. The risk of mother-to-child transmission is around 7 percent.

21. Paterson, *AIDS Related Stigma*, 2.

22. Ibid., 9.

23. Ibid., 11.

24. Soelle with Cloyes, *To Work and to Love*, 130.

25. Cochrane, "Of Bodies, Barriers, Boundaries, and Bridges," 19.

26. Olivier, "Where Does the Christian Stand?" 97–98.

27. Sexual conservatives use the suffering and anguish caused by the pandemic to bolster cynical views of contemporary sexuality as a whole. See John Grabowski, *Sex and Virtue: An Introduction to Sexual Ethics* (Washington, DC: Catholic University of America Press, 2003), 4–9.

28. See Paul Thomas and Jon W. Foster, *AIDS, Development, and Canadian Policy: Achieving Universal Access by 2010* (Ottawa: North-South Institute, 2007).

29. Babalwa Cekiso, in Morgan et al., *Long Life*, 170.

30. Soelle with Cloyes, *To Work and to Love*, 154–55.

Agnes M. Brazal

1. See Marilen J. Dañguilan, MD, *Women in Brackets: A Chronicle of Vatican Power and Control* (Metro Manila: Philippine Center for Investigative Journalism, 1997).

2. Ibid., 114. Par. 7.45 states, "Recognizing the rights, duties and responsibilities of parents[,] . . . countries should, where appropriate, remove legal, regulatory and social barriers to reproductive health information and care for adolescents."

3. These statistics are from "Philippine Religion," from the Web site of Dog Meat Trade.com: http://www.dogmeattrade.com/library_articles/philippine_religion.html.

4. The number of cases is difficult to identify. A 2005 UNAIDS update of adults aged 15 to 49 with HIV/AIDS reports 12,000. See "HIV/AIDS in Philippines," http://hivinsite.ucsf.edu/global?page=cr08-rp-00. The Philippines NGO Support Program estimates 25,000, according to the Web site of the Alliance Linking Organisation, http://www.aidsalliance.org/sw7228.asp. The government HIV/AIDS registry reports 2,719 (December 2006).

5. This survey included only one other Asian country, Thailand. Cecile C. A. Balgos, *Drugs, Death, and Disease: Reporting on AIDS in Southeast Asia* (Quezon City, Philippines: Philippine Center for Investigative Journalism and United Nations Educational, Scientific, and Cultural Organization, 2001).

6. UNAIDS and WHO, *AIDS Epidemic Update* (2006), 36, http://data.unaids.ord/pub/EpiReport/2006/05.Asia_2006_EpiUpdate_eng.pdf.

7. HIV/AIDS Registry, Department of Health, National Epidemiology Center, Philippines (2006).

8. UNAIDS, *HIV/AIDS in the Philippines: Keeping the Promise—Primer on the UNGASS Declaration of Commitment on HIV/AIDS*, UN General Assembly, Special Session on HIV/AIDS, June 25–27, 2001 (Makati: UNAIDS, 2001), 7.

9. Corazon M. Raymundo and Grace T. Cruz, eds., *Youth Sex and Risk Behaviors in the Philippines: A Report on a Nationwide Study—2002 Young Adult Fertility and Sexual Study (YAFS 3)* (Quezon City, 2004). From various ethno-linguistic groups and religious and socioeconomic backgrounds, the study adhered to the international definition of adolescents as 15 to 24 but included those from 25 to 27 to further the analysis.

10. The first study was in 1982, the second in 1994.

11. *Fourth AIDS Medium Term Plan 2005–2010 Philippines* (Philippine National AIDS Council supported by UNAIDS, 1992), 9. YAFS I (1982) reported an estimated 12 percent of young women engaged in premarital sex; no data was given for men. *Sexual and Reproductive Health of Adolescents and Youths in the Philippines: A Review of Literature and Projects 1995–2003* (World Health Organization Western Pacific Region, 2005), 33.

12. Raymundo and Cruz, *Youth Sex and Risk Behaviors in the Philippines*, 81.

13. *Fourth AIDS Medium Term Plan*, 9.

14. Raymundo and Cruz, *Youth Sex and Risk Behaviors in the Philippines*, 80.

15. More than 20 percent of HIV cases in the Philippines were due to male-to-male transmission. The rate is probably higher, but social stigma prevents men from admitting homosexual activity. *HIV/AIDS Country Profile Philippines 2002* (Manila: Philippine National AIDS Council, 2003), 10.

16. Ibid., 89.

17. *Sexual and Reproductive Health of Adolescents and Youths*, 41.

18. Carolina Ruiz-Austria, "Say It Isn't Sex: The Politics of Sex Education in the Philippines," *Public Policy* 10, no. 2 (July–December 2006): 113.

19. Peter J. Smith, "Philippines Scraps Sex Education in Schools after Catholic Opposition," http://www.lifesite.net/ldn/2006/jun/06061205.html.

20. Ibid.

21. Health Action Information Network (HAIN), *A Study on the Knowledge, Attitudes, Practices, and Behavior toward HIV/AIDS and Sexual Health Practices among Filipino Youth* (Makati City, Philippines: UNICEF, 2006), 15, 20. This study, more recent than YAFS III, is based on a smaller sample (4,111), and though wide enough to cover the entire country, it may not be considered entirely representative.

22. Raymundo and Cruz, *Youth Sex and Risk Behaviors in the Philippines*, 46–49.

23. "Republic Act 8504—The Philippine AIDS Prevention and Control Act of 1998," *HIV/AIDS in the Philippines: Keeping the Promise; Primer on the UNGASS Declaration of Commitment on HIV/AIDS*, UN General Assembly, Special Session on HIV/AIDS (25–27 June 2001), 44–45. Also on artificial contraception, see Robert Blair Kaiser, *The Encyclical That Never Was: The Story of the Pontifical Commission on Population, Family, and Birth, 1964–66* (London: Sheed & Ward, 1987). On HIV prevention, see James Keenan and Jon Fuller, introduction to *Catholic Ethicists on HIV/AIDS Prevention*, ed. James Keenan with Jon Fuller, Lisa Cahill, and Kevin Kelly (Quezon City: Claretian Publications, 2001), 22–24.

24. For a background on the Philippine church's intervention in policy making pertaining to reproductive health issues, see Dañguilan, *Women in Brackets*; Reynaldo H. Imperial and Diane G. Mendoza, *Sex, Church, and a Free Press: Safe Sex and the Media in Southeast Asia* (Manila: AIDS Society of the Philippines, 2004), 2–9; and Ruiz-Austria, "Say It Isn't Sex," 113–33.

25. Frances Kissling and Geoffrey Clifton-Brown, "The Vatican and the Politics of Reproductive Health," http://www.catholicsforchoice.org/topics/politics/documents/1996houseoflords.pdf. While I engage the proposals of Kissling and Clifton-Brown, I do not necessarily agree fully with their stance on abortion.

26. Imperial and Mendoza, *Sex, Church, and a Free Press*, 6.

27. Kissling and Clifton-Brown, "Vatican and the Politics of Reproductive Health."

28. John Paul II, *Centesimus annus* (1991), 46.

29. Pontifical Council for Justice and Peace, *Compendium of the Social Doctrine of the Church* (Vatican City: Librería Editrice Vaticana, 2004), 191.

30. "Pulse Asia's March 2007 Ulat ng Bayan Survey: Media Release on Family Planning," http://pulseasia.newsmaker.ph/main.asp?mode=&page=article&articleID=7413186670&sec.

31. On *sensus fidelium* and "reception," see Paul Crowley, "Catholicity, Inculturation, and Newman's *Sensus Fidelium*," *Heythrop Journal* 33 (1992): 161–74; and Hervé Legrand, "Reception, *Sensus Fidelium* and Synodal Life: An Effort at Articulation," *Jurists* 57, no. 1 (1997): 405–31.

32. Pontifical Council for Justice and Peace, *Compendium of the Social Doctrine of the Church*, 414.

33. Dañguilan, *Women in Brackets*, 5; Imperial and Mendoza, *Sex, Church, and a Free Press*, 76. In 1995, pro-life Philippines, with the support of the hierarchy, alleged that the tetanus toxoid used in immunization programs worldwide for the past fifty years is an abortifacient. The strong pressure from the hierarchy caused its temporary

withdrawal from use in the Philippines, despite the scientific validation of safety, thus depriving many women and children of protection from tetanus. The controversy ceased when John Paul II wrote to the Catholic hierarchy to desist from issuing statements against the toxoid until proven scientifically that it is an abortifacient. Dañguilan, *Women in Brackets*, 129–37.

34. Centers for Disease Control and Prevention, "How Effective Are Latex Condoms in Preventing HIV?" http://www.cdc.gov/hiv/pubs/faq/faq23.htm.

35. Jon Fuller, "AIDS Prevention: A Challenge to the Catholic Moral Tradition," *America* 175, no. 20 (December 28, 1996): 13–20.

36. *The Training Manual on HIV and AIDS for Catholic Church Pastoral Workers Resource Book*, endorsed by Bishop Angel Lagdameo, president of the Catholic Bishops Conference of the Philippines, states that should HIV-discordant couples "decide to continue their sexual relationship, consistent and correct condom use can help minimize the risk of transmission." (UNAIDS, 2008), 38.

37. See Vatican Council II, *Gaudium et spes* (1965).

38. Dañguilan, *Women in Brackets*, 107.

39. Kissling and Clifton-Brown, "Vatican and Politics of Reproductive Health."

40. Pontifical Council for Justice and Peace, *Compendium of the Social Doctrine of the Church*, 346.

41. "Based on the Research, Comprehensive Sex Education Is More Effective at Stopping the Spread of HIV Infection, Says APA Committee: Research Shows That Abstinence-Only Programs Have Limited Effectiveness and Unintended Consequences," http://www.apa.org/releases/sexeducation.html. A UN review of 68 studies worldwide likewise showed that a comprehensive sex education leads to delayed first sexual intercourse and fewer partners, unexpected pregnancies, and STDs. "Sex Ed Does Not Encourage Promiscuity, Study Says," http://www.feminist.org/newsbyte/uswirestory.asp?id=2659.

42. Raymundo and Cruz, *Youth Sex and Risk Behaviours in the Philippines*, 106–7.

Elizabeth Hepburn, IBVM

1. "Gender Equality in Australia's AIDS Program—Why and How," http://www.ausaid.gov.au/publications/pdf/gender_policy.pdf.

2. Australian Medical Association Code of Ethics, 2005, Section 1.11, http://www.ama.com.au/web.nsf/doc/WEEN-5PF8DV.

3. See http://www.hivaids.webcentral.com.au/text/st453.html.

4. *Sydney Morning Herald*, April 20, 2007, 5.

5. http://www.unaids.org/en/Regions_Countries/Regions/Asia.asp.

6. "HIV/AIDS: Australia's Response," http://www.ausaid.gov.au/keyaid/hivaids/default.cfm.

7. J. Grierson, R. Thorpe, and M. Pitts, *HIV Futures 5: Life as We Know It*, monograph series 60 (2006), The Australian Research Centre in Sex, Health, and Society, La Trobe University, Melbourne, Australia.

8. This figure is from "UNAIDS Fact Sheet: Oceania," http://data.unaids.org/pub/EpiReport/2006/20061121_epi_fs_o_en.pdf.

9. Grierson et al., *HIV Futures 5*, 49.

10. Ibid., 68.

11. Stephen A. Schmidt, "When You Come into My Room," *Journal of the American Medical Association* ("A Piece of My Mind") 276, no. 7 (1996): 512.

12. R. M. Zaner, "A Meditation on Vulnerability and Power," in *Health and Human Flourishing*, ed. Carol R. Taylor and Roberto Dell'Oro (Washington, DC: Georgetown University Press, 2007), 156.

13. Margaret A. Farley, *Compassionate Respect* (New York: Paulist Press, 2002), 60–62.

14. Martha C. Nussbaum, *Upheavals of Thought: The Intelligence of Emotions* (New York: Cambridge University Press, 2001), 306.

15. *Code of Ethical Standards for Catholic Health and Aged Care Services in Australia* (Canberra: Catholic Health Australia, 2001), 36.

16. Ibid., 37.

17. Martha C. Nussbaum, *Love's Knowledge* (New York: Oxford University Press 1990), 78–79.

18. Matthew Fox, *A Spirituality Named Compassion* (Minneapolis: Winston Press, 1979), 10.

Elsie M. Miranda

1. Originally AIDS (acquired immuno-deficiency syndrome) was named GRIDD (gay-related immuno-deficiency disorder). Medical terminology changed as more became known about the virus.

2. Benedict XVI, "World Day of Peace Message 2007," *Origins* 36, no. 28 (2006): 437.

3. Foucault recognized that some of the most significant obstacles to achieving transformational education came from those systems of power that delegitimized the narratives and voices of the subjugated. People who dominated systems that promoted discourses of right never allowed countering viewpoints any form of expression, let alone legitimacy. See Michel Foucault, *Knowledge/Power: Interviews and Other Writings, 1972–1977*, ed. Colin Gordon (New York: Pantheon Books, 1980).

4. Jurgen Habermas, *Moral Consciousness and Communicative Action*, trans. Christian Lenhardt and Shierry Weber Nicholsen (Cambridge, MA: MIT Press, 1990), 116–44.

5. In 2005 Florida ranked behind New York and California (first and second) in a list of the states with the highest number of new HIV infections in the country. See http://www.cdc.gov/hiv/stats.

6. Drew Christiansen, SJ, "Commentary on *Pacem in terris*," in Kenneth Himes, ed., *Modern Catholic Social Teaching* (Washington, DC: Georgetown University Press, 2005), 217.

7. Paul VI, *Populorum progressio*, section 5, quoting Apostolic letter motu proprio, *Catholicam Christi Ecclesiam*, AAS 59 (1967), 27.

8. See Walter Brueggemann, *The Prophetic Imagination* (Minneapolis: Fortress Press, 2001), 1–37. The prophetic imagination gives apostolic witness to gospel values, with a bold sensitivity to the conversations in the arena of the institutional Church as well as among the people of God.

9. *Baptism, Eucharist, and Ministry*, Faith and Order Paper No. 111 (Geneva: WCC Publications, 1982), 1.

10. Ibid., 3.

11. See, for example, the Gates Foundation, http://www.gatesfoundation.org, and Partners in Health, http://www.pih.org/issues/hivaids.html.

12. Paul VI, *Populorum progressio*, 47.

13. I have been blessed to witness bishops who are true shepherds of God's reign, who know how to "be with" and listen to the harsh and hopeful narratives of people's lives. To date, however, their prophetic witness remains the exception.

14. Michel Foucault, "The End of the Monarchy of Sex," trans. Dudley M. Marchi, in *Foucault Live: Interviews, 1966–1984*, ed. Sylvère Lotringer (New York: Semiotext, 1989), 137–38. Foucault's epistemological studies recognize the changing frameworks of production of knowledge through the history of science, philosophy, and literature. In his later genealogical studies, he argues that institutional power, intrinsically linked with knowledge, forms individual human "subjects" and subjects them to disciplinary norms and standards.

15. Ibid., 138.

16. See Michel Foucault, *The History of Sexuality: An Introduction* (New York: Random House, 1978); Foucault, *The Archaeology of Knowledge and The Discourse on Language* (New York: Pantheon Books, 1972); and Foucault, *Power/Knowledge*.

17. Judith Butler, "Sexual Inversion," in *Feminist Interpretations of Michel Foucault*, ed. Susan J. Hekman (University Park, PA: Penn State University Press, 1996), 64–68. Butler uses Luce Irigaray to challenge the limits of Foucault's argumentation; his categories of sex and the principle of intelligibility sanctioned male sex as universal, disqualifying female sexual constructions and erasing the feminine.

18. *Baptism, Eucharist, and Ministry*, 8.

19. Adrienne Rich, "The Photograph of the Unmade Bed," in *The Fact of a Doorframe* (London: W. W. Norton & Co., 1984), 134–36.

20. Paul VI, *Populorum progressio*, 1.

21. See Deuteronomy 31.

22. Shepherds traditionally straddled the gate of the corral and counted each head of sheep as it rubbed against their legs upon entering or exiting the corral. The use of the shepherd metaphor, referring to spiritual leaders, denotes the type of intimacy where firsthand knowledge, love, and care of each head in the community is counted.

Anna Kasafi Perkins

1. Paula Clifford, "Theology and the HIV/AIDS Epidemic," *Christian Aid*, August 2004, http://www.e-alliance.ch/stigmacd/docs/2.27ChristianAidTheologyandHIV.doc.

2. Enda McDonagh, "Theology in a Time of AIDS," *Irish Theological Quarterly* 60, no. 2 (1994), http://www.cafod.org.uk/var/storage/original/application/phpb 27ZGZ.pdf.

3. Rosie Stone, *No Stone Unturned: The Carl and Rosie Story* (Kingston: Ian Randle Publishers, 2007), 64–65.

4. Caribbean Conference of Churches (CCC), "Guidelines for Caribbean Faith Based Organisations' Response: Policies and Action Plans to Deal with HIV/AIDS" (2004), appendix 1, www.ccc-caribe.org/eng/releases/faithresponse_0105.htm.

5. Janet Brown and Jurgen Hendriks, as quoted in Arnau VanWyngaard, "Towards a Theology of HIV/AIDS," *Reformed Ecumenical Council Focus* 6, nos. 1–2 (July

2006): 51–75, http://rec.gospelcom.net/files/resourcesmodule/@random45c78e42
bcfcd/1170706469_Towards_a_Theology_of_HIV_AIDS.pdf.

6. Kemala Kempadoo, *Sexing the Caribbean: Gender, Race, and Sexual Labour* (New York: Routledge, 2004), 178–97.

7. Glenda Simms, "What Can the Dear Wives Do? . . . Being Vulnerable to HIV Can Simply Mean Marriage," *Jamaica Gleaner* online, December 19, 2004, http://www.jamaica-gleaner.com/gleaner/20041219/focus/focus1.htm.

8. Isabel Apawo Phiri, "HIV/AIDS: An African Theological Response in Mission," *Ecumenical Review*, October 2004, http://findarticles.com/p/articles/mi_m2065/is_4_56/ai_n15944461.

9. Clifford, "Theology and the HIV/AIDS Epidemic."

10. "In its prophetic mission [the Church] is called to announce the Kingdom of God to the sick and those who suffer, keeping watch that their rights are recognized and respected, and to also denounce the sin and its historical, social, political and economic roots which lead to ills such as the illness HIV-AIDS." CELAM, "La Iglesia Católica Latinoamerica y del Caribe frente a la pandemia del VIH/Sida," *Dia Mundial de Lucha Contra el SIDA*, December 1, 2005, 36; author's translation.

11. Quoted in Solangre De Santis, "In the Age of AIDS, Can Theology Kill? Religious Leaders Debate Moral Aspect of Disease," *Anglican Journal*, http://www.anglicanjournal.com/hivaids/xvi-international-aids-conference/051/article/in-the-age-of-aids-can-theology-kill.

12. Ruth Faden, Nancy Kass, and Deven McGraw, "Women as Vessels and Vectors: Lessons from the HIV Epidemic," in *Feminism and Bioethics: Beyond Reproduction*, ed. Susan M. Wolf (New York: Oxford University Press, 1996), 252–81.

13. Graham Pembrey, "HIV and AIDS in the Caribbean," at http://www.avert.org/aids-caribbean.htm. These statistics are from the April 19, 2007 update.

14. Tracey-Ann Wisdom, "Poor Attitude toward HIV among Youth," *Sunday Gleaner*, July 1, 2007, B8.

15. Lesley Doyal, "HIV and AIDS: Putting Women on the Global Agenda," in *AIDS: Setting a Feminist Agenda*, ed. Lesley Doyal et al. (London: Taylor & Francis, 1994), 13.

16. Ibid.

17. Michelle Davis, "Gender and the HIV/AIDS Epidemic in the Caribbean," *Gender in the 21st Century: Caribbean Perspectives, Visions, and Possibilities*, ed. Barbara Bailey and Elsa Leo-Rhynie (Kingston: Ian Randle, 2004), 564–82.

18. "From the Courts," *Daily Observer*, April 23, 2007, 5.

19. Wisdom, "Poor Attitude toward HIV among Youth."

20. Davis, "Gender and the HIV/AIDS Epidemic in the Caribbean," 575.

21. Eudine Barriteau, cited in Davis, "Gender and the HIV/AIDS Epidemic," 546.

22. Davis, "Gender and the HIV/AIDS Epidemic," 569.

23. Kempadoo, *Sexing the Caribbean*, 178–79.

24. Robert Turner, "Two Juveniles Arrested," *The Star*, June 19, 2007, http://www.jamaica-star.com/thestar/20070619/news/news8.html.

25. Clifford, "Theology and the HIV/AIDS Epidemic," 9.

26. Ibid.

27. Désirée Bernard, "Confronting Gender-Based Violence in the Caribbean," the 2006 Lucille Mathurin Mair Lecture (Kingston: Centre for Gender and Development, University of the West Indies, November 2006), 5.

28. Quoted in Simms, "What Can the Dear Wives Do?"

29. Ibid.

30. Ibid.

31. CCC, "Guidelines for Caribbean Faith Based Organizations' Response."

32. "To educate women to be more conscious of their vulnerable condition and to be able to be more self-protecting." CELAM, "La Iglesia Católica Latinoamerica y del Caribe," 67; author's translation.

33. Clifford, "Theology and the HIV/AIDS Epidemic," 9.

34. Jon Sobrino, *The Principle of Mercy: Taking the Crucified People from the Cross* (Maryknoll, NY: Orbis Books, 1994), 28.

35. Samuel E. Carter, "God and Natural Disasters: A Pastoral Letter from Archbishop Samuel E. Carter" (Kingston, Jamaica: Roman Catholic Archdiocese of Kingston, 1988).

36. National Conference of Catholic Bishops, *Called to Compassion and Responsibility: A Response to the HIV/AIDS Crisis* (Washington, DC: USCCB, 1990).

37. Kristin Jack, "Micah: Towards a Christ-Centered Theology of HIV/AIDS," discussion paper drafted following the 2002 Chiang Mia Micah consultation on HIV/AIDS, September 2005, http://en.micahnetwork.org/hiv_aids__1/christian_response.

38. Gustavo Gutierrez, *The God of Life*, trans. Matthew J. O'Connell (Maryknoll, NY: Orbis Books, 1991), 146–47.

39. Reformed Ecumenical Council, "Towards a Theology of Hope in a Time of HIV/AIDS," July 2005, http://rec.gospelcom.net/files/resourcesmodule/@random45ad 2258292e0/1168974651_Towards_a_Theology_of_Hope_in_a_time_of_HIV.pdf.

40. Antilles Bishops Conference, "A Statement of the Antilles Episcopal Conference on HIV/AIDS" (Paramaribo, Suriname, April 14, 2005).

41. McDonagh, "Theology in a Time of AIDS."

42. Wendy Farley, *Tragic Vision and Divine Compassion: A Contemporary Theodicy* (Louisville, KY: Westminster/John Knox Press, 1990), 21.

43. Ibid., 21.

44. Ibid., 29.

45. See the USAID Web site, http://www.usaid.gov/our_work/global_health/aids/ News/abcfactsheet.html; and Share the World's Resources, "Dialogue on AIDS Prevention," http://www.stwr.org/health-education-shelter/dialogue-on-aids-prevention .html.

46. CELAM speaks of prevention as being one of the most difficult areas for those who want to be loyal to the church. CELAM, "La Iglesia Católica Latinoamerica y del Caribe," 66.

47. Jack, "Micah: Towards a Christ-Centred Theology of HIV/AIDS."

48. McDonagh, "Theology in a Time of AIDS."

Marie-Jo Thiel

1. Aquilino Morelle, "L'institution médicale en question," *Esprit*, October 1993.

2. According to a report of the Cour des comptes studying the activities of the French agency against AIDS during the years 1989 to 1991, neither drug addicts nor immigrant populations were addressed with prevention messages. See Jérôme Duck, "Le fonctionnement du dysfonctionnement," *Le Canard enchaîné*, November 10, 1993.

3. The statistics in this paragraph are from the Web sites of these two organizations: http://www.invs.sante.fr; and http://www.insee.fr/fr/ffc/chifcle_fiche.asp?tab_id=217, update March 2007, *Tableaux de l'Économie Française*, Édition INSEE 2006.

4. "Sub Saharan Africa: HIV and AIDS Statistics," http://www.avert.org/subaadults .htm. Sub-Saharan Africa is the region most harshly hit by the pandemic. See "The Point," http://www.who.int/mediacentre/news/releases/2004/pr_unaids/fr.

5. See Hélène Jaccomard, *Lire le sida: Témoignages au féminin* (Bern: Peter Lang, 2004).

6. See Bernard Paillard, *L'Epidémie: Carnets d'un sociologue* (Paris: Stock, 1994).

7. Quoted in Eric Favereau, *Nos années SIDA: 25 ans guerres intimes* (Paris: La Découverte, 2006), 147–48 (Iozzio trans.).

8. INVS and the National Agency of Research on AIDS and Viral Hepatitis, press communiqué, June 22, 2005, http://www.invs.sante.fr/recherche/index2.asp?txtQuery =sida+hepatitis&Submit.x=15&Submit.y=11.

9. Eric Favereau, "Quand la contamination devient crime," *Libération*, April 12, 2007, 30–31.

10. This reference is a French juridical concept used to determine the extent or legitimacy of damages resulting in a disability that prevents someone from work. Cases leading to this 2006 indictment had little by little moved to specify the crime. See Mélanie Heard, "Pénalisation de la transmission du VIH: quelle responsabilité pour les personnes séropositives?" *Esprit*, December 2005, 102–26.

11. Ibid

12. Favereau, *Libération*, 31 (Iozzio trans.).

13. Claudine Herzlich, "Vingt ans après . . . L'évolution d'une epidémie," *Etudes*, February 2002, 188.

14. I refer only to the perspective of the Catholic Church; references to "the Church" are to be understood accordingly.

15. The three official texts of the French bishops are found in "Commission sociale de l'Episcopat," Albert Rouet (ed.), *Le Sida: La Société en question* (Paris: Bayard éditions & Centurion, 1996).

16. Ordinarily in English, the term "protect" would be used; however, the French term for "preserve" is deliberate here in order to maintain a connection with the *préservatif*, that is, the condom.

17. Laurence Monroe, "Réactions contrastées au texte des évêques sur le sida," *La Croix*, the Catholic newsjournal, February 16, 1996, and the days following through the end of the month.

18. Henri Tincq, "Le risque assumé d'une crise ouverte avec Rome," *Le Monde*, February 14, 1996.

19. Cardinal Joseph Bernadin, "A Challenge and a Responsibility," October 1986, *La Documentation Catholique* 1935 (March 1, 1987): 255–59.

20. John Paul II, "Speech to the participants in the International Conference sponsored by the Pontifical Council for the Pastoral Assistance to Health Care workers," November 15, 1989, *La Documentation Catholique* 1998 (January 21, 1990): 57.

21. Déclaration des évêques du Congo (RDC), "Combattre et prévenir le sida," *La Documentation Catholique* 2383 (July 1, 2007): 640.

22. In 2005, three quarters of sexually active French women aged 15 to 54 used contraception: first, the pill (close to 60 percent of all women and 88 percent for the 20–24 age group); second, the intrauterine device (24.2 percent of women older than 30).

The usage of nonmedical contraception methods (e.g., preservatives, natural methods, spermicides) is minor and depends especially upon social and emotional position. Nevertheless, since 2000, the condom has been used in a more systematic manner at the time of the first sexual experience (close to 85 percent of the young women reporting); see http://www.avenirsdefemmes.com/content/view/411/290.

23. See Cardinal Joseph Ratzinger, "Letter from the Bishops of the Catholic Church on the Pastoral in regard to Homosexual Persons," Acta Apostolicae Sedis 79 (1987): 543–54; reprinted in La Documentation Catholique 83 (1986): 1160–64. The bishops' proposal rectifies a possible interpretation as too "benevolent."

24. Pascal Hintermeyer et al., Un voile sur l'amour (Strasbourg: Presses Universitaires de Strasbourg, 1994), 94.

25. "Le sida: le problème pastoral de l'Église," La Documentation Catholique 2176 (February 15, 1998), 194 (Iozzio trans.).

26. National Institutes of Health, "Scientific Evidence on Condom Effectiveness for Sexually Transmitted Disease Prevention," seminars held in Herndon, Virginia, June 12–13, 2000.

27. See J. Suaudeau, "Le 'sexe sûr' et le préservatif face au défi du sida," Medicina e Morale 4 (1997): 689–726.

28. Patrick Verspieren, "L'Eglise catholique face à l'épidémie de sida," Études (February 2007): 233.

29. "Sida: l'Eglise fait scandale," Républicain Lorrain (October 11, 2003), 38.

30. A. Rouet et al., "Le sida interroge la sociéte," in Le Sida, 192.

31. Dionigi Tettamanzi, Nouvelle Bioéthique Chrétienne, t. 3 (Paris: Salvator, 2004), 113–54. See also Cardinal J. M. Lustiger, and the theologian O. de Dinechin, among others.

32. "The Holy See to the XXVI Special Session of the UN," La Documentation Catholique 2258 (November 18, 2001): 977.

33. "Le préservatif a sa place dans le contexte de la prévention intégrale et globale du sida," La Croix, January 20–21, 2005. On January 18, 2005, P. Martinez Camino met Helena Salgado, minister of health of Spain, in order to envision a better collaboration in the framework of the fight against AIDS. The Episcopal Conference was obliged the following day to specify the position of the Church in Spain.

34. Maurice E. Piat, "Sida: conscientiser et agir ensemble," Bémoi, La Documentation Catholique 2354 (March 19, 2006): 289–90.

35. Of the women questioned, 9.5 percent experienced domestic violence (physical, sexual, verbal, and psychological abuse) during the previous twelve months; 1.1 percent of women 20 to 24 experienced at least one rape attempt or actual rape in the last twelve months in the public, professional, or private spheres; and 18 percent were victims of physical aggression at some point during their adult lives (since the age of 18). See http://www.femmes-egalite.gouv.fr/grands_dossiers/dossiers/violences/ENVEFF.htm.

Hille Haker

1. Catholic Information Service for Africa (CISA), "Zambia: Archbishop Urges West to Do More to Combat Diseases in Africa, July 2007, http://www.cisanewsafrica.org/story.asp?ID=2362.

2. CISA, "Malawi: Catholic Group Okays HIV Initiative, but Rejects Condoms," http://www.cisanewsafrica.org/story.asp?ID=2423.

3. Traditional Catholic sexual morality rules out all forms of homosexuality, all forms of premarital sex, all forms of marital sex that are not, in principle, directed toward procreation, and all forms of sex with more than one partner. For a short overview of moral-theological and social ethics responses to HIV/AIDS over the last twenty years, see Frank Sander, "AIDS—God's punishment?" *Concilium* 43, no. 3 (2007).

4. Among others and in addition to the UN Development Reports, see Thomas Pogge, *Global Justice* (Oxford: Blackwell, 2001); and Pogge, *World Poverty and Human Rights: Cosmopolitan Responsibilities and Reforms* (Malden, MA: Blackwell, 2002).

5. See Lisa Cahill, "Aids, Global Justice, and Catholic Social Ethics," *Concilium* 43, no. 3 (2007).

6. CISA, "Zambia: Archbishop Urges West to Do More."

7. Christian theology is based on the unconditional affirmation and dignity of every individual, as realized by God's grace. Homosexuality is not against human nature but is a variant.

8. Female infection rates in discordant marriages are much higher than was expected, taking for granted that women were infected by their husbands. "The Not-So-Fair Sex," *Economist*, July 27, 2007.

9. See Gillian Paterson, "Escaping the Gender Trap: Unravelling Patriarchy in a Time of AIDS," *Concilium* 43, no. 3 (2007).

10. CISA, "Zimbabwe: Catholic Woman Gets Top Job at Non-Catholic Association," July 16, 2007, http://www.cisanewsafrica.org/story.asp?ID=2387.

11. Avishai Margalit, *The Decent Society* (Cambridge, MA: Harvard University Press, 1998).

12. The implementation of the UN's Millennium Development Goals comes to mind. Obviously, within the narrower context of health policies, changes need to be advocated and promoted, particularly with respect to patents and public access to decision-making procedures when policies with public interest (and public funding) are concerned.

13. See Paul Ricoeur, *Oneself as Another* (Chicago: University of Chicago Press, 1992); Alan Gewirth, *Reason and Morality* (Chicago: University of Chicago Press, 1978); Gewirth, *The Community of Rights* (Chicago: University of Chicago Press, 1996); and Hille Haker, *Moralische Identität: Literarische Lebensgeschichten als Medium ethischer Reflexion: Mit einer Interpretation der "Jahrestage" von Uwe Johnson* (Tübingen: Francke, 1999).

14. Regina Ammicht-Quinn and Hille Haker, "HIV/AIDS: A Commentary," *Concilium* 43, no. 3 (2007).

Gillian Paterson

1. I am grateful to Lesley Doyal, Alice Welbourn, and Maria Schleger for sharing their wisdom with me.

2. Figures change rapidly; see http://www.avert.org/uksummary.htm.

3. A social construction is a concept, practice, or way of shaping reality that may appear natural and obvious to those who accept it; nevertheless, it is an invention or artifact of a particular culture or society.

4. Names and some details have been changed to protect identities.

5. See Malidoma Somé, "Gays: Guardians of the Gates," *M.E.N. Magazine* (1993), www.menweb.org/somegay.htm.

6. L. Doyal, S. Paparini, and J. Anderson, "'Elvis Died and I Was Born': Black African Men Negotiating Same-Sex Desire in London," *Sexualities* 11, no. 1 (2008): 171–92.

7. Paul Ricoeur, *From Text to Action: Essays in Hermeneutics* (Evanston, IL: Northwestern University Press, 1991), 145–50.

8. Paul A. Bové, "Discourse," in *Critical Terms for Literary Study*, ed. F. Lentricchia and T. McLaughlin (Chicago: University of Chicago Press 1995), 57.

9. Augustine of Hippo, *De consensu evangelistarum* 4.10.20, in Augustine of Hippo, *Anti-Pelagian Writings*, ed. P. Schaff (Edinburgh: T&T Clark, 1997).

10. G. and A. Scambler, "Social Change and Health Promotion among Women Sex Workers in London," *Health Promotion International* 10, no. 1 (1995): 17–24.

11. Erving Goffman, *Stigma: Notes on the Management of Spoiled Identity* (London: Penguin, 1990).

12. John Paul II, *Fides et ratio* (1998), 2.

Suzanne Mulligan

1. UNAIDS, "2008 Report on the Global AIDS Pandemic," www.unaids.org/en/KnowledgeCentre/HIVData/GlobalReport/2008/2008_Global_report.asp.

2. Ibid., 30.

3. Ibid., 33.

4. See the UNAIDS's "AIDS Epidemic Update," December 2006, at http://www.unaids.org.

5. See Catholic Institute for International Relations (CIIR), *Tamar's Cry: Re-reading an Ancient Text in the Midst of an HIV/AIDS Pandemic* (London: CIIR, 2002), 17; and PACSA (the Pietermaritzburg Agency for Christian Social Awareness), "Rape," PACSA Factsheet no. 44 (June 1998), 1.

6. South African law defines rape very narrowly. "Rape" refers to unlawful and intentional sexual intercourse with a woman without her consent. It applies only to sexual intercourse between a man and woman, and there must be penetration by the penis into the vagina. Acts of forced oral or anal sex do not qualify, nor does penetration by foreign objects such as bottles or sticks. These acts are criminalised instead as "indecent assault," but are not defined as rape. The South African Law Commission is working to amend this narrow definition, but at the time of this writing the definition remains so confined.

7. See Binaifer Nowrojee, *Violence against Women in South Africa: The State Response to Domestic Violence and Rape* (New York: Human Rights Watch, 1995), 90.

8. Considerable efforts have been made recently to improve the police service's handling of rape cases through special training of police personnel, additional resources for rape investigation, and training in forensic-gathering techniques.

9. Rachel Jewkes, Lorna Martin, and Loveday Penn-Kekana, "The virgin cleansing myth: cases of child rape are not exotic," *Lancet* 359 (February 23, 2002): 711.

10. Ibid.

11. Ibid., 711.

12. See Jewkes et al., "Virgin Cleansing Myth," 711. There are two types of HIV: HIV-1 and HIV-2. Both are transmitted through sexual intercourse, blood products, and through mother-to-child transmission. They both lead to AIDS. However, HIV-1 is the most common type of the virus, and when people refer to "HIV" it is usually HIV-1 that they have in mind. HIV-2 is less easily transmitted, and the period between infection and illness is longer. HIV-2 is concentrated in West Africa and is rarely found elsewhere in the world.

13. The Human Development Index records levels of development and inequality within countries and between countries. Tony Barnett and Alan Whiteside explain that "the Human Development Index (HDI) introduced in 1990 is designed to capture as many aspects of human development as possible in one simple composite index, producing a ranking of human development achievements. . . . The HDI determines how nations and regions of nations compare with each other and over time." Tony Barnett and Alan Whiteside, *AIDS in the Twenty-First Century: Disease and Globalization* (New York: Palgrave Macmillan, 2002), 276–77.

14. For the Gini coefficient, see the South African government's report *Poverty and Inequality in South Africa* (May 1998). The Gini coefficient measures economic inequality. If income is perfectly distributed and no inequality exists, the coefficient will be zero. If all the income goes to one person, the number will be 1. The higher the coefficient, the greater the economic inequality. South Africa's is very high; developed countries, in comparison, average 0.34. See the Southern African Catholic Bishops' Conference Pastoral Letter, *Economic Justice in South Africa: A Pastoral Statement* (Pretoria: SACBC, 1999), 18.

15. Fantu Cheru, "Overcoming Apartheid's Legacy: The Ascendancy of Neoliberalism in South Africa's Anti-Poverty Strategy," *Third World Quarterly* 22, no. 4 (2001): 505–6.

16. At the time of writing the commission has not yet pronounced on this matter.

17. For further reading on this point, see Nawaal Deane, "The Political History of AIDS Treatment," in *HIV/AIDS in South Africa*, ed. S. S. Abdool Karim and Q. Abdool Karim (New York: Cambridge University Press, 2005), 538–45; and Pieter Fourie, *The Political Management of HIV/AIDS in South Africa* (New York: Palgrave Macmillan, 2006).

18. Kevin Kelly, *New Directions in Sexual Ethics: Moral Theology and the Challenge of AIDS* (London: Geoffrey Chapman, 1998), 8–9.

19. Amartya Sen has written extensively on the idea of development as freedom. Economic factors such as poverty take away a person's basic freedoms and limit the choices that he or she can make. See Sen, *Development as Freedom* (Oxford: Oxford University Press, 1999).

20. Quoted in J. Michael Kilby, "The Legacy of the Global HIV/AIDS Epidemic for Public Health," *Lancet* 362 (October 18, 2003): 1339.

Mary M. Doyle Roche

1. UNAIDS, *AIDS Epidemic Update 2006*, http://www.unaids.org/en/HIV_data/epi2006/default.asp.

2. "Global Summary of the AIDS Epidemic 2005," in UNAIDS, *AIDS Epidemic Update*, December 2005, 1, http://www.unaids.org/Epi2005/doc/EPIupdate2005_pdf

_en/Epi05_02_en.pdf. By the time this goes to press updated statistics are likely. For current information see http://www.unaids.org. The figure of 2.3 million children living with AIDS is from 2006.

3. See UNICEF, *Africa's Orphaned Generations*, http://www.unicef.org/publications/files/africas_orphans.pdf.

4. See UNAIDS and UNICEF, *A Call to Action: Children—the Missing Faces of AIDS*, http://www.uniteforchildren.org/knowmore/files/U77HIV_letter.pdf.

5. UNAIDS, *AIDS Epidemic Update*, 2006, 13.

6. UNAIDS and UNICEF, *Call to Action*, 14.

7. Ibid., 7.

8. Lisa Sowle Cahill, "AIDS, Justice, and the Common Good," in *Catholic Ethicists on HIV/AIDS Prevention*, ed. James F. Keenan, SJ, Jon D. Fuller, SJ, MD, Lisa Sowle Cahill, and Kevin Kelly (New York: Continuum, 2000), 282.

9. UNAIDS and UNICEF, *Call to Action*, 3.

10. Lisa Sowle Cahill has brought the tradition of the common good to bear on the epidemic in the developing world in "AIDS, Justice and the Common Good." This essay follows in that trajectory by exploring specific implications for children and young people.

11. John XXIII, *Pacem in terris* (1963), sections 57–58.

12. See James F. Keenan and Jon D. Fuller, "The International AIDS Conference in Bangkok: Two Views," *America* 191, no. 5 (August 2004): 13–16; and Keenan and Fuller, "The Language of Human Rights and Social Justice in the Face of HIV/AIDS," *BUDHI* 1–2 (2004): 211–31.

13. See Lanie Friedman Ross, *Children, Families, and Health Care Decision-Making* (Oxford: Clarendon Press, 2002).

14. See Bruce C. Hafen and Jonathan O. Hafen, "Abandoning Children to Their Rights," *First Things* (August–September 1995): 18–24.

15. The Convention on the Rights of the Child was ratified by the General Assembly on November 20, 1989.

16. For more information on the session, see http://www.un.org/ga/children.

17. For a recent, sustained theological treatment of children's innocence, see Bonnie J. Miller-McLemore, *Let the Children Come: Reimagining Church from a Christian Perspective* (San Francisco: Jossey-Bass, 2003).

18. See Julia O'Connell Davidson, *Children in the Global Sex Trade* (Cambridge: Polity Press, 2005); and Donald Dunson, *No Room at the Table: Earth's Most Vulnerable Children* (Maryknoll, NY: Orbis Books, 2003).

19. While the focus on children and young people remains a priority for the world community, the 2006 Global Report from UNAIDS attends to four at-risk and "neglected" populations: sex workers, men who have sex with men, injection drug users, and prisoners. Compassionate response to these groups often falters because communities pass moral judgment. These are not HIV/AIDS's "innocent victims." Children and young people are found in each of these four demographics. See chap. 5, "At Risk and Neglected," in UNAIDS, *Report on the Global AIDS Epidemic 2006*, http://data.unaids.org/pub/GlobalReport/2006/2006_GR_CH05_en.pdf. The full report is available at http://www.unaids.org/en/HIV_data/2006GlobalReport/default.asp.

20. Legislation for AIDS relief continues to bear Ryan White's name. The Ryan White HIV/AIDS Treatment Modernization Act was reauthorized by Congress in

December 2006. See US Department of Health and Human Services, http://hab.hrsa
.gov/treatmentmodernization/default.htm.

21. See Maura Ryan, "Preventing Transmission to Neonates in the United States,"
in Keenan et al., eds., *Catholic Ethicists on HIV/AIDS Prevention*, 120–28.

22. See Gurinder Gulati, "Young peer educators raise awareness of HIV/AIDS prevention in Gujarat youth," 2007, http://www.uniteforchildren.org/knowmore/know
more_39975.htm.

23. Yvonne Duncan, "UNICEF Executive Director Meets with Children Orphaned
by AIDS in South Africa, http://www.unicef.org/infobycountry/southafrica_41142
.html.

24. Nattha Keenapan, "Thai Children Unmask the Stigma of Living with HIV/AIDS,"
http://www.uniteforchildren.org/knowmore/knowmore_40297.htm.

Mary Jo Iozzio

1. http://www.census.gov.

2. This number is a gross estimate gleaned from a crude analysis and conglomer-
ate projections from the National Center for Health Statistics found at http://www
.cdc.gov/nchs/fastats/disable.htm.

3. http://factfinder.census.gov/servlet/ADPTable?_bm=y&-geo_id=01000US&
-qr_name=ACS_2004_EST_G00_DP1&-ds_name=ACS_2004_EST_G00_&-redoLog=
false&-_scrollToRow=5&-format.

4. See Wolf Wolfensberger, "Social Role Valorization News and Reviews," *International Social Role Valorization Journal* 1, no. 2 (1994), http://www.socialrole
valorization.com/journal/Q-The%20Wolfensberger%20Column.pdf.

5. http://www.cdcnpin.org/scripts/population/disable.asp.

6. Disabilities that arise from HIV/AIDS can qualify individuals as people with disabilities and thus eligible for protections under the Americans with Disabilities Act
(1990); see the Rehabilitation Act of 1973 for other services and protections for people with disabilities. The remarks that follow apply only to persons who had disabilities before infection.

7. http://www.cdcnpin.org/scripts/population/elderly.asp.

8. I am particularly interested in the older elder population. Like people with disabilities, older elders tend to be missed as a population to consider for risky behaviors
—regardless of the nature of risk, for example, sky-diving, motorcycling, and mountain-
climbing as well as recreational drug use and multiple sex partners.

9. These statistics are from the CDC; see http://www.cdc.gov/hiv/stats/hasrlink.htm;
and http://www.cdc.gov/hiv/topics/surveillance/resources/reports/2005report/table7.htm.

10. Health Resources and Services Administration (HRSA), "HIV/AIDS in the Deaf
and Hard of Hearing," April 2001, http://hab.hrsa.gov/publications/hrsa401.htm.

11. HRSA, "Mental Illness and HIV Disease," January 2001, http://hab.hrsa.gov/
publications/hrsa101.htm.

12. United Nations, "HIV/AIDS and Older People," March 2002, http://www.global
aging.org/waa2/articles/hivolder.htm.

13. AARP, "Sexuality at Midlife and Beyond: 2004 Update of Attitudes and Behaviors," May 2005, http://www.aarp.org/research/family/lifestyles/2004_sexuality.html.

14. http://hab.hrsa.gov/publications/hrsa401.htm.

15. "Older People and HIV," May 5, 2007, http://www.thebody.com/nmai/elderly .html.

16. This list of symptoms is from the CDC, http://www.cdc.gov/hiv/pubs/faq/ faq5.htm.

17. See Krisann K. Oursler, Joseph L. Goulet, David A. Leaf, et al., "Association of Comorbidity with Physical Disability in Older HIV-infected Adults," *AIDS Patient Care and STDs* 20 (11) (November 1, 2006): 782–91.

18. "The AIDS epidemic poses a serious threat to people with developmental disabilities, the magnitude of which has not yet been fully realized by many professionals working with this population." Raymond Jacobs, Perry Samowitz, Joel M. Levy, and Philip H. Levy, "Developing an AIDS Prevention Education Program for Persons with Developmental Disabilities," *Mental Retardation* 27 (1989) 233. Further, in reference to older elders, "health providers often fall into the trap of age stereotypes . . . [and] are less likely to ask older patients about their sexual behavior." United Nations, "HIV/AIDS and older people."

19. Nora E. Grace, "HIV/AIDS and People with Disability," *Lancet* 361 (2003): 1401–1402.

20. "HIV/AIDS in the Deaf and Hard of Hearing."

21. Marilyn M. Irwin, "Sexuality and People with Disabilities," http://www.iidc .indiana.edu/cedir/sexuality.html.

22. United Nations, "HIV/AIDS and Older People."

23. "What are HIV Prevention Needs of Adults over 50?" Center for AIDS Prevention Studies, University of California, San Francisco (1997), www. Caps.ucsf.edu/ pubs/FS/over50.php.

24. I am especially indebted to the insights of James F. Keenan, SJ, who brings Thomas Aquinas's thinking on mercy to the contemporary world. See Keenan, *The Works of Mercy: The Heart of Catholicism* (Lanham, MD: Rowman & Littlefield, 2005).

25. Thomas Aquinas, *Summa theologiae* 2.2.30.3c.

26. Ibid., 2.2.30.4.ad2 and ad3.

27. See Maria Cimperman, OSU, *When God's People Have HIV/AIDS* (Maryknoll, NY: Orbis Books, 2005).

Emily Reimer-Barry

1. HIV-positive Catholics are a "primary source" for the Catholic moral tradition today. "It can even be said that such people are the tradition," writes Nicholas Peter Harvey in "Listening in England to a Woman's Life Experience," in *Catholic Ethicists on HIV/AIDS Prevention*, ed. James F. Keenan, SJ, with Jon D. Fuller, Lisa Sowle Cahill, and Kevin T. Kelly (New York: Continuum, 2000), 75.

2. On ethnography, see Robert S. Weiss, *Learning from Strangers: The Art and Method of Qualitative Interview Studies* (New York: Free Press, 1994), and James P. Spradley, *The Ethnographic Interview* (New York: Holt, Rinehart & Winston, 1979). For theologians who use ethnography, see Ada Maria Isasi-Diaz, *En La Lucha: Elaborating a Mujerista Theology* (Minneapolis: Fortress Press, 2004), and Aana Marie

Vigen, *Women, Ethics, and Inequality in U.S. Healthcare: To Count among the Living* (New York: Palgrave Macmillan, 2006).

3. I interviewed these women in person between March and October 2006 in Chicago. IRB Approval #73475, Loyola University Chicago. Pseudonyms are given for each of the women I interviewed. Some women chose their own pseudonym; others did not.

4. By "church" I mean the people of God, individual parish communities, and the institutional Roman Catholic Church.

5. These statistics are from the U.S. Census Bureau, http://quickfacts.census.gov/qfd/states/17/1714000.html; and http://www.census.gov/population/cen2000/phc-t29/tab03a.csv.

6. "Demographic Profile of the Archdiocese," http://www.archchicago.org/about_us/statistics.shtm. There are 47 Catholic hospitals in Illinois.

7. Chicago Department of Public Health, *STD/HIV/AIDS Chicago Winter Report 2006*, 2–3, http://egov.cityofchicago.org/webportal/COCWebPortal/COC_EDITORIAL/StdHivAidsChgoWinter06.pdf.

8. Ibid., 6. Men having sex with men remains the leading cause of HIV infection for males. For non-Hispanic blacks and Hispanic women, heterosexual transmission is the highest mode of infection. For non-Hispanic whites, the numbers of cases attributed to heterosexual transmission and injection drug use are nearly even.

9. These research centers are the University of Chicago, Northwestern University, Loyola University Chicago, University of Illinois at Chicago, and the Ruth M. Rothstein CORE Center, a partnership between Rush Medical Center and Cook County Hospital.

10. U.S. Census Bureau, http://quickfacts.census.gov/qfd/states/17/1714000.html.

11. Their stories appear in Emily Reimer-Barry, *In Sickness and in Health: Towards a Renewed Roman Catholic Theology of Marriage in Light of the Experiences of Eight Catholic Married Women Living with HIV*, dissertation, Loyola University Chicago, August 2008.

12. See Patricia D. Siplon, *AIDS and the Policy Struggle in the United States* (Washington, DC: Georgetown University Press, 2002).

13. The Centers for Disease Control and Prevention (CDC) tracks HIV prevalence by geography, gender, age, sexual orientation, and ethnicity; a growing number of social scientists point out that socioeconomic status has a greater impact on HIV risk. Paul Farmer and colleagues claim that women are vulnerable to AIDS through *social* processes. See Paul Farmer, Margaret Connors, and Janie Simmons, eds., *Women, Poverty, and AIDS: Sex, Drugs, and Structural Violence* (Monroe, ME: Common Courage Press, 1996), xix, 23, 33; United Nations Department of Economic and Social Affairs, *Population, Development, and HIV/AIDS with Particular Emphasis on Poverty: The Concise Report* (New York: UN Publications, 2005), 49; UNAIDS, UNFPA, and UNIFEM, *Women and AIDS: Confronting the Crisis* (Geneva, Switzerland: UNAIDS, 2004).

14. Rodrick Wallace, "A Synergism of Plagues: 'Planned Shrinkage,' Contagious Housing Destruction, and AIDS in the Bronx," *Environmental Research* 47 (1988): 1–33; Mindy Thompson Fullilove, "Death and Life in the Great American City," *International Journal of Mental Health* 28, no. 4 (1999–2000); Robert E. Fullilove and Mindy Thompson Fullilove, "HIV Prevention and Intervention in the African-American Com-

munity: A Public Health Perspective," in *The AIDS Knowledge Base*, 3rd ed., ed. P. T. Cohen, M. A. Sande, and P. A. Volberding (Philadelphia: Lippincott Williams & Wilkens, 1999); Jon C. Teaford, "Urban Renewal and Its Aftermath," *Housing Policy Debate* 11, no. 2 (2000): 443–65. Even as I write, the *Chicago Tribune* reports that thirty-four Chicago public school students have been killed since the start of the 2006–2007 school year. The latest victim, Schanna Gayden, 13, was buying a snack from a vendor at the Funston Elementary School playground; rival gangs began to fire against each other across Central Park Avenue, and Schanna was fatally struck. See John Keilman, "Church Packed for Slain Girl's Funeral," *Chicago Tribune* online edition, July 1, 2007, http://www.chicagotribune.com/news/local/chi-both_gayden.

15. For a database of reported crime in Chicago, see the Chicago Police Department's CLEAR (Citizen Law Enforcement Analysis and Reporting) Geographic Information System, http://gis.chicagopolice.org. For crime and development trends focusing on race and ethnicity, see William Julius Wilson and Robert J. Sampson, "Toward a Theory of Race, Crime, and Urban Inequality," in *Crime and Inequality*, ed. John Hagan and Ruth D. Peterson (Stanford, CA: Stanford University Press, 1995); Jeffrey Morenoff and Robert J. Sampson, "Violent Crime and the Spatial Dynamics of Neighborhood Transition: Chicago 1970–1990," *Social Forces* 76 (1997): 31–64; Arnold Hirsch, *Making the Second Ghetto: Race and Housing in Chicago, 1940–1960* (Cambridge: Cambridge University Press, 1983); John M. Hagedorn and Paul J. Goldstein, "Murder and Drugs in the Information Age: An Urban Political Economy Approach to Variation in Homicide Rates" (Chicago: Great Cities Institute, University of Illinois-Chicago, 1999).

16. Robert J. Sampson, Jeffrey D. Morenoff, and Stephen Raudenbush, "Social Anatomy of Racial and Ethnic Disparities in Violence," *American Journal of Public Health* 95 (2005): 114–32.

17. Eileen Stillwaggon, *Ecology of AIDS* (New York: Oxford University Press, 2006), 120. "During a time of economic collapse and social disintegration, it is easier to see that epidemic increases in the numbers of injecting drug users and commercial sex workers certainly signal that they are members of a crumbling society and their situation arises from the crisis in that society" (121–22). See also Margaret Connors, "Sex, Drugs, and Structural Violence: Unraveling the Epidemic among Poor Women in the United States," in Farmer et al., eds., *Women, Poverty, and AIDS*, 96; Brian R. Edlin et al., "Intersecting Epidemics—Crack Cocaine Use and HIV Infection among Inner-City Young Adults," *New England Journal of Medicine* 331, no. 21 (1994): 1442.

18. See UN Millennium Project, *Taking Action: Achieving Gender Equality and Empowering Women: Task Force on Education and Gender Equality* (Sterling, VA: Earthscan, 2005).

19. See L. Heise, M. Ellsberg, and M. Gottemoeller, "Ending Violence against Women," *Population Reports*, series L, no. 11 (Baltimore: Population Information Program, Johns Hopkins University School of Public Health, 1999).

20. Cristina L. H. Traina, *Feminist Ethics and Natural Law: The End of the Anathemas* (Washington, DC: Georgetown University Press, 1999), 44.

21. Ibid. See also Lisa Sowle Cahill, *Sex, Gender, and Christian Ethics* (Cambridge: Cambridge University Press, 1996); and Martha Nussbaum, *Women and Human Development: The Capabilities Approach* (Cambridge: Cambridge University Press, 2000).

Shawnee Marie Daniels-Sykes, SSND

1. The Centers for Disease Control and Prevention (CDC) and the 2000 census note that African-Americans make up approximately 13 percent of the U.S. population. In 2005, African-Americans accounted for 18,510 (49 percent) of the estimated 38,096 new HIV diagnoses in the United States. Of all African-American men with HIV, the primary transmission category is men having sex with men (MSM), followed by injection drug use (IDU) and high-risk heterosexual contact. Of all African-American women with HIV, the primary transmission category is high-risk heterosexual contact, followed by IDU. Of the estimated 141 perinatal infections of HIV, 91 (65 percent) were African-Americans. See "Fact Sheet: HIV/AIDS among African Americans," www.cdc .gov/hiv/topics/aa/resources/factsheets/aa.htm.

2. CDC, *Morbidity and Morality Weekly Report* 55 (February 10, 2006), 124.

3. This essay provides an overview of what the literature reveals thus far, but additional empirical research is necessary to expose or determine the extent of the problem of HIV/AIDS in the older African-American population.

4. I coined the term "Roman Catholic social bioethics" in my doctoral dissertation; see Shawnee Daniels-Sykes, *Roman Catholic Social Bioethics Critiques Secular Bioethics: Fetal Tissue Research and Vulnerable Populations* (dissertation, Marquette University, Milwaukee, Wisconsin, 2007). This term is one way to move beyond the physicalism and personalism that traditionally characterize Catholic bioethics to a position that views the importance of Catholic bioethics in addressing social justice concerns in the public square.

5. Kelly A. Gebo and Richard D. Moore, "Treatment of HIV Infection in the Older Patient," *Expert Review of Anti-Infective Therapy* 2 (2004): 733.

6. Makebra Anderson, "HIV/AIDS and the Elderly," May 24, 2005, http://www .finalcall.com/artman/publish/article_2010.shtml.

7. See Allen S. Funnye, Abbasi J. Aktar, and Gisele Biamby, "Acquired Immunodeficiency Syndrome in Older African Americans," *Journal of the National Medical Association* 94 (April 2002): 209–14.

8. The literature on HIV and older adults is based on data about AIDS cases and not actual HIV infection; AIDS is suggestive of the advanced stages in which older people are diagnosed. The number of older people living with HIV is difficult to ascertain because it is not readily talked about in this population.

9. Mary Brophy Marcus, "Aging of AIDS: The Silent Risk Group for HIV Infection: Senior Citizens," *U.S. News & World Report* 133 (August 12, 2002), 2.

10. "Older People Vulnerable to HIV/AIDS," *Population Today* 30 (May–June 2002): 7.

11. See Funnye et al., "Acquired Immunodeficiency Syndrome in Older African-Americans," 209–14.

12. See the NBCC Congress IX Pastoral Plan of Action, Principle: HIV/AIDS, 2002, www.nbccongress.org/aboutus/nbcc-congresses/congress-09-PRINCIPLE-RACISM-AFRICA.asp#hw-ads.

13. See Robert L. Miller, "Legacy Denied: African American Gay Men, AIDS, and the Black Church," *Social Work* 52 (January 2007): 52; see also J. David Kennamer, Julie Honnold, Judith Bradford, and Michael Hendricks, "Differences in Disclosure of Sexuality Among African American and White Gay/Bisexual Men: Implications for HIV/AIDS Prevention," *AIDS Education and Prevention* 12 (December 2000): 522–23.

14. W. Michael Byrd and Linda A. Clayton, *An American Health Dilemma: Race, Medicine, and Health Care in the United States*, vol. 2, *1900–2000* (New York: Routledge, 2002), 541.

15. Kelly Brown Douglas, *Sexuality and the Black Church: A Womanist Perspective* (Maryknoll, NY: Orbis Books, 1999), 87–108.

16. CDC, *A Heightened National Response to the HIV/AIDS Crisis among African Americans*, 2007, 2, http://www.cdc.gov/hiv/topics/aa/resources/reports/heightened response.htm.

17. Judith A. Levy, "HIV and AIDS in People over 50," *SIECUS Report* 30 (December 2001–January 2002): 10.

18. See J. L. King, *On the Down Low: A Journey into the Lives of "Straight" Black Men Who Sleep with Men* (New York: Broadway Books, 2004).

19. Stacy Tessler Lindau, Sara A. Leitsch, Kristina L. Lundberg, and Jessica Jerome, "Older Women's Attitudes, Behavior, and Communication about Sex and HIV: A Community-Based Study," *Journal of Women's Health* 15 (2006): 747–48.

20. See Vicki Freimuth, Sandra Crouse Quinn, Stephen B. Thomas, Galen Cole, Eric Zook, and Ted Duncan, "African Americans' View on Research and the Tuskegee Syphilis Study," *Social Science and Medicine* 52 (2001): 797–808; Peter A. Clark, "Prejudice and the Medical Profession: Racism, Sometimes Overt, Sometimes Subtle, Continues to Plague U.S. Health Care," *Health Progress* (September–October 2003): 12–23.

21. See Barbara L. Bernier, "Class, Race, and Poverty: Medical Technologies and Socio-Political Choices," *Harvard Blackletter Law Journal* 115 (1994): 115–43.

22. See Vanessa Northington Gamble, "A Legacy of Distrust: African Americans and Medical Research," *American Journal of Preventive Medicine* 9 (1993): 35–38, and Gamble, "Under the Shadow of Tuskegee: African Americans and Health Care," *American Journal of Public Health* 87 (November 1997): 1775.

23. CDC, *Heightened National Response to the HIV/AIDS Crisis*, 2; Douglas, *Sexuality and the Black Church*, 97–99.

24. See Pope Paul VI, *Humanae vitae*.

25. See Vincent J. Genovesi, "Marital Sexuality: Contraception and Beyond," in *Pursuit of Love: Catholic Morality and Human Sexuality* (Wilmington, DE: Michael Glazier, 1987).

26. See United States Conference of Catholic Bishops (USCCB), *The Many Faces of AIDS: A Gospel Response* (Washington, DC: United States Catholic Conference, 1987), http://www.usccb.org/sdwp/international/mfa87.shtml; USCCB, *A Call to Compassion and Responsibility: A Response to the HIV/AIDS Crisis* (Washington, DC: United States Catholic Conference, 1990), http://www.usccb.org/sdwp/international/ctoresp.shtml.

27. Catholic social teaching includes a large body of literature that delineates the Church's moral stance on social issues. These teachings draw on the natural law tradition, the heritage of Catholic thought, and the Hebrew and Christian Scriptures.

28. See Shawnee Daniels-Sykes, *Roman Catholic Social Bioethics Critiques Secular Bioethics*, 128–33, 160–62; Charles Curran, *Catholic Social Teaching: A Historical, Theological, and Ethical Analysis, 1891–Present* (Washington, DC: Georgetown University Press, 2002); and David J. O'Brien and Thomas A. Shannon, *Catholic Social Thought: The Documentary Heritage* (Maryknoll, NY: Orbis Books, 1992).

29. See Anthony R. Geonnotti and David F. Katz, "Dynamics of HIV Neutralization by a Microbicide Formulation Layer: Biophysical Fundamentals and Transport Theory," *Biophysical Journal* 91 (September 15, 2006): 2121–30; Robin Shattock and

Suniti Solomon, "Commentary: Microbicides—AIDS in Safer Sex," *Lancet* 363 (March 27, 2004): 1002–3; Jan Balzarini and Lust Van Damme, "Microbicide Drug Candidates to Prevent HIV Infection" *Lancet* 369 (March 3–9, 2007): 787–97.

30. USCCB, *Call to Compassion and Responsibility*, 12.

Ma. Christina A. Astorga

1. These statistics are from UNAIDS and WHO and can be found at http://www .avert.org/worldstats.htm.

2. Jose Narciso and Melchor C. Sescon, "Fighting Stigma and Discrimination against People Living with HIV and AIDS in the Philippines," http://www.hurights.or .jp/asia-pacific/046/04.html. Further, "Today's teenagers are getting hotter and wilder . . . as far as sex is concerned. . . . Some 4.9 million young adults, ages ranging from 15–24 lost their virginity before marriage, 1.6 million with multiple partners and 400,000 with someone of the same sex." Christine Herrera, "Youths Getting 'Hotter and Wilder,'" *Manila Standard*, February 14, 2006, http://fromthenews.ripchordweb solutions.com/?p=2928.

3. Ibid.

4. Ambika Bhushan, "AIDS Creeps Up on Unsuspecting Philippines," Reuters New Media, 2005, http://www.aegis.com/news/re/2005/RE050917.html.

5. Ibid. See also Teodora Tiglao, Ma. Sandra B. Tempongko, and Duce Gust, "AIDS: Knowledge, Awareness, and Attitude in Metro Manila," *UPM Journal* 2, no. 4 (October–December 1996): 33. The Country Report of the Philippines states that "the country's archipelagic nature may have helped slow down the spread of HIV/AIDS." Philippine National AIDS Council, Country Report of the Philippines, January 2003 to November 2005, Manila, http://www.unaids.org/pub/Report/2006/2006_country _progress_report_philippines_en.pdf.

6. Sally Baden, *Women, HIV/AIDS, and Development: Towards Gender Appropriate Prevention Strategies in South-East Asia and the South Pacific*, report prepared for Women, Health, and Population Division, Australian International Development Assistance Bureau (report no. 5).

7. The text of the Philippine AIDS Control and Prevention Act can be found at http://www.mars.dti.ne.jp/~frhikaru/philippine/ra8504AIDS.html; see also "HIV/AIDS in Philippines and USAID Involvement," September 2001, http://www.synergyaids.org/ documents/2983_Philippines_Brief_rev_5.pdf; and Anthony R. Roda, "Fidel V. Ramos Signs the Philippine AIDS Prevention Act of 1998," *Health Beat* (1998): 11–13.

8. Marites Sison, "Health-Philippines: HIV/AIDS Caregivers Need Care Too," http://ipsnews.net/aids2002/asia.shtml.

9. Michael Tan and Manuel Dayrit, "HIV/AIDS in the Philippines," *AIDS* 8, supplement 2 (1994): 125–30. See also Johanna Son, "Philippines: Church, a Goliath against Reproductive Health," IPS-Inter Press Service News Agency, November 11, 2006, http://www.ipsnews.net.

10. Rhea Agnes Alburo, "The Single Most Effective Technology against Sexual Transmission of Human Immunodeficiency Virus," in *The Country Report of the Philippines, January 2003 to November 2005*, prepared by the Philippine National AIDS Council, with support from the UN Theme Group on HIV/AIDS, December 2005, 34, 36.

11. David Morley, "Papal Policy, Poverty, and AIDS," *British Medical Journal* 300 (1990): 1705. See also Human Rights Watch, "Religion and Human Rights Movement Tensions Today," January 2005, http://hrw.org/wr2k5/religion/10.htm.

12. "What's Culture Got to Do with HIV and AIDS?" *Findings*, February 2007, 2, accessible at http://www.healthlink.org.uk.

13. World Health Organization (WHO), "Women, Girls, HIV and AIDS: Why Women?" 2004, http://www.wpro.who.int/NR/rdonlyres/F1F88521-518C-4EAC-AF7E-1F07A4E9FF0B/0/WAD2004_Women_Girls_HIV_AIDS.pdf.

14. See WHO, "Women, Girls, HIV and AIDS"; Lory Ann B. Bilbao, "Women Most Vulnerable to HIV," *Sun Star Iloilo*, November 24, 2005, www.sunstar.com.ph/static/ilo/2005/11/24/news/women.most.vulnerable.to.hiv.council.htm; and International Planned Parenthood Foundation, "Report Card: HIV Prevention for Girls and Young Women," http://www.unfpa.org/hiv/docs/report-cards/philippines.pdf.

15. UN WomenWatch, "Women and HIV/AIDS Concerns: A Focus on Thailand, Philippines, India, and Nepal," http://www.un.org/womenwatch/daw/csw/hiv.htm.

16. Ibid.

17. Ibid.

18. Aida F. Santos, "Patriarchy, Poverty, Prostitution, and HIV/AIDS: The Philippine Experience," Fourth International Congress on AIDS in Asia and Pacific, October 25–29, 1997, Manila, http://www.catw-ap.org/patri.htm. "The number of prostituted persons in the Philippines is about the size of the country's manufacturing workforce. There are about 400,000 to 500,000 prostituted persons in the Philippines. . . . A recent study showed there are 75,000 children, who were forced into prostitution due to poverty." Coalition against Trafficking in Women, "The Philippines: Trafficking," http://www.catwinternational.org/factbook/philippines.php.

19. UN WomenWatch, "Women and HIV/AIDS Concerns."

20. Quoted in "What's Culture Got to Do with HIV and AIDS?" 2.

21. Quoted in ibid.

22. Ibid., 5.

23. Ibid., 3.

24. Ibid.

25. Fatima A. Castillo and Cynthia M. Villamor, "The Social Component of AIDS Prevention in the Philippines: Training the Female Commercial Sex Workers to Become Change Advocates, Phase I," *UPM Journal* 2, no. 4 (October–December, 1996): 86.

26. Ibid., 89–93. See also Laufred Hernandez, Reynaldo Imperial, Nymia Simbulan, Cynthia Dominguez, Charles Carpenter, "An Ethnography of Male Sex Workers in the Philippines," *UPM Journal* 2, no. 4 (October–December, 1996), 1–6; and Justin Eusebio, "Condoms, HIV/AIDS, and Perceived Sexual Risk among Young Adult Urban Males in the Philippines," http://www.focusanthro.org/archive/2006-2007/Eusebio%20-%20Condoms%20and%20HIV%20in%20the%20Philippines.pdf.

27. Tan and Dayrit, "HIV/AIDS in the Philippines," 130.

28. Carolina Austria, "Positive Influences: RH Reality Check Asia," http://www.rhrealitycheck.org/blog/2007/06/18/positiveinfluences.

29. Dennis A. Ahlburg, Eric Jensen, and Aurora E. Perez, "Determinants of Extramarital Sex in the Philippines," *Health Transition Review*, Supplement 7 (1997): 467–79. See also "Consensus Report on STI, HIV and AIDS Epidemiology, Philippines, 2000," World Health Organization (Regional Office for the Western Pacific) and

Department of Health, Philippines, http://www.wpro.who.int/NR/rdonlyres/ B1D6D9DB-B27D-4BC4-A382-AF16A42E4E16/0/Consensus_Report_PHL_2000.pdfy Philippines2000.

30. UNESCO/UNAIDS Project, "Women Migrants and HIV/AIDS: An Anthropological Approach," Studies and Reports, Special Series issue no. 22, Division of Cultural Policies and Intercultural Dialogue (2005), 2. See also CARAM-ASIA, "AIDS and Migration Are Global Issues: Coordination of Action Research on AIDS and Mobility," *IAC Newsletter* 14 (2004): 1.

31. CARAM-ASIA, "AIDS and Migration Are Global Issues," 16.

32. Population Reference Bureau, "Media Coverage of Women and HIV/AIDS," 2000, www.prb.org/pdf/ConveyConcerns3_Eng.pdf.

33. Irene Fernandez, "Migration and HIV/AIDS Vulnerability in South East Asia," paper presented at the Twelfth World AIDS Conference, Geneva, July 1998.

34. Ibid., 4.

35. UNESCO/UNAIDS Project, "Women Migrants and HIV/AIDS," 21. See also Narciso and Sescon, "Fighting Stigma and Discrimination."

36. UNESCO/UNAIDS Project, "Women Migrants and HIV/AIDS, 21–22."

37. UNESCO/UNAIDS Project, "Women Migrants and HIV/AIDS, 23–24."

Maryanne Confoy, RSC

1. My interest in this region is from meetings with members of the South Pacific Association of Theologians and with women engaged in theological education both in their local area and in the regional context.

2. Many groups in Oceania work on behalf of those with HIV/AIDS. "TEAR Australia is a movement of Christians . . . responding to the needs of poor communities around the world. . . . We support the initiatives of other Christian groups, including churches, relief and development agencies and community-based organizations, which are working with the poor in their communities," http://www.tear.org.au. The work of Caritas Internationalis is also significant.

3. Paul Farmer, *AIDS and Accusation: Haiti and the Geography of Blame*, updated ed. (Berkeley: University of California Press, 2006), 259.

4. The particular problems of indigenous people and HIV/AIDS are only acknowledged here. The concerns of indigenous people are appropriately addressed by the people themselves and by those who work and minister in close association with them. See H. Hughes, *Lands of Shame: Aboriginal and Torres Strait Islander "Homelands" in Transition* (St. Leonards, Australia: Centre for Independent Studies, 2007).

5. The Catholic Church, along with the many Western nations and medical and pastoral professionals, is involved in extraordinary ways in terms of HIV/AIDS care, research initiatives, international aid programs, and sharing of resources.

6. See Dorothee Soelle, *The Strength of the Weak: Toward a Christian Feminist Identity* (Philadelphia: Westminster Press, 1984); and Paul Farmer, *Pathologies of Power: Health, Human Rights, and the New War on the Poor* (Berkeley: University of California Press, 2005).

7. The term "Oceania," coined by Pacific anthropologist Epeli Hau'ofa, refers to the world where "ancestors made their homes and bred their generations of seafarers,

and where they mingled unhindered by boundaries." Lisa Meo, "Feminist Theologies, Pacific Islands," in *Dictionary of Feminist Theologies*, ed. Letty M. Russell and J. Shannon Clarkson (Louisville, KY: Westminster John Knox Press, 1996), 108.

8. Oceania has the smallest fraction of the world's population—about half of 1 percent. Australia, New Zealand, and Papua New Guinea dominate the region politically and demographically, as together they contain approximately 90 percent of the region's population. UNAIDS/WHO, "AIDS Epidemic Update," December 2005, http://www.thebody.com/content/world.art26437.html.

9. In Samoa, 43 percent of women attending antenatal services in the capital Apia are found infected with at least one STD. Of sex workers in East Timor, 25 percent had gonorrhea and/or chlamydia, and 60 percent were infected with HSV2, according to research in 2003. These rates stand in sharp contrast to westernized areas of the region such as Australia and New Zealand. See Pisani and Dili survey team, *HIV, STIs and Risk Behaviour in East Timor* (Durham, NC: US Family Health International, 2004).

10. "Throughout Melanesia, women are recognised for their critical contributions to local production and for exercising practical and moral authority in the domestic economy, as well as in situations of conflict, fighting, peacemaking and reconciliation, such as in Bougainville and the Solomon Islands." Australian Council for Overseas Aid 2000, *Manmade Disaster in the Solomons* (Deakin, ACT, AU: ACOA, 2000), 28.

11. U.S. CDC International News, "UN Says Pacific Faces New Wave of HIV, with Papua New Guinea on the Brink of Epidemic," March 22, 2004, www.thebody.com/content/world/art26437.html.

12. Kelly Brown Douglas, "Why Religion, Race, and Gender Matter in Pacific Politics," *Development Bulletin* 59 (2002): 11.

13. Meo, "Feminist Theologies, Pacific Islands," 109.

14. Quoted in Global HIV Prevention Working Group, *HIV Prevention in the Era of Expanded Treatment Access*, June 2004, http://www.kff.org/hivaids/upload/HIV-Prevention-in-the-Era-of-Expanded-Treatment-Access.pdf.

15. See Nicola Slee, *Women's Faith Development: Patterns and Processes* (Aldershot, UK: Ashgate, 2004), 173–75; and Jean Baker Miller, "The Development of Women's Sense of Self," in Judith V. Jordan et al., *Women's Growth in Connection: Writings from the Stone Center* (New York: Guilford Press, 1991), 11–26.

16. Javier Cardinal Lozano Barragán, "Message for World AIDS Day," December 1, 2004, http://www.zenit.org/article-11627?l=english.

17. See Slee, *Women's Faith Development*, 22–24; and Mary F. Belenky, B. M. Clinchy, N. R. Goldberger, and J. M. Tarule, *Women's Ways of Knowing: The Development of Self, Voice, and Mind* (New York: Basic Books, 1986), 15.

18. "Two-thirds of the 23 countries and territories of Oceania have minority Catholic populations." Bryan T. Froehle and Mary L. Gautier, *Global Catholicism: Portrait of a World Church* (Maryknoll, NY: Orbis Books, 2003), 115.

19. Meo, "Feminist Theologies, Pacific Islands," 109.

20. Ibid.

21. Quoted in Slee, *Women's Faith Development*, 1.

22. M. Shawn Copeland, "On the Body: An(other) Theological Anthropology," paper presented at the Academy of Catholic Hispanic Theologians in the United States and the Black Catholic Theological Symposium, San Antonio, Texas, June 5, 2006.

23. Douglas, "Why Religion, Race, and Gender Matter in Pacific Politics," 11.

24. Ibid., 10.

25. See Belenky et al., *Women's Ways of Knowing*; Slee, *Women's Faith Development*; and Meo, "Feminist Theologies, Pacific Islands."

26. Slee, *Women's Faith Development*, 65.

27. Douglas, "Why Religion, Race, and Gender Matter in Pacific Politics," 9.

28. Enda McDonagh, "Theology in a Time of AIDS," *Irish Theological Quarterly* 60 (1994): 99, http://www.cafod.org.uk/var/storage/original/application/phpb27ZGZ.pdf.

29. I received this prayer during a visit to a women's group led by Lisa Meo in Fiji.

Metti Amirtham, SCC

1. Quoted in V. Suja, "Epidemiology of HIV/AIDS: Women's Perspectives," *Samyukta: A Journal of Women's Studies* 11, no. 1 (2002): 90.

2. Ibid., 92.

3. UNAIDS, *2006 Report on the Global AIDS Epidemic*, http://data.unaids.org/pub/GlobalReport/2006/2006_GR-ExecutiveSummary_en.pdf.

4. Ibid.

5. NACO, *Technical Report, India, HIV Estimates 2006* (New Delhi: National Institute of Medical Statistics, 2006), www.nacoonline.org/upload/NACO%20PDF/Technical%20Report%20on%20HIV%20Estimation%202006.pdf.

6. UNAIDS, *2006 Report on the Global AIDS Epidemic*.

7. Gracious Thomas, *AIDS in India: Myth and Reality* (New Delhi: Rawat Publications, 1994), 39.

8. Elizabeth Reid, "Challenges for UNDP in a Changing World, 1990–2000: Social Trends," *International Encyclopaedia of AIDS*, vol. 2, ed. Digumarti Bhaskara Rao (New Delhi: Discovery Publishing House, 2000), 779.

9. Khorshed M. Pavri, *Challenges of AIDS* (New Delhi, India: National Book Trust, 1996), 99.

10. "HIV is currently spreading at the rate of one new infection every fifteen seconds, primarily due to ignorance." Thomas, *AIDS in India*, 7.

11. Renée Sabatier for Panos Dossier, *AIDS and the Third World* (London: Panos Institute, 1988), 55–60.

12. Elizabeth Reid, "Towards an Ethical Response to the HIV Epidemic," in Rao, ed., *International Encyclopaedia of AIDS*, vol. 2 (New Delhi: Discovery Publishing House, 2000), 401.

13. Pavri, *Challenges of AIDS*, 104.

Therese Tinkasiimire, DST

1. N. Kaleeba, *Taso News Letter* (Kampala), May 1999, 3.

2. See Ministry of Health, The Republic of Uganda, "AIDS Situational Summary" (June 2003), 8, http://www.health.go.ug/hiv.htm.

3. See Symposium of Episcopal Conferences of Africa and Madagascar, "A Proposed HIV/AIDS Plan of Action," http://www.sceam-secam.org/showpdfs.php?id=11;

also M. Czerny, "The Church in Africa in the Face of the HIV/AIDS Pandemic," *AJA News*, no. 24 (November 2004), 8.

4. This study was entitled, "The Catholic Church's Responses to HIV/AIDS Prevention and Care in Hoima of Western Uganda." Funding was provided by Yale University, Center for Interdisciplinary Research on HIV/AIDS.

5. Caroline O. N. Moser, *Gender Planning and Development: Theory, Practice & Training* (New York: Routledge Press, 1993), 29–31.

6. Ibid., 27.

7. Ministry of Health, The Republic of Uganda, "AIDS Situational Summary."

8. J. S. Mbiti, *Introduction to African Religion* (London: Heinemann Educational Books, 1978), 111.

9. N. Kaleeba, J. D. Kadowe, D. Kalinaki, W. Glen, *Open Secret: People Facing Up to HIV and AIDS in Uganda* (London: ACTION AID, 2000), 23.

10. Paul Kasozi, "Changes in Public Attitude," quoted in Kaheeba et al., *Open Secret*, 28.

11. WHO, http://www.aidsuganda.org 2005, 10.

12. See "HIV/AIDS in Uganda," Uganda AIDS Commission Official Web site, http://www.aidsuganda.org/.

13. Maureen Farrell, "Condoning or condemning the condom: Lessons learned from Uganda," *Sexual Health Exchange* (2004), a themed issue on Faith-Based Responses to HIV AIDS, www.kit.nl/exchange/html/2004-1_condoning_or_condemning.asp.

14. Ibid.

15. Kaleeba et al., *Open Secret*, 19.

16. Ibid, 11.

17. G. Bantebya, "A Gender Analysis of the Health Sector: Practice, Policy, and Budget," in *The Gender Budget 1998/9: HIV/AIDS Situation*, ed. R. Mukama (Kampala: FOWODE, 2000), 165–66.

18. See Akinyele E. Dairo, "*Partnership with Male Cultural Leaders for ASRH and Prevention of HIV Infection Among Young People*" (New York: United Nations Population Fund, 2001), www.ayaonline.org/CDWebDocs/AYAResources/Toolbox/Case Studies/UG-CS-PartnershipWithMaleLeaders.pdf.

19. Michael Fleshman, "Women: The Face of AIDS in Africa," *Africal Renewal* 18 (October 2004), 6, quoting Kathleen Cravero, "AIDS may wipe out Women," *The New Vision*, Uganda's leading website, www.newvision.co.ug (2004).

20. Ibid.

21. UNAIDS, "A global overview of the AIDS epidemic," *2004 Report on the global AIDS epidemic*, www.unaids.org/bangkok2004/GAR2004_html/GAR2004_03_en.htm.

22. Ibid, 11.

23. John Mary Waliggo, "A Woman Confronts Social Stigma in Uganda," in *Catholic Ethicists on HIV/AIDS Prevention*, ed. J. F. Keenan et al. (New York: Continuum, 2000), 48.

24. Ibid., 56.

25. John Mary Waliggo, *Struggle for Equilty: Women and Empowerment in Uganda* (Eldoret, Kenya: AMECEA Gaba Publications, 2002), 9.

26. Czerny, "Church in Africa in the Face of the HIV/AIDS Pandemic," 12.

27. UNAIDS/UNFPA/UNIFEM, "Women's Rights, Recommendation: Promote and Protect the human rights of women and girls," *Women and HIV/AIDS: Confronting the Crisis* (2005), http://www.unfpa.org/hiv/women/report/chapter7.html.

Pushpa Joseph, FMM

1. Mary (pseudonym) is a young woman, a high school teacher in South India who was infected with HIV by her husband. She is yet another victim of the gendered nature of the epidemic. K. Mayer et al., "Marriage, Monogamy, and HIV: A Profile of HIV-infected Women in South India," *International Journal of STD and AIDS* 11, no. 4 (April 1, 2000): 250–53.

2. Remani (pseudonym) is a housewife who suffers from extreme isolation as a result of the stigma associated with HIV. She is an educated Hindu woman, a zoology graduate.

3. Rita (pseudonym) is from a poor family; her husband is a truck driver. The National AIDS Control Organization identifies truck drivers as a high-risk group accounting for a vast percentage of the HIV-infected population in India. The number of women infected is steadily rising: one in every four AIDS cases reported in India involves a woman. Four million HIV-infected individuals live in India, and up to 46 percent of these are women.

4. Women especially resort to spirituality as a healthy way of coping with HIV. See Sian Cotton et al., "Changes in Religiousness and Spirituality Attributed to HIV/AIDS: Are There Sex and Race Differences?" *Journal of General Internal Medicine* 21 (December 2006): S14–S20, http://www.pubmedcentral.nih.gov/articlerender.fcgi ?artid=1924779; and N. G. Mathew, *Spirituality/Religiosity as a Resource in Coping with Terminal Illness: A Study among HIV/AIDS Adults in Chennai*, M.Phil. diss., University of Madras, October 2004.

5. India's first cases of HIV were diagnosed among sex workers in Chennai, South India, in 1986. For recent statistics see "Overview of HIV and AIDS in India," http://www.avert.org/aidsindia.htm.

6. Mary Elizabeth O'Brien, *Spirituality in Nursing: Standing on Holy Ground*, 3rd ed. (Sudbury, MA: Jones & Bartlett Publishers, 2008), 5. See also M. Burkhardt, "Spirituality: An Analysis of the Concept," *Holistic Nursing Practice* 3, no. 3 (1989): 69–77; and K. Litwinczuk and C. Groh, "The Relationship between Spirituality, Purpose in Life, and Well-Being in HIV-Positive Persons," *Journal of the Association of Nurses in AIDS Care* 18, no. 3 (2007): 13–22.

7. Peter Aggleton et al., "HIV-Related Stigma, Discrimination, and Human Rights Violations: Case Studies of Successful Programmes," UNAIDS Best Practice Collection, 2005, http://data.unaids.org/publications/irc-pub06/JC999-HumRightsViol_en.pdf.

8. White Robed Monks of St. Benedict, "Religion and Spirituality: Unity in Difference," http://www.whiterobedmonks.org/schem3.html.

9. See Devan Nambiar, "Heart to HAART," http://www.thebody.com/content/treat/art14292.html.

10. Ronald Rolheiser, *The Holy Longing: Guidelines for a Christian Spirituality* (New York: Doubleday, 1999), 7.

11. See Augustine Meier et al., eds., *Spirituality and Health: Multidisciplinary Explorations* (Waterloo, Ontario: Wilfrid Laurier University Press, 2005).

12. See Stanley J. Grenz, "Christian Spirituality and the Quest for Identity: Toward a Spiritual-Theological Understanding of Life in Christ," *Baptist History and Heritage* 37, no. 2 (2002), http://findarticles.com/p/articles/mi_m0NXG/is_2_37/ai_94160844.

13. See Mark Cichocki, "The Role of Religion and Spirituality in HIV," http://aids .about.com/od/spirituality/a/religion.htm.

14. O'Brien, *Spirituality in Nursing*, 5.

15. This understanding is from the Royal College of Psychiatrists in the United Kingdom, http://www.rcpsych.ac.uk/mentalhealthinformation/therapies/spirituality andmentalhealth.aspx.

16. Kenneth T. South, "AIDS and American Religion: An Issue of Blood," http://www.thebody.com/content/living/art32943.html. See also Albert Jewell, *Ageing, Spirituality, and Well-Being* (London: Jessica Kingley Publishers, 2004).

17. Michel Foucault, "The Subject and Power," in *Power*, trans. Robert Hurley et al. (New York: New Press, 1994), 337–42.

18. See Nalini Tarakeshwar et al., "A Relationship-Based Framework of Spirituality for Individuals with HIV," *AIDS and Behaviour* 10, no. 1 (January 2006): 59–70.

19. See Anne Bayley, *One New Humanity: The Challenge of AIDS* (New Delhi: ISPCK, 1999), 129; Joann Butrin, *Who Will Cry for Me: Pastoral Care for Persons with HIV/AIDS* (Springfield, MO: Health Care Ministries, Assemblies of God, 1996), 47.

20. Quoted in Judith B. Kendall et al., "Doing Well with AIDS: Three Case Illustrations," *Archives of Psychiatric Nursing* 3 (1989): 161.

21. F. P. Lamendola and M.A. Newman, "The Paradox of HIV/AIDS as Expanding Consciousness," *Advances in Nursing Sciences* 16, no. 3 (1994): 159–65.

22. Cichocki, "Role of Religion and Spirituality in HIV."

23. Ibid. Moreover, India has an estimated population of 2.25 to 5 million injecting drug users. See Jummy Dorabjee, Gary Reid, and Suresh Kumar, *Capacity Building for HIV/AIDS Prevention among Injecting Drug Users in India* (2003), http://www.youandaids.org/unfiles/capacity_building_for_hivaids_prevention_among _injecting_drug_users_in_india.pdf.

24. Deepti Priya Mehrotra, "Walking on the Path with Women," http://www.life positive.com/mind/philosophy/feminism/women-spiritual.asp.

25. Ibid.

26. Maria Cimperman, *When God's People Have HIV/AIDS: An Approach to Ethics* (New York: Orbis Books, 2005), 35.

27. "Herbal Medicine May Improve Blood Count in AIDS Patients," *Indian News Health*, December 11, 2005. See Paul Sachdev, "AIDS/HIV and social work students in Delhi, India: an exploratory study of knowledge, beliefs, attitudes and behaviors," *International Social Work* 41.3 (1998): 293–310.

28. Despite the effectiveness of antiretroviral drugs, the cost prevents many from undergoing treatment.

29. Nambiar, "Heart to HAART."

30. James Gillett, Roy Cain, and Dorothy Pawluch, "How People with HIV/AIDS Manage and Assess Complementary Therapies: A Qualitative Analysis," *Journal of the Association of Nurses in AIDS Care* 13, no. 2 (2002): 17–27.

31. Nambiar, "Heart to HAART."

32. South, "AIDS and American Religion."

33. Ravi Shanker, yoga instructor at one of the AIDS centers in South Tamil Nadu, believes there are four poses individuals with HIV should do everyday: the headstand, shoulder stand, the bridge, and the plow. These postures increase strength, decrease stiffness, relieve pressure on the abdominal organs, and increase the circulation of blood.

34. Rashani, "There Is a Brokenness," in *WomanPrayers: Prayers by Women Throughout History and Around the World*, by Mary Ford-Grabowsky (New York: HarperCollins, 2003), 141.

Maria Clara Lucchetti Bingemer

1. In 1873, Dr. Armauer Hansen of Norway uncovered *Mycobacterium leprae*, the bacterium that caused what, until the twentieth century, was known as leprosy. "Hansen's disease, also known as leprosy, is a chronic bacterial disease that primarily affects the skin, peripheral nerves and upper airway. . . . The stigma long associated with the disease still exists in most of the world and the psychological and social effects may be more difficult to deal with than the actual physical illness." Health Resources and Services Administration, "National Hansen's Disease (Leprosy) Program," http://www.hrsa.gov/hansens.

2. See Exod 7–11 for the plagues in Egypt.

3. An earlier translation of the RSV renders the passage in legal terms: "This is the law for any leprous disease: for an itch, for leprosy in a garment or in a house, and for a swelling or an eruption or a spot, to show when it is unclean and when it is clean. This is the law for leprosy."

4. See W. Kasper, *Le Dieu des chrétiens* (Paris: Cerf, 1985), 250–55; and B. Forte, *Jesus of Nazaré: História de Deus, Deus da História* (Sao Paulo: Paulinas, 1985), 217–32.

5. Walter Kasper, *Introduzione Alla Lede* (Brescia, IT: Queriniana, 1972), 58–59.

6. Rinaldo Fabris, "O Evangelho de Marcos," in *Os Evangelhos* (volume I) (Sao Paulo: Paulus, 1990), 44.

7. On this point, see Mark 1:25, 34, 44; 3:12; 5:43; 7:36; 8:26, 30; and 9:9.

8. Fabris, "O Evangelho de Marcos," 442.

9. "The Legend of the Three Companions (Leg3C) 11, Test 3," http://www.pro-casp.org.br/paragrafo_capitulo.php?indice=10&titulo=Legenda%20dos%20Três%20Companheiros&cParagrafo=417&cCapitulo=20#LTC%2011; see also Rosalind B. Brooke, *The Image of St. Francis: Responses to Sainthood in the Thirteenth Century* (Cambridge: Cambridge University Press, 2006), chap. 6.

10. Leg3C 11.

11. See James Broderick, *A Biography of St. Francis Xavier* (New York: Wicklow Press, 1952).

12. See Gavan Daws, *Holy Man: Father Damien of Molokai* (Oahu: University of Hawaii Press, 1989); and Irene Caudwell, *Damien of Molokai 1840–1889* (Oxford: Blackwell Press, 2007).

13. When Hawaiians were looking to symbolize the formation of their statehood (1959), they chose Damien to represent them in the Statuary Hall of the Capitol in Washington, D.C. The statue of the missionary, a work of New York artist Marisol Escobar, of Venezuelan origin, has stood there since 1969.

14. See 1 Cor 12:9. On the implications of God's solidarity with human suffering, see Jürgen Moltmann, *The Crucified God* (Minneapolis: Fortress Press, 1993).

15. Quoted by Benedict XVI in his address for World AIDS Day, December 1, 2007.

16. "Pope Urges Every Effort to Stop the Spreading of AIDS and the 'Scorn' of Those Who Suffer from It," November 28, 2007, http://www.asianews.it/index.php?l=en&art=10912&size.

17. Benedict XVI, General Audience, November 30, 2005, http://www.vatican.va/holy_father/benedict_xvi/audiences/2005/documents/hf_ben-xvi_and_20051130_en.html.

18. Ibid.

19. Ibid.

20. John Paul II, *Salvifici doloris* (1984), 29.

21. Conferencia Nacional dos Bispos do Brasil, *Diretrizes Gerais da Ação Evangelizadora da Igreja no Brasil* (2003–2006), #123.e, http://www.cnbb.org.br/ns/modules/mastop-publish/files/files_48a048722815a.pdf. These instructions were promulgated by the Bishop's Conference of Brazil for the organization of all pastoral plans in the dioceses of Brazil.

22. "Pastoral de DST/AIDS—CNBB," http://www.pastoralaids.org.br/index1.php.

Contributors

Metti Amirtham, SCC, is from Tamil Nadu, India. She has a doctorate in feminist theology. She is involved in theologizing feminist concerns in various theological seminaries and formation houses and works at the grassroots level, especially among movements and NGOs that work for women's empowerment. She regularly writes both in English and Tamil on social issues.

Ma. Christina A. Astorga is associate professor and the inaugural director of the Center for the Study of Catholic Social Thought at Duquesne University. Formerly she was chairperson of the Theology Department at the Ateneo de Manila University-Loyola Schools; a visiting scholar at Weston Jesuit School of Theology; a Fellow at the Jesuit Institute, Boston College, and at Woodstock Theological Center, Georgetown University; and a visiting professor at the University of San Diego and Canisius College.

Maria Clara Lucchetti Bingemer is a Brazilian lay theologian, professor of theology at the Catholic University of Rio de Janeiro, and dean of the Center of Theology and Human Sciences. Among her publications are, in English, *Mary, Mother of God and Mother of the Poor*, with Ivone Gebara (Orbis Books, 1999); in Spanish, *Mujeres de palabra/Women of the Word*, with Elian Yunes (Obra Nacional de La Buena Prensa, 2005); and in Portuguese, *O segredo feminino do misterio: Ensaios de teologia na otica de mulher* (Vozes, 1991).

Agnes M. Brazal is a professor at Maryhill School of Theology, Philippines. She co-edited the books *Body and Sexuality: Theological-Pastoral Perspectives of Women in Asia* (2007) and *Faith on the Move: Toward a Theology of Migration in Asia* (2008). She was a visiting fellow in 2006 at the Katholieke Universiteit Leuven, Belgium, where she obtained her licentiate and doctorate in sacred theology.

Lisa Sowle Cahill is the J. Donald Monan, SJ, Professor at Boston College. She is past president of the Catholic Theological Society of America and the Society of Christian Ethics, and a fellow of the American Academy of Arts and Sciences. Her works include *Theological Bioethics: Justice, Participation, and Change* (Georgetown University Press, 2005), *Bioethics and the Common Good* (Marquette University Press, 2004), *Family: A Christian Social Perspective* (Fortress Press, 2000), and *Sex, Gender, and Christian Ethics* (Cambridge University Press, 1996). She is the editor of *Genetics, Theology, Ethics: An Interdisciplinary Conversation* (Crossroad, 2005), and *Sexuality and the U.S. Catholic Church: Crisis and Renewal* (Herder & Herder, 2006).

Maria Cimperman, OSU, is assistant professor of moral theology and social ethics at Oblate School of Theology in San Antonio, Texas. She has written *When God's People Have HIV/AIDS: An Approach to Ethics* (Orbis Books, 2005) and finds ways to integrate the reality of HIV into all of her courses and presentations on many different topics.

Maryanne Confoy, RSC, is professor of pastoral theology at Jesuit Theological College and United Faculty of Theology in Melbourne, Australia, and an international consultant. She is visiting professor at Institute of Religious Education and Pastoral Ministry, Boston College. She has authored and edited several books, including *Freedom and Entrapment: Women Thinking Theology* and *Religious Life and Priesthood: Vatican II Rediscovered*.

Shawnee Marie Daniels-Sykes, SSND, is assistant professor of theology at Mount Mary College, Milwaukee. She received her PhD in religious studies from Marquette University, her MA in pastoral studies from Saint Francis Seminary, St. Francis, Wisconsin, and two bachelor's degrees: in nursing from the University of Wisconsin–Milwaukee, and in biology and biochemistry from Spelman College in Atlanta. She is the first black Catholic theological bioethicist in the United States.

Mary M. Doyle Roche is assistant professor of religious studies and the Edward Bennett Williams Faculty Fellow at the College of the Holy Cross in Worcester, Massachusetts. In addition to HIV/AIDS, her primary interests are ethical issues regarding children and families.

Margaret A. Farley is Gilbert L. Stark Professor Emerita of Christian Ethics at Yale University Divinity School. She is a past president of the Society of Christian Ethics and the Catholic Theological Society of America, and a recipient of the CTSA's John Courtney Murray Award for Excellence in Theology. Her publications include *Personal Commitments: Beginning, Keeping, Changing* (HarperCollins, 1990), and *Just Love* (Continuum, 2006), for which she received the Grawemeyer Award in Religion.

Hille Haker is professor of moral theology and social ethics at the Catholic Faculty of Frankfurt, and is a member of the European Group on Ethics in Sciences and New Technologies. Formerly an associate professor of Christian ethics at Harvard University, staff member of the Center for Ethics in the Sciences and Humanities, and lecturer in the department of ethics and social ethics at the Catholic Theological Faculty, University of Tübingen. Her books include *Moralische Identität* (1999), *Ethik der genetischen Frühdiagnostik* (2002), and the following co-edited volumes: *Ethics of Human Genome Analysis: European Perspectives* (1993), *The Ethics of Genetics in Human Procreation* (2000), and *Ethik-Geschlecht-Wissenschaften* (2006). She is a director of *Concilium, International Journal of Theology*, and co-editor of *Other Voices: Women in World Religions* and *HIV/AIDS* (Concilium 3-2006 and 4-2007).

Elizabeth Hepburn, IBVM, is author of a number of journal articles and *Of Life and Death* (Dove Books, 1996), as well as other titles published through the Catholic Health Association. Formerly principal of Santa Sophia College, University of Sydney, she now serves as principal of St. Mary's College at the University of Melbourne. Previously she served as faculty and mission director at institutions in Canberra, Brisbane, and Papua New Guinea.

Mary Jo Iozzio is professor of moral theology and director of the graduate program in theology and ministry at Barry University. She is co-editor of the *Journal of the Society of Christian Ethics*. She has edited *The Other Casualties of War: Disabilities in the Armed Services* (Haworth Press, 2008) and *Considering Religious Traditions in Bioethics* (University of Scranton Press, 2001), and has authored *Self-Determination and the*

Moral Act (Peeters Press, 1995) and *Radical Dependence: Theological Anthropology and Bioethics in the Key of Disability* (University of Notre Dame Press, forthcoming).

Pushpa Joseph, FMM, teaches in the School of Religion at the University of Madras, South India, and is a member and former lead coordinator of Ecclesia of Women in Asia. She is a feminist theologian with a specialization in Indian feminist hermeneutical methodologies. Her research interests are in the area of women's issues in society and religion, bioethics, and HIV/AIDS. She recently published "But Why Aren't We Listening? When Silence Speaks" in the *Jnandeepa Journal of Philosophy and Religion* (January 2007).

Anna Kasafi Perkins is former dean of studies and lecturer at St. Michael's Theological College, an institute of the Roman Catholic Archdiocese of Kingston and an affiliated institution of the University of the West Indies (UWI). She is the program officer in the Quality Assurance Unit at UWI and part-time lecturer and editor of the journal for St. Michael's Theological College.

M. Bernadette Mbuy Beya, CSU, is former mother superior of the Compagnie de Sainte Ursule and former director of the Institut Superieur des Sciences Religieuses in Lubumbashi, Congo. As a member of EATWOT (Ecumenical Association of Third World Thologians) and a founding member of the Circle of African Women Theologians, she was president of the Commission of African Women and secretary general for Francophones, traveled extensively, and published widely in French and English on the condition of women in Africa. Many of her publications are found in *Voices from the Third World*, a biannual journal of theology developed by EATWOT.

Elsie M. Miranda is assistant professor of theology and director of the MA in Practical Theology and ministerial formation at Barry University in Miami Shores, Florida. Currently she is working on education and formation for professional lay ecclesial ministers in a multicultural church.

Suzanne Mulligan holds the Finlay Post-Doctoral Fellowship in Theology at the Milltown Institute in Dublin, Ireland, and is a lecturer in moral theology. Her publications include "Moral Discourse in a Time of AIDS," in *Contemporary Irish Moral Discourse: Essays in Honour of Patrick Hannon*, edited by Amelia Flemming (Columba Press, 2007), and "A Strange Sort of Freedom: Moral Agency and HIV/AIDS," in *Moral Theology for the 21st Century: Essays in Honour of Kevin Kelly*, edited by Julie Clague, Bernard Hoose, and Gerard Manion (T&T Clark, 2008).

Gillian Paterson is a theologian, writer, and consultant living in Britain. She is currently a Research Fellow at Heythrop College, University of London. Her specialty is the responses of churches to the HIV epidemic. Her published works include *Women in the Time of AIDS* (Orbis Books, 1996), *AIDS and the Churches in Africa* (Christian Aid, 2001), *AIDS-Related Stigma: The Theological Challenge* (EAA and WCC, 2005), and "Escaping the Gender Trap: Unravelling Patriarchy in a Time of AIDS" (*Concilium*, 2007).

Emily Reimer-Barry earned her doctorate in the Department of Theology at Loyola University Chicago. While an instructor there she developed the university's first undergraduate theology course focusing on HIV/AIDS and Catholic moral theology. Now she is an assistant professor of theology and religious studies at the University of San Diego.

Carolyn Sharp is associate professor of ethics in the Faculty of Theology at Saint Paul University in Ottawa. She holds an interdisciplinary PhD in theology and women's studies from the University of Saint Michael's College, Toronto. From 1992 to 1999, she edited the Jesuit monthly journal *Relations*. She is active in the women's movement and in various community organizations and is a member of the Conseil du statut de la femme du Québec and the theology committee of the Quebec Assembly of Catholic Bishops.

Marie-Jo Thiel is a professor in the Catholic Theology Faculty of Marc Bloch University in Strasbourg, France, director of the European Center for the Study and Teaching of Ethics (CEERE) of the Universities of Strasbourg, and director of the research group "Bioethics and Religion." She holds PhDs in moral theology and medicine. She has authored and edited several books, including: *Avancer en vie. Le troisième âge* (1993/1998), *Pratiquer l'analyse éthique* (1999), *Éduquer à la beauté, Eduquer aux valeurs* (2000), *Où va la médecine?* (2003), *Le pouvoir de maîtriser le vivant* (2003), *Europe, spiritualités et culture face au recisme* (2004), *Entre Malheur et espoir: Annoncer la maladie, le handicap, la mort* (2006), *Les rites autour du mourir* (2008), *Ethique et santé* (2008); and she has written many journal articles and essays in other collections. She is involved extensively in ethics committees in France and in the EU.

Therese Tinkasiimire, DST, of Fort-Portal, Uganda, is senior lecturer in the Department of Religious Studies at Makerere University in Kampala, Uganda. She holds a master's degree from the University of Portland, and a PhD from Gonzaga University in Spokane, Washington. At Makerere University she teaches religious ethics and religion and gender.

Y-Lan Tran, CND, teaches moral theology at St. Joseph Scholasticate (Vietnamese Jesuit Scholasticate) and at the Inter-Congregation Institute for Woman Religious in Ho Chi Minh City, Vietnam. She also works as medical doctor at Medical Diagnostic Center in Ho Chi Minh City.

Index